CAMPAIGN CRAFT

Recent Titles in the
Praeger Series in Political Communication
Robert E. Denton Jr., General Editor

The Rhetoric of First Lady Hillary Rodham Clinton: Crisis Management Discourse
Colleen Elizabeth Kelley

The Clinton Scandals and the Politics of Image Restoration
Joseph R. Blaney and William L. Benoit

The Idea of Political Marketing
Nicholas J. O'Shaughnessy, editor, and Stephan C. M. Henneberg, associate editor

The Primary Decision: A Functional Analysis of Debates in Presidential Primaries
William L. Benoit, P. M. Pier, LeAnn M. Brazeal, John P. McHale, Andrew Klyukovski, and David Airne

Notable Speeches in Contemporary Presidential Campaigns
Robert V. Friedenberg

Global Political Campaigning: A Worldwide Analysis of Campaign Professionals and Their Practices
Fritz Plasser

The 2000 Presidential Campaign: A Communication Perspective
Robert E. Denton Jr., editor

Press Bias and Politics: How the Media Frame Controversial Issues
Jim A. Kuypers

The Media and Neo-Populism: A Contemporary Comparative Analysis
Gianpietro Mazzoleni, Julianne Stewart, and Bruce Horsfield

Grim Fairy Tales: The Rhetorical Construction of American Welfare Policy
Lisa M. Gring-Pemble

Elizabeth Hanford Dole: Speaking from the Heart
Molly Meijer Wertheimer and Nichola D. Gutgold

CAMPAIGN CRAFT

The Strategies, Tactics, and Art of Political Campaign Management

Third Edition

DANIEL M. SHEA AND
MICHAEL JOHN BURTON

Praeger Series in Political Communication
Robert E. Denton Jr., General Editor

Westport, Connecticut
London

Library of Congress Cataloging-in-Publication Data

Shea, Daniel M.
  Campaign craft : the strategies, tactics, and art of political campaign management /
Daniel M. Shea and Michael John Burton.—3rd ed.
      p.   cm.—(Praeger series in political communication, ISSN 1062-5623)
  Includes bibliographical references and index.
  ISBN 0–275–98903–8 (hard copy : alk. paper)—ISBN 0–275–99004–4 (pbk. : alk.
paper)   1. Campaign management—United States.   I. Burton, Michael John.
II. Title.   III. Series.
  JK2281.S49   2006
  324.70973—dc22   2006001245

British Library Cataloguing in Publication Data is available.

Library of Congress Catalog Card Number: 2006001245
ISBN: 0–275–98903–8 (cloth)
      0–275–99004–4 (paper)
ISSN: 1062–5623

First published in 2006

Praeger Publishers, 88 Post Road West, Westport, CT 06881
An imprint of Greenwood Publishing Group, Inc.
www.praeger.com

Printed in the United States of America

The paper used in this book complies with the
Permanent Paper Standard issued by the National
Information Standards Organization (Z39.48–1984).

10   9   8   7   6   5   4   3   2

For our mothers,
Rosemary Bowers Shea
1937–2005
Grace M. Burton
1939–2005

Contents

Series Foreword

Those of us from the discipline of communication studies have long believed that communication is prior to all other fields of inquiry. In several other forums I have argued that the essence of politics is "talk" or human interaction.[1] Such interaction may be formal or informal, verbal or nonverbal, public or private, but it is always persuasive, forcing us consciously or subconsciously to interpret, to evaluate, and to act. Communication is the vehicle for human action.

From this perspective, it is not surprising that Aristotle recognized the natural kinship of politics and communication in his writings *Politics* and *Rhetoric.* In the former, he established that humans are "political beings [who] alone of the animals [are] furnished with the faculty of language."[2] In the latter, he began his systematic analysis of discourse of proclaiming that "rhetorical study, in its strict sense, is concerned with the modes of persuasion."[3] Thus, it was recognized over twenty-three hundred years ago that politics and communication go hand in hand because they are essential parts of human nature.

In 1981, Dan Nimmo and Keith Sanders proclaimed that political communication was an emerging field.[4] Although its origin, as noted, dates back centuries, a "self-consciously cross-disciplinary" focus began in the late 1950s. Thousands of books and articles later, colleges and universities offer a variety of graduate and undergraduate coursework in the area in such diverse departments as communication, mass communication, journalism, political science, and sociology.[5] In Nimmo and Sanders's early assessment, the "key areas of inquiry" included rhetorical analysis, propaganda analysis, attitude change studies, voting studies, government and the news media, functional and systems analyses, technological changes, media technologies, campaign techniques, and research techniques.[6] In a survey of the state of the field in 1983, the same authors and Lynda Kaid found additional, more specific areas of concerns such as the presidency, political polls, public opinion, debates, and advertising.[7] Since the first study, they have also noted a shift away from the rather strict behavioral approach.

A decade later, Dan Nimmo and David Swanson argued that "political communication has developed some identity as a more or less distinct domain of scholarly work."[8] The scope and concerns of the area have further expanded to include critical theories and cultural studies. Although there is no precise definition, method, or disciplinary home of the area of inquiry, its primary domain comprises the role, processes, and effects of communication within the context of politics broadly defined.

In 1985, the editors of *Political Communication Yearbook: 1984* noted that "more things are happening in the study, teaching, and practice of political communication than can be captured within the space limitations of the relatively few publications available."[9] In addition, they argued that the backgrounds of "those involved in the field [are] so varied and pluralist in outlook and approach, . . . it [is] a mistake to adhere slavishly to any set format in shaping the content."[10] More recently, Swanson and Nimmo have called for "ways of overcoming the unhappy consequences of fragmentation within a framework that respects, encourages, and benefits from diverse scholarly commitments, agendas, and approaches."[11]

In agreement with these assessments of the area and with gentle encouragement, in 1988 Praeger established the series entitled "Praeger Series in Political Communication." The series is open to all qualitative and quantitative methodologies as well as contemporary and historical studies. The key to characterizing the studies in the series is the focus on communication variables or activities within a political context or dimension. As of this writing, over seventy volumes have been published and numerous impressive works are forthcoming. Scholars from the disciplines of communication, history, journalism, political science, and sociology have participated in the series.

I am, without shame or modesty, a fan of the series. The joy of serving as its editor is in participating in the dialogue of the field of political communication and in reading the contributors' works. I invite you to join me.

Robert E. Denton, Jr.

NOTES

1. See Robert E. Denton Jr., *The Symbolic Dimensions of the American Presidency* (Prospect Heights, IL: Waveland Press, 1982); Robert E. Denton Jr. and Gary Woodward, *Political Communication in America* (New York: Praeger, 1985; 2nd ed., 1990); Robert E. Denton Jr. and Dan Hahn, *Presidential Communication* (New York: Praeger, 1986); and Robert E. Denton Jr., *The Primetime Presidency of Ronald Reagan* (New York: Praeger, 1988).

2. Aristotle, *The Politics of Aristotle*, trans. Ernest Barker (New York: Oxford University Press, 1970), 5.

3. Aristotle, *Rhetoric,* trans. W. Rhys Roberts (New York: The Modern Library, 1954), 22.

4. Dan Nimmo and Keith Sanders, "Introduction: The Emergence of Political Communication as a Field," in *Handbook of Political Communication,* ed. Dan Nimmo and Keith Sanders (Beverly Hills, CA: Sage, 1981), 11–36.

5. Ibid., 15.

6. Ibid., 17–27.

7. Keith Sanders, Lynda Kaid, and Dan Nimmo, eds., *Political Communication Yearbook: 1984* (Carbondale: Southern Illinois University Press, 1985), 283–308.

8. Dan Nimmo and David Swanson, "The Field of Political Communication: Beyond the Voter Persuasion Paradigm," in *New Directions in Political Communication,* ed. David Swanson and Dan Nimmo (Beverly Hills, CA: Sage, 1990), 8.

9. Sanders et al., *Political Communication Yearbook,* xiv.

10. Ibid.

11. Nimmo and Swanson, "The Field of Political Communication," 11.

Acknowledgments

The authors are indebted to all who helped them produce the first and second editions of *Campaign Craft*. For the third edition, Hilary Claggett and her team at Praeger were instrumental to our efforts to keep the book current. Moreover, Daniel M. Shea would like to acknowledge the support of the Center for Political Participation at Allegheny College and student assistants Diana Warth, Craig Berger, Dominic Ionta, and Kevin Wahlmark. Michael John Burton gives his sincere thanks to William J. Miller, Mark Ondrejech, and Nicholas Garlinghouse. We offer great appreciation to all who helped us with this book, but any mistakes we will keep for ourselves.

List of Figures and Tables

FIGURES

TABLES

Chapter One

Introduction: Consultant-Centered Campaigns

The presidential election of 1896 was among the most intensely fought races in American history. It pitted Democrat William Jennings Bryan, a fiery ex-congressman from Nebraska, against Republican William McKinley, who had served in Congress prior to being elected governor of Ohio. Bryan was a gifted orator in the classical tradition. At the time, economic misfortune was dividing the nation by region and class, and many saw the gold standard as a threat to debtors and a boon to financiers. Bryan delivered an impassioned speech at the Democratic convention. In defiance of his adversaries, Bryan declared, "You shall not press upon the brow of labor this crown of thorns, you shall not crucify mankind upon a cross of gold" (Bryan 1913, 249). Taking his "Silver Democrat" message to 26 states, talking to an estimated 5 million people, distancing himself from the failures of the incumbent Democratic administration, Bryan cast himself as the champion of the "common man" (Dinkin 1989, 114).

Sensing trouble, McKinley harnessed the talents and ingenuity of his longtime friend and political godfather Marcus A. Hanna—arguably the first modern campaign consultant. Hanna fashioned the McKinley race along "business principles," putting together an elaborate organization designed to handle every phase of the race (Troy 1991, 105). He created different bureaus for different constituencies—Germans, African Americans, wheelmen, merchants, and even women, who did not yet enjoy universal suffrage. Hundreds of speakers were deployed, and countless pamphlets were distributed, many of them printed in foreign languages for use in ethnic neighborhoods. To finance this high-priced strategy, Hanna systematically approached captains of industry, raising more money than had ever been raised for a presidential race—estimated at $3.5 million to $4.0 million (Glad 1964, 169; Jones 1964, 283). Mark Hanna's spending record would stand for nearly a quarter century.

Bryan's travels notwithstanding, the customs of the 1800s held that presidential candidates actively campaigned only if they were in trouble. McKinley rightly feared that campaigning would make him look weak and, more important, that it would give Bryan a chance to upstage him. Hanna therefore orchestrated a series of finely tuned "pilgrimages." The candidate did not go to the people; the people went to the candidate.

Hanna enlisted the aid of leading GOP railroad moguls who offered excursion passes to those wishing a journey to McKinley's front porch in Canton, Ohio (Jamieson 1984, 18). Once these delegations reached the candidate, every step was choreographed, and the press was given prime seating. Introductory speeches delivered by supporters were carefully scrutinized by Hanna's team to ensure consistency of message. McKinley's front-porch campaign captured the attention of the nation: "The desire to come to Canton has reached the point of mania," reported Francis Loomis (Troy 1991, 105). From midsummer until the election, McKinley gave more than 300 speeches and had perhaps 1 million callers at his door. Such a phenomenon had the ordeal become that many people snatched twigs, grass, stones, and even pieces of the famous porch as souvenirs.

Election Day saw one of the largest voter turnouts in history. McKinley won with just 51 percent of the vote, thanks, in large measure, to the skill of his top aide, Mark Hanna.

Hanna's accomplishment was a low-tech affair. Telephone communication was still novel. A couple decades after the McKinley victory, wireless radio was accelerating communication and setting the stage for astonishing technological change in the second half of the century. Television was introduced following World War II and, within 10 years, fully two-thirds of the nation's households had at least one television set. Satellite communications soon became a standard part of local television newscasts. The Cable News Network (CNN) took its place in the White House, often reporting international news to the president's staff before the intelligence agencies could. In the first years of the twenty-first century, nearly every home had a television, more than 80 percent of American households have cable or satellite, and just about as many American adults had access to the Internet—a technology that few could have imagined as recently as the early 1990s. College students walk around campus with digital phones, radio stations broadcast on the Internet, and start-up businesses issue email-capable phones to incoming employees. Deejays are "podcasting" and consumers are equipping their cars with satellite receivers. One can only imagine what Hanna would have dreamed up for the new technologies of the World Wide Web.

The technological revolution is changing education, transportation, personal communications, the job market, and the way that people think about the future. Less obvious but no less profound are the corresponding adjustments made to the American system of governance. Government at all levels is going online. Voters are tracked by ever-growing databases and through evermore sophisticated micro targeting programs. Large campaigns simply cannot survive without hiring someone who knows how to uplink video to a satellite and set up blogs and Web sites, features unheard of only a few years ago.

Howard Dean, the former governor of Vermont and later the chair of the Democratic National Committee, ran for the presidency in 2004. His campaign manager during that race was longtime consultant and high-tech entrepreneur Joe Trippi. Not long after the race, Trippi recounted how he believes elections will be forever changed. In *The Revolution Will Not Be Televised,* Trippi writes,

> In 1956, it was 45 million people watching *The Wizard of Oz* on TV, Elvis appearing on Ed Sullivan, and the networks covering the Democratic National Convention for the first time. Today, 75 percent of Americans are online, eBay draws forty-five million bidders a year to its auctions, hundreds of millions of songs are downloaded from music web sites, and the Dean campaign has shown how a candidate could ride the Net from obscurity to the verge of a party's presidential nomination. . . . The Internet is like an eight-year-old child, growing in leaps and bounds, giddy with possibilities. (2005, 201)

In the recent past, campaigns were conducted by armies of volunteers, usually local party activists and the candidate's network of friends and family. Time-honored methods were used, mostly face-to-face canvassing and the distribution of printed material (e.g., pamphlets, posters, and newspaper advertisements). In the 1950s, "retail" politics was the way of the world. Massachusetts pol Tip O'Neill, who would later make his mark as Speaker of the House, could view politics as a sociable affair: hands are shaken, deals are made, and no one gives his or her vote until asked (O'Neill 1987). As a retired legislator, O'Neill lamented, "If I were running today, I probably would have to use all the modern techniques of political campaigning: hiring a political consultant, polling extensively and making ads targeted to TV audiences" (1994, xi–xii).

O'Neill was living in the twilight of retail campaigns. The shift toward professional campaigning that began with Mark Hanna's work in 1896 was hastened by Dwight D. Eisenhower's 1952 campaign for president. Eisenhower hired an advertising team that produced some of the first television campaign commercials. Using the product-tested technique of name repetition, Eisenhower's jingle went, "Ike for President, Ike for President; You like Ike, I like Ike, Everybody likes Ike." By the mid-1960s, the skills and tactics used by product marketing specialists had moved down to the realm of congressional elections. Carefully constructed, random-sample surveys, for example, proved to be a better and more cost-effective means of identifying the wishes of voters than just walking around and consulting other party leaders. In this transformation, Joe McGinniss, who detailed Richard Nixon's 1968 advertising strategy, saw a loss of innocence: "With the coming of television, and the knowledge of how it could be used to seduce voters, the old political values disappeared" (1969, 28).

Today, pure grassroots campaigning seems archaic for all but the humblest races. Political operatives dismiss it as "old style." Even city council races are starting to use expensive, high-tech methods, and the newfound tricks of the 1980s were considered passé a decade later. Instead of large-scale polls, narrowly targeted focus groups came into vogue. By the mid-1990s, it was normal to see videotapes distributed en masse. Satellite feeds were replacing smoke-filled rooms, and blast faxes rendered hand-distributed press releases obsolete. Of course, the advent of the World Wide Web brought about fundamental changes in daily campaign communications. Every position paper, every ad, every news release can be posted for all to see at minimal cost. No other area of American politics has so drastically changed over the past few decades than the manner in which candidates pursue voters.

The revolution in campaign technology has had and will continue to have a substantial effect on elections. It intensifies the importance of money in the election process. Candidates with access to financial resources can bypass traditional party screening mechanisms, which once began with loyalty and hard work. Traditional political parties, the center of campaign activity for more than 150 years, have lost ground to campaign consultants, political action committees (PACs), and independent 527 committees, though the parties have maintained relevance by adopting the ways of these upstart competitors. The parties, which once served as the organizational foundation of American politics, have become "service-oriented" organizations that allocate financial resources and expertise to candidates (White and Shea 2004, 101–26). The money that a candidate receives from a political party and other sources is spent on a variety of specialized services, from sophisticated polling to high-budget media production. All politics may be local, as Tip O'Neill often said, but the campaign industry has become distinctly national in its scope and power.

Inevitably, the types of campaign information provided to voters have also changed. Viewers now see 30-second television spots and six-second sound bites. In 1994, three years after Arnold Schwarzenegger's *Terminator 2* thrilled audiences with a new cinematic effect—image morphing—Republican candidates ran ads that showed the faces of Democratic candidates slowly dissolving into that of President Bill Clinton. The technique was roundly criticized as an oversimplification of serious issues, but it was effective.

Some have argued that, with the new media, "style becomes substance" (see McGinniss 1969, 30). The volume of negative campaign advertising now runs at a fever pitch. The media often seem more interested in who is ahead in the polls and in how each campaign is being run than in the policy stands of the candidates. There is even some evidence to suggest that the type of person willing to undergo the rigors of modern campaigning has changed, leading to a much different crop of public officials and a new approach to governance (Ehrenhalt 1991).

THE STUDY OF CONTEMPORARY ELECTIONS

Do campaigns matter? That is, can campaign tactics and strategy actually win elections? Several of the earliest election studies, conducted in the 1950s and 1960s (e.g., Berelson, Lazarsfeld, and McPhee 1954), found little evidence that they did. Voters, it was believed, vote according to party affiliation rather than campaign message. The authors of these early studies concluded that the principal effect of campaigns is to pressure people toward a predisposition. "As time goes on ... we find that people abandon deviant opinions on specific issues to agree with the position taken by their party" (Berelson et al. 1954, 285). Only when a dramatic, cross-cutting issue divided the electorate would voters be swayed by candidate appeals. Partisan stability was believed to be especially strong at the local level. Scholars found little value in studying individual campaigns because electioneering seemed to have little bearing on election outcomes.

The scholarly struggle to find the true weight of short-term factors, such as campaign tactics, did not end in the 1950s. In 1966, political scientist V. O. Key suggested that voters are inclined to use past events as a guide to their behavior on Election Day; in other words, they are willing to vote against their own party if the party has not performed well: "As voters mark their ballots they may have in their minds impressions of the last TV political spectacular of the campaign, but, more important, they have in their minds recollections of their experiences of the past four years" (1966, 9). Morris Fiorina (1981) built on Key's argument, maintaining that voters typically compile a "running tally of retrospective evaluations" and that this calculation directly shapes their partisan orientation, which, in turn, plays a powerful role in determining future voting decisions. People look at the candidate's records of accomplishment and failure. Alternatively, perhaps the strongest voting cue is simple incumbency. Yale scholar David Mayhew (1974a, 1974b) suggested that because members of Congress want to be reelected, they spend a great deal of time working toward that end. The "electoral connection," as described by Mayhew, emphasizes the power of incumbency over the noise and fanfare of campaigns.

Elsewhere (Burton and Shea, in press), we review an assessment of the forecasts offered in 2004 by seven teams of scholars, finding that they missed the final vote tally by an average of just 2.6 percentage points. Four of these teams were within two points of perfection—a remarkable feat given that the predictions were made nearly a year in advance. Some models were off the mark by three or four percentage points, an error margin that was attributed to "unexpected developments," such as developments in Iraq, or to measurement error and the failure to consider all significant variables. Overall, though, campaign effects in the race between George W. Bush and John Kerry seemed to be minimal (see also American Political Science Association 2005). So maybe campaigns don't matter.

At the same time, however, we know that numerous contextual changes since the 1980s have pushed scholars to take a second look at campaign effects. These changes included a trend where fewer voters seemed guided by party preference alone. Perhaps campaign effects are strongest for alienated, nonpartisan voters. Data from the 2004 election seem to suggest that partisanship may be on the rise, but it is hard to imagine that it will return to post–World War II levels anytime soon. Surely the amount of money spent by candidates at all levels has skyrocketed, and reams of studies conclude that the candidate with the most money usually wins. These findings suggest that campaign tactics and high-priced consultants do matter. Although the machinery of urban party organizations has broken down, parties are providing candidates with greater and greater assistance. Several studies during the past decade have underscored the growing import of party organizations at all levels of electoral politics (see, e.g., Frendries and Gitelson 1999). Each of these trends (and many others) underscored the need for shifting the analysis from the voter to the campaign process itself.

Indeed, scholarly findings are starting to emerge. Steven Finkel (1993) examined changes in voter intention during the 1980 campaign, finding that about five percent changed their minds. Obviously, five percent can be critical to the outcome of a competitive race, but even still Finkel argued that campaign effects would have to be much more substantial to be considered meaningful (as noted in Holbrook, in press). Bartels also focused on the 1980 presidential campaign and found that "while candidate support was highly stable over time, exposure to the campaign via mass media was an important predictor of the changes that did occur. "Exposure to the media is likely to be most important when people have relatively weak ties to the candidates, and when one of the candidates is relatively unknown" (as noted in Holbrook, in press).

Scholars point to the accuracy of forecasting models, but practitioners are sure that their handiwork matters. Looking back at the 2004 election, Kerry campaign manager Bob Shrum declared, "Everything mattered—everything they did, everything we did, and a series of external events all mattered" (Institute of Politics 2006, 134). Likely the most accurate perspectives take into account both long-term forces, such as the partisan disposition of the electorate and the state of the economy, and short-term effects, such as campaign tactics. One scholar to merge both long- and short-term forces into a model of campaign effects is Thomas Holbrook. He argues that "election outcomes and voting behavior are easily explained with just a few variables, none of which are related to the campaign," and yet, according to Holbrook, "campaigns do matter." "Prevailing attitudes about the economy and the incumbent administration" merely create a predicted "equilibrium"—the outcome that would be expected without campaign effects (1996, 156–57). Candidate support at the beginning of a race is often *out* of equilibrium, failing to match predictions. A predicted front-runner who has somehow fallen behind expectations has a mission: "move public opinion toward the expected outcome" (157). Campaign effects might be small, but they are real. Likewise, scholar James Campbell (2000) argues that precampaign "fundamentals"—such as incumbency and the election-year economy—frame the general structure of campaigns, but they do not always determine the outcome. In every election, idiosyncratic campaign effects, such as candidate gaffes, strategic blunders, and campaign events, can shift voter attitudes (Burton and Shea 2003, 30). The net effect of campaign effects at the presidential level has been roughly 1.5 percent of the popular vote. Given that seven outcomes since 1876 were within this (not including the 2000 race) 1.5 percent range, Campbell concludes that "a significant number of presidential elections have been. . .close enough that some unsystematic factors of particular campaigns may have made the difference to the election's outcome" (182).

Other scholars have found limited campaign effects as well. Paul R. Abramson, John H. Aldrich, and David W. Rohde found that a great deal of the party defection in 1996 occurred just prior to Election Day, seeming to suggest that "the choices for some voters were affected by the campaign" (1999, 40). Stephen Medvic has found that campaigns that hire a wide range of consultants tend to do better than campaigns that do not—a conclusion that holds particularly true for challengers (2003, 104). He writes,

> The level of professionalization proved a significant influence on a candidate's percent of the vote received. . . . Campaigns run by professional consultants benefit not only from the experience of the consultants but from the unique approach to campaigning that consultants bring to an organization. It stands to reason that the more campaign activities handled by consultants, the greater the candidate's share of the vote will be. (101)

In sum, although disentangling the impact of campaign maneuvers and events from long-term forces is a difficult task, there seems little doubt that both come together on Election Day. Given the rather even polarization of the electorate following the 2004 elections—where the number of citizens identifying with either of the major parties is nearly the same as those without a party identification—the weight of campaign tactics may be accentuated in the years ahead. Of course, no campaign team, even the very best, can make a silk purse out of a sow's ear. Long-term forces sometimes dominate the playing filed, but they do not always decide the outcome of the game. It is here—in the slack and uncertainty of most electoral contests—that the art and craft of modern electioneering can make the difference.

CAMPAIGN MANAGEMENT LITERATURE

Campaign management and technology have not been altogether neglected by scholars. Several books emerged in the 1970s, most notably those of Robert Agranoff (1972), Joseph Napolitan (1972), and James Brown and Philip M. Seib (1976). In the 1980s, Larry Sabato (1981) drew attention to the emerging campaign profession. Marjorie R. Hershey (1984), Ann Beaudry and Bob Schaeffer (1986), and Barbara L. Salmore and Stephen A. Salmore (1989) shed much-needed light on the inner workings of electioneering. Later, Edwin Diamond and Stephen Bates (1992) and Karen S. Johnson-Cartee and Gary A. Copeland (1991) provided in-depth examinations of campaign advertising; Kathleen Hall Jamieson (1992) explored the rise of "dirty politics," and Gary W. Selnow (1994) took account of computer technology in elections.

Two books on the effects of negative campaigning are worth noting. Steven Ansolabehere and Shanto Iyengar (1997) analyzed negative advertising using a series of randomized experiments, and Richard Lau and Gerald Pomper (2004) offer a sharp, comprehensive look at numerous data sets. Several new works have examined the growing importance of consultants in the process, including those of Johnson-Cartee and Copeland (1997) and Kerwin C. Swint (1998). James A. Thurber and Candace Nelson edited two volumes (1995, 2000), both of which provide a mix of theoretical and applied material. David Dulio (2004) provides a thorough and comprehensive look at how consultants continue to change the electoral process. Robert V. Friedenberg (1997) has outlined an important segment of the campaign industry, communications consultancy, and Candice Nelson (and others) edited a provocative volume on campaign ethics (2002). Thurber, Nelson, and Dulio (2000) provide a timely look at television advertising.

Richard J. Semiatin (2005) follows the campaign process from start to finish, Cherie Strachan (2003) explores the growing professionalization of campaigns at the local level, and Ronald Keith Gaddie (2004) recently penned a provocative work that contemplates why anyone would want to run for office in the first place. Focusing on 16 different congressional races in 2002, L. Sandy Maisel and Darrell West (2004) provide an edited volume on campaign discourse—that is, the types of information voters hear during campaigns. One of the most difficult obstacles that candidates confront is knocking off an incumbent. Edward Sidlow's (2004) recent book explores this issue in detail. Jeff Stonecash (2003) does an excellent job demystifying the nuances of the modern campaign polling process, and Michael Malbin (2003) continues to produce the most important book on campaign finance laws and how they affect candidates, parties, and consultants.

Strategy has received less scholarly attention than one might have guessed. A few years ago, the authors of this volume wrote *Campaign Mode: Strategic Vision in Congressional Elections* (2003). One goal was to chart how top-end consultants confront the myriad choices in every election, suggesting in the end that "campaign mode" is a "state of mind that combines a visceral drive to win elections with a deep-seated habit of strategic thinking" (4). Few can reach this level, but those who do can turn the outcome of an election. Although not a scholarly work per se, the Institute of Politics at Harvard University pulled together the top consultants from the 2004 presidential campaign and published a provocative account of the proceedings (2006). Much of the discussion is, obviously, on the importance of campaign strategy. Larry Sabato's edited book (1989a) was one of the earliest of this sort, a collection of reprinted articles from *Campaigns and Elections,* a trade magazine for campaign consultants. *Campaigns and Elections* also produced *The Road to Victory,* another compendium of past articles (Faucheux 1998). Bruce Newman penned *The Handbook of Political Marketing* (1999), which offers a wealth of information for the practitioner and provides keen scholarly insight, and Faucheux and Herrnson (2002) provided similarly important guidance.

Beyond edited collections, there are a variety of campaign manuals, usually written by elected officials and campaign professionals, that give readers a sense of ground-level campaign tactics. These books, such as the *Campaigns and Elections* articles, are strong on detail. Judge Lawrence Grey's *How to Win a Local Election,* for example, tells campaign operatives, "A clear coat of varnish can extend the life of a sign, and one good tip is to take the stack of signs as they come from the printer and use a roller with varnish to seal all the edges" (1999, 194–95). Dick Simpson, an academician and former campaign consultant, penned a venerable handbook dubbed *Winning Elections* (1996). Robert Thomas and Doug Gowen have written a short work on running for local office (1999).

Dennis Johnson's *No Place for Amateurs* (2001) offers a detailed look at new-style electioneering, as does Catherine Shaw's volume *The Campaign Manager* (2004). Campaign manuals such as these explore strategic issues, but they do so in the absence of a larger theoretical construct. It is not their mission to locate new-style politics in the broader context of the digital age.

This book is designed to merge theory and practice and to help fill a gap in the campaign management literature. It is meant for students of new-style electioneering, combining theoretical knowledge with practical information about the nature and function of "real-world" election activities. Each chapter reviews a segment of the new campaign craft and its logic and importance as well as relevant tactics, technologies, and illustrations. More than anything else, the goal of the book is to help take the mystery out of this enigmatic piece of American politics.

NEW-STYLE CAMPAIGNING

The term "new-style" campaigning is used frequently in the pages that follow. Originally advanced by Robert Agranoff (1972), it continues, with some modification, to symbolize the state of modern electioneering. The distinctions between "old-style" and "new-style" campaigning can be drawn along four dimensions: (1) new players, (2) new incentives, (3) new tactics, and (4) new resources.

New Players

The exact role of candidates in elections has changed a great deal in the past few decades. Each party offers a candidate, the person with the most votes wins, and the candidates remain the stars—but the supporting cast of contemporary campaigns is vastly different from what it was in the "golden age of parties."

From the 1830s into the 1960s, candidates did not run for office by themselves—they stood for election with their campaigns driven largely by party organizations and their fortunes linked to the success or failure of the party. Candidates were expected to contribute to their election effort, of course—often a donation to party coffers was a precondition of nomination—but a great deal of voter contact was left to party activists. If there were people who could be called "professionals," they were professionals only in the sense that they were the most seasoned party workers. Training was provided by the party as operatives moved up the organizational ladder. Formal education was no match for trial by fire. George Washington Plunkitt, a powerful Democratic leader in New York City's old Tammany Hall organization, was clear on this point:

> We ain't all bookworms and college professors. If we were, Tammany might win an election once in four thousand years. Most of the leaders are plain American citizens, of the people and near the people, and they have all the education they need to whip the dudes who part their name in the middle and to run City Government. We got bookworms, too, in the organization. But we don't make them district leaders. We keep them for ornaments on parade days (Riordon 1995, 45).

Experience, not scientific outlook, was the organizing force of Tammany politics.

Tammany and other political machines drew their power largely from the distribution of government jobs and other benefits to new immigrants in return for demonstrated party loyalty. But at the turn of the twentieth century, the Progressive movement began to hammer away at city machines. Progressive reformers pushed for civil service rules (which reduced opportunities for patronage), the secret ballot (which rendered vote promises unenforceable), and direct primary elections (which removed the selection of nominees from party leaders and gave it to the voting electorate). In some states, good-government groups even pressed for nonpartisan municipal elections. Decreased immigration, increased mobility, broad-based education, and changing family patterns all worked to reduce the power of political parties.

Old connections were fading. Of John F. Kennedy, O'Neill wrote, "I'd have to say that he was only nominally a Democrat. . . .To work for Jack [in his congressional races], the Kennedys recruited a group of energetic and talented volunteers, most of whom had never worked in a political campaign" (1987, 76). It was a pattern that would repeat itself time and again for one candidate after another. By the 1970s, presidential nomination reforms had stripped party leaders of the role they once played in selecting their party's candidate, and campaign finance reform led to the proliferation of labor, business, and ideological PACs, further diminishing the relative weight of party assistance to candidates. In effect, the smoke-filled rooms were taken out of the process. Some observers were left to conclude that "the party's over" (Broder 1971).

Without parties, it was assumed that candidate "image" would replace party-based appeals. Beginning first at the presidential level, students of American elections noticed a growing number of candidates running without benefit of significant party help. "Candidate-centered" politics was said to have emerged. Television was perfectly suited to campaign appeals based on individual candidates. With television ads being purchased by individual contributions, candidates at all levels soon found that they could go it alone. It became common for people to say, "I vote for the candidate, not the party," even when they consistently voted for one party or another. Voters, like candidates, surrendered much of their overt party allegiance.

New-style election consultants quickly emerged, responding to the new demands of candidates—and in some ways fueling that demand (Sabato 1981). Familiar with the tools of public relations and product marketing, campaign professionals met the needs of a changing campaign environment. Consultants were able to measure voter preferences and then aim specific campaign messages toward specific groups. Strategy was mapped on slide rules, then on calculators, then on desktop computers, and now on the omnipresent notebook computers one sees in political campaigns. As the campaign industry began to take off in the early 1970s, one scholar counted some 30 branches of the campaign profession (Agranoff 1972, 17). The number soared over the next three decades. By the spring of 2006, *Campaigns and Elections* magazine boasted nearly 75 different categories of campaign professionals, including crisis management, grassroots strategy, digital mapping, media and speech training, online information services, referendum consulting, and more. One estimate holds that there are now some 7,000 consultants making all or part of their living running campaigns (Johnson 2001, xiii).

New Incentives

Incentives for helping candidates prior to the 1970s were manifold. Party organizations controlled the reins of government—regulating patronage disbursement and managing government contracts. Some people would assist a candidate because they believed in the person or the party, while others were family friends showing personal loyalty. It was also common to find campaign workers expecting that after the election they would get a job on the elected official's staff.

More recently, although volunteers continue to help and while some people are surely hoping for a government job, independent professionals are the core of the campaign team. It is gainful employment. Top consultants can earn hundreds of dollars per hour, often charging a sizable percentage on media expenditures. At the very top of the profession, where consultants compete for a slice of the presidential campaign pie, the numbers are astronomical. Dick Morris, who advised the 1996 Clinton campaign, told the *Washington Post*, "I made about $500,000 in 1995 . . . and I made about a million in 1996" (Harris 1998). Consultants strongly differentiate themselves according to party (Thurber, Kolodny, and Dulio 2000). There are Democratic media consultants and Republican media consultants, if for no other reason than because candidates do not trust freelancers willing to serve both sides of the aisle. (Morris is an exception to that rule.) But consulting is a profit-based enterprise. Consultants might believe in their candidates or in particular causes, but they do it to collect a paycheck.

New Tactics

If the medium is the message, the technology is the tactic. Television and radio allow candidates to enter more living rooms in 30 seconds than party foot soldiers might have reached in a month. Computers are used in direct mail, survey research, list development, fund-raising, targeting, and just about every other campaign function. About the only thing that computers do not do is directly ask for votes—but this may be changing as well. New technologies allow a candidate to simultaneously meet with several groups of voters via satellite hookups, and "actualities" can be fed to radio news stations digitally. The Internet allows voters to see policy papers, family photographs, and even television ads.

The difference is not just the medium of message dissemination but the strategy that new-style electioneering sustains. Early uses of mass media took a shotgun approach. The candidate's media strategy—to the extent that it had any well-planned line of attack—would seek to broadcast the message widely. The goal was to reach as many people as possible. This meant getting the message out through newspapers, rallies, and districtwide, door-to-door canvassing. Each of these tactics was effective in contacting people, though not always in reaching the most persuadable voters. Little was done to link the right message with the right person. In the new millennium, scrupulous efforts are made to discover voter preferences through survey research. A carefully honed message is directed to each persuadable voter group. Contemporary electioneering uses a rifle, not a shotgun. It is the art and science of modern campaign "targeting."

New Resources

New-style campaigns survive on money. Nearly all the tactics of this emerging profession hinge on financial resources. Some candidates have found ways to win despite lagging funds, but examples are rare. There is a startlingly close correlation between campaign money and electoral success. Few new-style consultants would trade cash for volunteers. The reason is simple: if a campaign is short on volunteers for a phone bank, it can buy the services of a telemarketing firm; if, however, the campaign is short on money, surplus volunteers will not pay the long-distance bills.

The weight of financial necessity on recent elections has created a plethora of new questions. Where should the money come from? What do contributors expect? How are the funds to be raised? And how much is enough? The rising cost of elections and the growth of special-interest money have astounded observers of the democratic process. Agranoff, for example, seemed surprised in 1972 when he noted that state legislative campaigns might cost between $10,000 and $20,000 (1972, 27). By the late 1990s, 10 times this amount was customary in some states. In the 1998 Democratic three-way gubernatorial primary in California, business executive Al Checchi spent $40 million, only to finish last, and in 2000, Jon Corzine spent $60 million to become the junior senator from New Jersey. By 2004, 10 races for the Senate saw expenditures of more than $16 million, and 10 House races spent more than $5 million (Opensecrets.org 2005). In South Dakota, where incumbent Senator Tom Daschle confronted a vigorous challenge from John Thune in 2004, more than $36 million was spent. This came out to a whopping $71 per vote. Moreover, national and state parties (and even outside interest groups) are spending increasingly large amounts on television advertising and mobilization efforts. Six independent 527 committees each spent more than $25 million in 2004, with the highest spending coming from Americans Coming Together ($79 million) and Joint Victory Campaign 2004 ($71 million) (Opensecrets.org 2005).

CONSULTANT-CENTERED CAMPAIGNS

Agranoff's view of new-style campaigning goes a long way toward describing the state of affairs at the beginning of the new millennium, but it is not a perfect fit. Two adjustments must be made to the traditional view: in some ways, the party organizations have made a comeback and that, at the same time, the modern campaign, often called a candidate-centered operation, might actually be "consultant centered."

The Resurgence of Party Organizations

It was taken for granted by the mid-1970s that political parties barely mattered in electoral politics. Voter partisanship was down, presidential candidates ran on their own hook—sometimes blasting the official party apparatus—and legislators were inclined to stray from the wishes of the party leaders. Nevertheless, the national party organizations and thousands of state and local party units throughout the nation hung on. They did not completely disappear, as many expected.

The Party Transformation Study (PTS), undertaken by Neil Cotter and his colleagues in 1984, systematically surveyed thousands of party leaders across the nation. Their principal finding was that, contrary to popular wisdom, most party organizations remained vibrant and, in fact, were often stronger than at the turn of the twentieth century. Although the relative weight of party activity had declined in light of PACs, parties were by far the largest single source of assistance to candidates. Office seekers relied on parties to carry petitions, organize volunteers, give money, make telephone calls, and canvass door to door. The PTS was followed up by a number of other studies, all of which found basically the same thing—"the party goes on" (Kayden and Mahe 1985).

At first, the contradiction seemed puzzling. How could it be that fewer voters tied themselves to a partisan label and that legislators saw fit to abandon the party at will when, at the same time, party organizations were expanding? Joseph Schlesinger (1991) has provided a possible answer: it is precisely because partisanship does not matter among the voters, he argued, that elections have become more competitive and less predictable; party organizations have been forced to adapt, and adaptation has taken the form of greater campaign service. Moreover, because candidates face uncertain elections, they look to merge with others in the same predicament as a form of collective protection.

Today, aggressive local party organizations can be found across the nation. Many have moved into the digital age and boast computer targeting systems, direct-mail operations, survey apparatus, and telemarketing centers. The same 1970s-era campaign finance reform measures that gave limited direct party payments to candidates also opened up the soft-money loophole. Direct donations to federal candidates were tightly regulated, but money given to the parties was not. As a result, political parties at all levels could make big-money media buys promoting their party and its members. Even after the Bipartisan Campaign Reform Act of 2002 (discussed in the pages to follow), which was intended to limit soft-money contributions, parties have thrived.

The national and state party organizations have developed new structures specifically designed for legislative elections. These "campaign committees," such as the National Republican Campaign Committee (for Republican members of Congress) or the Democratic Legislative Campaign Committee (for Democratic state legislatures), serve as leading-edge consultancy operations. Now found in almost every state, legislative campaign committees (LCCs) provide a host of campaign services (Shea 1995). Some of the newest players are the Democratic and Republican governors' associations. In a move to stay clear of soft-money limits, activists on both sides of the partisan divide have set up these "independent" units, organized as 527s. They are flush and use their funds strategically. In 2004, for example, Missouri had open seats for governor, lieutenant governor, and secretary of state and two congressional seats. The Missouri Democratic Party took in $3 million from the Democratic Governors' Association (DGA) to help with these races, and the Republican state committee received some $2 million from their governors' association. In all, the DGA raised $24 million in 2004, and the RGA raised some $34 million (Center for Public Integrity 2005). There is no doubt that there will be much organizational innovation in the coming years.

The services and resources provided to candidates by national and state committees are vast. They give money, but, more important, they provide expertise and assistance. Promising congressional candidates can expect to be invited to Washington, D.C., or the state capital to attend training sessions. They can use media studios to make radio and television spots, and they receive professional assistance on their direct mail. In some states, LCC staff operatives join candidates in the field, essentially running the show. Moreover, the party committees serve as "brokers" linking candidates with potential contributors and offer discounts for service vendors. Candidates interested in a survey can be put in contact with a top-notch pollster—and receive the benefits of volume pricing. In a kind of matchmaking service, campaign committees bring PAC decision makers and candidates together to see if the relationship will work.

Campaign committees are cold-blooded. Unlike many "leadership PACs," which help candidates friendly to prominent party members, the purpose of campaign committees is to build legislative majorities. They target their efforts on only the most competitive races (Shea 1999). If a candidate's chances are good, significant help might be forthcoming, but a long-shot candidate will get little support beyond basic guidance and a few referrals, if that. As one would-be congressional candidate described his first encounter with the Democratic Congressional Campaign Committee, "All they did. . .was show me a list of PACs and then tell me that the PACs wouldn't talk to me until I was the designated candidate. They promised me nothing. I could count on no help from them at all" (Fowler and McClure 1989, 37). For some candidates, the money game has become one of the most frustrating aspects of new-style campaigning—how does one become competitive without first getting assistance? Fund-raising requires funds. The trip to the campaign committee has become a critical part of a candidate's bid for office.

The Rise of Consultant-Centered Campaigns

Even with this new infusion of party resources, the value of the party label per se is in sharp decline. Fewer candidates overtly link themselves to a party ticket. It is sometimes difficult to discern a candidate's party from his or her campaign ads, and party signifiers have fallen from many campaign posters. Character, not party, is what candidates emphasize, and consultants sometimes advise clients to distance themselves from party leaders. "The candidate, rather than the party," writes Agranoff, "tends to be the chief focus of today's campaign communication" (1972, 4).

The change has been rolling forward for decades. During the 1950s, Dwight Eisenhower demonstrated that Democratic voters could be unhitched from their partisan moorings by sheer personal appeal. In 1976, Jimmy Carter ran on honesty, not his Democratic credentials, and in 1980, Ronald Reagan showed strength of character, not just Republican ideals.

The shift from party to personality was made possible, in part, because the "image makers" began providing their services. Image-based campaigns emerged at the presidential level because survey and marketing experts pushed candidates in that direction. Only after persistent appeals from his new-style advisers did Richard Nixon make the transition from party to image—leading to his success in the 1968 presidential election. It was a two-way street. Consultants required candidates, and candidates required consultants. McGinniss wrote, "[Nixon] would need men of dignity. Who believed in him and shared his vision. But more importantly, men who knew television as a weapon: from broadest concept to most technical detail" (1969, 34). From this symbiotic relationship would emerge the "selling of the president." Years later, Bob Squier, who was once Washington's premier media consultant, could say in passing, "You'll find people in my business tend to use this word 'viewer' and 'voter' almost interchangeably" (1998).

While McGinniss viewed the use of campaign advertising with a mix of awe and contempt, few serious candidates above the local level try to run a campaign without professional consultancy services. Professionals measure public opinion, shape candidate appeals, raise funds, and implement the most efficient voter contact methods available. Contemporary campaigns are not party centered, nor are they strictly candidate centered—rather, they are consultant centered.

There is a bit of exaggeration but also some truth in Dan Nimmo's claim that campaigns may no longer be battles between candidates but between titans of the campaign industry, working on behalf of those personalities (Nimmo 1970). True, the candidate builds the campaign, hires the consultants, asks for money, and has his or her good name and reputation on the line. In this sense, modern elections *are* candidate centered. But if one looks at the campaign structure beneath the candidate to see who is running the show, one no longer finds a Tammany-style party operative promising government jobs. Campaigns are now staffed by people who know the strategies, tactics, and art of political campaign management—that is, by professionals.

Everything from fund-raising activities to direct mail to television advertising to grassroots work is now coordinated by well-paid campaign consulting firms. Significantly more people now make their living with campaign consulting firms than political parties, and most party organizations are assisted by campaign consultants. A state legislative campaign committee will, for example, target a winnable race, hire a consultant, and then send the consultant into the field to run the campaign. Plunkitt of Tammany Hall dismissed academics as party "ornaments," but in recent years the ranks of the campaign committees and the consultancy firms have been filled with alumni from graduate schools, such as the Bliss Institute of Applied Politics at the University of Akron or the Graduate School of Political Management at George Washington University. What would Plunkitt have thought of the American Association of Political Consultants, complete with dues, conferences, industry honors (the "Pollie" awards), and a professional code of ethics?

The recruitment of top consultants has become a campaign issue in itself. Journalists pay attention to the formation of each candidate's consulting team. With a strong corps in place, donors may start to open their checkbooks. A professional media consultant knows how to leverage press attention, and a professional fundraiser knows how to get the most money for the campaign. For a campaign on the move, the hiring of a strong consultancy team becomes something of a self-fulfilling prophecy. Few candidates fail to recognize the skills afforded by these new "wizards of American politics" (Luntz 1988).

ORGANIZATION OF THE BOOK

Each of the following chapters is designed to help students of American politics understand the history and logic of campaigns in this new age of high-tech, consultant-centered campaigning. The focus here is on subpresidential elections. Few consultants get the opportunity to plan media buys, organize direct mail, or raise funds in the higher echelons of a presidential campaign. State and local elections are most at issue here. While the book will feature presidential elections—they epitomize campaign strategy, and students of politics already know the plots and players—for the most part it addresses the strategies, tactics, and technologies appropriate for midlevel elections, such as those for Congress, state legislature, county executive, and city council. Chapter Two provides a glimpse into campaign plans at that level.

Part One investigates campaign context, beginning with Chapter Three, which looks at the mix of factors that defines a particular electoral race. This examination is followed by an extended look at demographic analysis in Chapter Four. Chapter Five examines opposition research—the collection of detrimental data on candidates.

Part Two looks at elements of strategic thinking. It begins with an overview of electoral targeting in Chapter Six, moving on to survey research in Chapter Seven and general strategy in Chapter Eight.

Part Three looks at voter contact techniques, beginning with campaign fund-raising in Chapter Nine, moving forward to communications in Chapter Ten (media strategy) and Chapter Eleven (news coverage) and grassroots voter contact techniques in Chapter Twelve. Finally, in a concluding chapter, the future of campaign organization is explored in light of new data management and voter contact technologies.

Throughout, the book maintains that a critical transformation of American elections is under way. New-style campaigning has taken hold from the presidential level down to town council contests. Political scientists have taken steps toward understanding many of the larger processes, but the details have been elusive. Gerald Pomper noted more than three decades ago that although Americans choose more than half a million public officials through the ballot, "elections are a mystery" (1974, 1). The intention of this book is to explain the basic operation of campaigns and, it is hoped, to underscore both the art and the science of professional electioneering.

Chapter Two

The Campaign Plan

Campaign manuals are unanimous on the importance of advance planning. One says, "Running for office requires extensive consultation and planning" (Semiatin 2005, 52), and another, "The need to make a plan and follow that plan is absolutely crucial" (Grey 1999, 96). From a third, "A flowchart (plan or calendar) is an essential tool in any successful campaign. Flowcharts keep the campaign organized and provide you and your team with a visual plan of the whole campaign" (Shaw 2004, 350). Yet another tells its readers, "Do not ever go into a campaign without some sort of plan" (Bike 1998, 176). Indeed, "A chart can have a calming effect on the candidate and staff because it clearly outlines exactly what needs to be done and when" (Shaw 2004, 350). S. J. Guzzetta talks about the shock of insight that accompanies forward thinking: "As you study this Manual, you will notice the enormous amount of work involved and its relatively high cost. Generally, the immediate reaction generally is 'Is all this really necessary to win?' The answer is an *emphatic* YES" (2002, 109).

Planning is critical. In Theodore White's classic book, *The Making of the President, 1960,* one sees how John F. Kennedy and his advisers spent three years planning their run for the presidency. A year before the election, a late October strategy session was held to lay out the "final assault plans" (White 1961, 53). In the morning, Senator Kennedy ticked off the strategy for each region, each state, even getting into the details of local political issues and factions. After lunch, with brother Bobby taking the lead, the day turned to "operational" matters, and "assignments were to be distributed and the nation quartered up by the Kennedy staff as if a political general staff were giving each of its combat commanders a specific front of operations" (1961, 56). Thus began one of the hardest-fought presidential campaigns in recent history.

In the early 1960s, Kennedy's brand of discipline was noteworthy. In the new millennium, it is routine. Contemporary campaign manuals offer sample work sheets, basic strategies, and even model campaign calendars to guide readers through the planning process. Every theater of operations presents unique challenges. Campaign planning is not a one-size-fits-all endeavor. But there are some overarching principles. This chapter discusses the main reasons to develop campaign plans, the contents of a typical plan, and some notes on strategy and timing that often guide the planning process.

THE NEED FOR CAMPAIGN PLANS

Consultants who expect to deal with problems on the fly will likely find themselves wishing that they had planned ahead of time. Open-ended assignments become failed expectations; undefined schedules become wasted time. Campaigns entail details and deadlines, not to mention ever-changing circumstances. Without written plans, campaigns founder, and in competitive races they tend to fail. A campaign plan, it has been said, is meant to "bring order out of that chaos we call the democratic process" (Grey 1999, 95).

A campaign plan defines *what* is to be done, *when* it should be done, *who* should be doing it, and *what* will be needed to finish the job. Good plans divide responsibility, integrate work, and offer a step-by-step blueprint of the election. With agendas and timetables in hand, everyone on the campaign has a job to do. A plan might be flexible; it might change; it might even require fundamental revision at the campaign's midpoint; yet the campaign plan remains a basic management tool for coordinating a diverse, concurrent, mutually dependent series of tasks.

Thoughtful campaign plans minimize uncertainty. A plan helps keep the candidate fixed on strategy, smoothing the impact of opposition attacks and tightening the focus on the endgame. As noted, the very existence of a campaign plan can go a long way toward assuaging the fears of an overly anxious candidate or staff. It is all too easy for volunteers and paid staffers to become fixated on day-to-day assaults that tempt the campaign team to get off message and reallocate resources away from mission-critical objectives. A campaign plan can help keep everyone on task and on schedule, or at least it can help maintain big-picture perspective on day-to-day volatility.

Uncertainty is minimized, in part, by weeding out redundancy. Establishing command authority and delegating staff responsibilities, a campaign plan can help conserve precious time and money. Canvassing the same neighborhood twice with the same flyer is a waste of resources. In some instances, duplication can be not just profligate but downright harmful. If more than one staff member is talking to reporters, conflicting messages might appear in the press, leaving the campaign in the embarrassing position of explaining what it was really trying to say. In a world where image tends to become substance, a confused campaign looks irresolute, perhaps too weak to govern.

Plans not only help guide internal campaign operations but also inspire confidence in potential supporters and the news media. The candidate starts to look like a winner—an invaluable attribute because one of the most difficult obstacles that a challenger has to overcome is public skepticism. People assume that incumbents are entrenched and that there is almost no point in supporting anyone crazy enough to buck the system. "Sure losers" are given scant attention by reporters and even less help from donors. A strong campaign plan leads influential people to see that the campaign is serious, that it will be conducted in an organized, efficient manner and will not waste resources or miss opportunities. The party faithful, prospective donors, and even media elites might start to think that there is a way to get to the front of the pack.

ELEMENTS OF A CAMPAIGN PLAN

The contours of a new-style campaign plan vary from candidate to candidate, campaign to campaign, and consultant to consultant. There is no single, step-by-step guide. Nevertheless, a core set of elements are addressed by serious campaign organizations. A strong plan lays out contextual information, voter summaries, strategies and tactics, as well as staffing and resource requirements. A brief listing illustrates some of the elements that typify a well-written plan.

District Profile. Campaigns must understand the district's geography, indus-try, housing patterns, community organizations, transportation infrastructure, and other fixed variables. This is the political terrain on which the candidate will maneuver. A campaign operation must chart the territory before the race begins. See Chapter Three.

Demographic Profile. Political professionals understand the close relationship between the characteristics of a voting population and electoral outcomes. For exam-ple, districts with a large number of union members tend to vote Democratic—and even a Republican candidate will have to pay attention to labor issues. A demographic profile sketches the characteristics of the voters, often including a narrative descrip-tion along with maps and summary tables. See Chapter Four.

Candidate and Opposition Profiles. Personal and professional qualifications are almost always highlighted in a campaign plan. Heavy emphasis is placed on a candidate's background, experience, committee posts, bill sponsorship, appoint-ments, and so on. The same goes for the opposition. As new-style campaigns have become increasingly "comparative," even "negative," it has become critical to research oneself and one's opponent. See Chapter Five.

Electoral History. One of the best ways to predict future voter behavior is to look at recent elections. The past truly is prologue. A ward that has voted Repub-lican in the past will likely vote Republican in the future. Even in the digital age, campaigns are tied to their geography—candidates are still expected to walk door to door—so it is useful to determine which parts of the district will be most recep-tive to the candidate's message. See Chapter Six.

Public Opinion. Campaigns have become increasingly reliant on polls. A sec-tion of the plan regarding public opinion might contain an overview of voter con-cerns and topics of interest to voters throughout the district. If a campaign expects to hire a pollster, some thought might be given to the types of information that will be sought—what sorts of questions should be asked and how the data should be used. See Chapter Seven.

General Strategy. Candidate positioning is a crucial part of any plan. The campaign must know where the candidate will appear on the political spectrum. A conservative candidate in a middle-of-the-road district might call attention to the moderate aspects of the campaign agenda. A liberal candidate might reword progressive issues in more conservative terms. Often, in an effort to clearly identify what the campaign is all about, a one-page rationale is in order, answering the question, Who will vote for this candidate, and why? See Chapter Eight.

Fund-Raising Plan. Strategies cost money to implement, and the money has to come from somewhere. This section discusses how the campaign war chest will be filled—who will give the money and when it can be expected to arrive. See Chapter Nine.

Communications Strategy. A strategic plan for campaign communications is commonly broken into subsections—one for each medium. There might be separate schedules for radio, television, and a campaign Web site. This section also lays out a strategy for news coverage—press events and meetings with editorial boards, for example. One-page summaries of the candidate's stand on all the expected issues of the race might be included, and a set of more detailed position papers with prepared questions and answers is often developed for rapid-response purposes. See Chapters Ten and Eleven.

Grassroots. Even as an increasing share of campaign spending is devoted to media outreach, campaigns continue traditional grassroots efforts, such as knocking on doors and putting up signs. Particularly important are "get-out-the-vote" drives, which professionals pronounce "G-O-T-V"—making sure that those who have committed themselves to voting for the candidate actually cast a ballot. See Chapter Twelve.

NOTES ON STRATEGY

In June 2002, a Democratic Senate staffer was walking Lafayette Park in Washington and discovered, sitting on ground, the Republican blueprint for the upcoming midterm elections. The strategy memorandum's author was none other than Karl Rove, senior adviser to President George Bush—the mastermind of Bush's victory in 2000 and later in 2004. The PowerPoint presentation, written for the Republican Party, reviewed the political context, outlined important demographic groups, mapped counterstrategies to the Democrats, and explained how GOP candidates should link their fortunes to George Bush. As recalled by one scholar, "The memorandum argued that the Republicans were the party of leadership and security, based on the events of 9/11" (Semiatin 2005, 87). As controversial as this document proved, given that it implied that the events of 9/11" could be used for political gain, it offered a glimpse of how top-end strategists weigh complex dynamics. Few doubted that the blueprint had merit.

At the same time, however, the memorandum seems to suggest that all GOP candidates in the 2002 midterm election should follow the same approach, that veering from this model would prove fatal. This is likely a mistake. According to Joseph Napolitan (1986), strategies must fit the candidates who use them.

Strategic plans often imply difficult choices. When the candidate is not comfortable with the plan, blunders tend to follow. A candidate who is disappointed with the plan can become hostile, second-guessing staff decisions. No campaign manager wants to hear the candidate ask, "Why am I doing this?" The ideal plan will be so well understood, so strongly documented, and so deeply ingrained in all campaign activities that the reason for every event will be obvious. The alternative is organizational chaos. "One of the worst things that can happen is to have a campaign go off in several different directions simultaneously" (1986, 27). If actions do not occur when and where they should, coordination is lost, resources are wasted, and the wrong message is sent.

Careful attention must be paid to message consistency. Throughout the race, a variety of messages may be put forth, but all must relate to a single core theme. Many campaigns have a message of the week. For each seven-day period, one aspect of the campaign theme will be hammered home—the expectation being that repetition helps the message break through. To avoid mixed messages, campaign managers insist that policy pronouncements not overlap. If, for instance, the campaign is interested in following a pro-environment track during a given week, all communications during this period should reinforce that theme, and nothing should be said regarding consumer protection. Later, if radio spots are aimed at consumer issues, the direct mailer should be sending the consumer protection letters just as the press secretary tries to get these same issues in the daily paper.

Careful media planning helps a campaign stay on message. One effective strategy is to get the campaign into the news and then use paid advertising to reinforce the news coverage. Before any candidate ran a paid ad touting the 1994 Republican Contract with America, GOP organizers ensured maximum attention on the airwaves. A massive event was held on the steps of the U.S. Capitol Building, with rows of GOP candidates pledging their allegiance to Republican principles. It was a show of unity and power. Live shots were beamed to local stations after news directors were consulted to find out what they wanted to air (Tron 1996, 50–52). In the weeks that followed, campaign advertisements bolstered the message of GOP unity planted in the minds of voters by a powerful news event.

Finally, successful campaigns try to think a few moves ahead, figuring out what the opposition will do and then developing options for dealing with the consequences. According to one strategist, "There's nothing more pleasing, from the point of view of a strategist, than to work against an incumbent who runs the same campaign again and again" (Shea and Brooks 1995, 24). Why? Because it is easy to predict what the opposition will do and far simpler to outmaneuver and disarm it. If the candidate's own record is vulnerable, then responses must be devised ahead of time. If there are weaknesses in some of the planned campaign promises, it is better to know what they are prior to the announcement. As consultant Mark Weaver suggests, the job of a campaign is "to predict the counter-attack and be ready—because it will come" (Shea and Brooks 1995, 29). Like chess, campaign politics is very much a game of predicting and defeating opposition tactics before they come into play. A campaign plan helps bring the future into view.

NOTES ON TIMING

The integration of tactical elements into a unified blueprint is difficult. The timing of each step often hangs on preceding steps. Fund-raising usually comes first, and voter contact might best proceed after the accumulation of survey data. Messages are most effective when they reinforce one another, so campaign ads should complement news coverage (and vice versa). The budgeting process must find a way to match income and outflow. Campaign literature should bear a strong resemblance to campaign signage, both of which are contingent on the general message of the campaign, which, in turn, depends on the strategic positioning of the candidate, which might not be known until after the opposition party has chosen its own candidate. The effort to assemble all the pieces into a consistent whole can be an organizational nightmare.

At the tactical level, some campaigns are urged to map their plans as a flow-chart. Starting with "about ten feet of butcher paper," operatives should attach colored sticky notes representing important events and functions (Shaw 2000, 350). Butcher paper and sticky notes are giving way to project management software—but the basic theory has not changed. Tasks must be divided into their constituent parts, arrayed one after the next, and organized so that everything can be completed by the time the election is held. Election Day being a hard-and-fast deadline, most political strategists think in reverse, starting with the last day of the campaign and moving toward the first. "For instance," it is suggested, "you know you will need to repair lawn signs the day after Halloween, so put that on a green Post-it above November 1. Lawn signs usually go up one month before the election, so put that up next" (Shaw 2000, 351). This sort of backward mapping ensures that campaigns will not run out of time at the end of the election cycle.

At the strategic level, some scholars see a three-stage evolution in voter attitudes: "cognition" (awareness of the candidate), "affect" (development of opinions about the candidate), and "evaluation" (the decision itself) (Salmore and Salmore 1989, 13–14). Political professionals think in terms of "name ID" (similar to "cognition"), "persuasion" (bringing people to believe in one's candidate), and "motivation" (getting them to go out and vote). For some voters, each phase follows the next in a matter of seconds. Strongly partisan voters know instantly who will get their votes and that they will, in fact, show up at the polls. For others, the process may take time as the candidates come to their awareness, as impressions are formed, and then as a decision is made—perhaps in the voting booth. Either way, campaign planners must know where the candidate stands at the outset of the campaign (Guzzetta 2002; Salmore and Salmore 1989).

Gordon Smith, an Oregon Republican, showed the value of name recognition in his U.S. Senate race when he flooded the television airwaves with ads early in his January 1996 special-election campaign, even though it temporarily depleted his treasury (Gruenwald 1995). Smith narrowly lost that race but won a bid for Oregon's other Senate seat a few months later, his name ID having been well established. In some campaigns, particularly those for lower-level posts, the first phase is not well achieved until late in the campaign—if at all. Consultants Ron Brown and Nello Giorgetti go so far as to suggest that

> for nine out of ten campaigns for local professional offices, the message is the candidate's name—repeated endlessly as election day draws near. It's more important to place the candidate's name before the voter, than a discussion of the office itself. (Brown and Giorgetti 1992, 51)

In high-profile races, however, where the candidates might already be well known, the shift from cognition to affect can begin early, thereby allowing a discussion of issues and other thematic messages.

Billboards, bumper stickers, and yard signs serve almost no function besides establishing name identification and perhaps party affiliation (if shown). There is some question as to whether the best approach is to get these materials out as early as possible—slowly building momentum as time goes by—or if a last-minute explosion will have greater impact (Shaw 2000, 120). In some jurisdictions, the choice is dictated by local ordinances regulating the number of days prior to an election that yard signs are allowable. In others, the fact that yard signs are vulnerable to late-campaign vandalism might force a decision to use billboards. In recent years, campaigns have refrained from using bumper stickers because they tend to become collectors' items, never entering the campaign at all.

Campaign themes occupy a prominent place at the planning roundtable as the candidate's strategic positioning is discussed and debated. Should the candidate be presented as a moderate, a liberal, or a right-wing conservative? Political professionals always want to control the positioning of the candidate. Political veteran Mary Matalin calls it "Cardinal rule 101 of politics: *Never let the other side define you*" (Matalin and Carville 1995, 72). When voters have no information about a candidate, they are susceptible to the first information that they hear. Research suggests that communications are most likely to be effective in the absence of "a nexus of mediating factors" (Whillock 1991, 9). In other words, people tend to first impressions, and voters pay more attention to messages that reflect their preexisting views (see also Diamond and Bates 1992). Sometimes the opposition is completely unknown and is therefore vulnerable. If the sponge is to be filled, the campaign wants to fill it. In fact, the corollary to cardinal rule 101 might well be, "Always define the opponent early."

Defining candidates requires money and media. Early money allows a campaign to attract more money, and, just as important, it lets the campaign get a jump on the opposition in the television air war. Timing is important because television is a limited commodity. Campaigns that fail to buy ad slots early see the best ones sold out from under them. Local affiliates can run out of choice pre–Election Day slots because the opposition has already bought up all available time.

End-of-the-campaign media runs are critical because campaigns are often won and lost during the final week. Scholarly evidence suggests that as much as 15 percent of the electorate makes its decision in the final few days of the campaign (Shea 1996b). Although 85 percent decides well ahead of Election Day, the undecided voters often determine the election. The final push is critical. When a consultant for Democrat Kathleen Brown's 1994 California gubernatorial campaign failed to keep any cash on hand for the standard end-of-the-cycle media blitz, a fellow professional was quoted as saying the consultant "should be tried for political malpractice" (Wallace 1994). The looming possibility that a campaign will run out of money terrifies campaign planners.

All are agreed that late-cycle ads are a good thing, but is this the only time for attack ads? Many challengers attack from the very beginning. Consultant Gary Nordlinger sees little choice: "When most challengers only have one-fourth the money that the incumbent has, he needs to concentrate on the sleeping giants" (Shea and Brooks 1995, 25). This, of course, means attacking early and attacking often. Other professionals suggest that a candidate's credibility must be established before the attack begins (Whillock 1991). Without the weight of a valid source behind it, charges may not stick—especially in today's political environment where charges and countercharges are commonplace. Incumbents must make a similar choice. The old rule was that a well-established incumbent should ignore challenger attacks. There is no point in giving them the dignity of a response. But after a series of elections in the 1980s, when several aloof incumbents went down to defeat, the conventional wisdom started to shift. Should incumbents sit idly by, knowing that the attack is coming? Perhaps "incumbents can no longer ignore attacks" (Shea and Brooks 1995, 25).

Whether attack ads work best at the beginning or at the end of a campaign cycle, the boundaries of that cycle are becoming blurred. Mail-in ballots and the loosening of absentee ballot rules change the timing of elections by allowing a larger number of people to vote early. Strategists must retime their tactics to fit the new environment. If Internet voting takes hold, the time frame of the cycle may be rendered even more vague, further complicating strategic plans.

CONCLUSION

Few battle plans survive their battles intact. Without perfect knowledge, mistakes will be made. "The best laid plans of mice and men," Robert Burns intoned, "gan aft agley"—that is, they "can go awry"—"and leave naught but grief and pain for promised joy." If a campaign plan is not premised on an accurate reading of the past, present, and future; of the candidate and the opponent; of the strengths and weaknesses of both campaign teams; and of the voting public, even the most detailed campaign plan will disappoint.

In 1991, those who planned George Bush Sr.'s reelection effort assumed—quite reasonably—that the economy would pick up, that there would be no opponent in the GOP primaries, that the White House and Bush's campaign organization would work cooperatively, and that the president would not have to hit the hustings in earnest until after the Republican Convention. Events unfolded differently. The economy continued to stagnate, conservative television commentator Pat Buchanan ran hard in the early primaries, coordination between the White House and the campaign operation was in constant disarray, and, because the president chose to govern instead of campaign, he fell so far behind Bill Clinton that recovery became all but impossible. The Bush campaign plan—thoughtful though it may have been—was doomed from the start.

Although this chapter has discussed general considerations used to devise campaign plans, a wise strategist knows that a plan is only as good as its assumptions and that assumptions can be terribly wrong. On one hand, the value of a campaign plan is that it keeps the organization focused in troubled times; on the other hand, however, sticking to a flawed plan extends the agony. Campaign strategists must decide when to cut the rope and when to hang on.

Part One

THE LAY OF THE LAND: UNDERSTANDING THE CAMPAIGN CONTEXT

Chapter Three

The Context of the Race

Reinhold Niebuhr, the American theologian, once wrote a prayer that cautioned against foolish thinking. Support groups of all description would later soften its meaning, but what is now called the "Serenity Prayer" was originally expressed in Old Testament prose. It read,

> God, give us grace to accept with serenity the things that cannot be changed, courage to change the things that should be changed, and the wisdom to distinguish between the two. (Sifton 1998)

The prayer was intended to focus the mind not on quietude but on stern wisdom—drawing attention to the rigors of differentiating the tractable from the intractable.

In a way, Niebuhr was describing an important part of political wisdom—the ability to look at a race, a district, or an opponent's popularity and then distinguish what can be changed from what cannot. The difference is not always clear. In some districts, the number of registered voters is something that cannot be modified, while in others, a strong voter registration drive can force a dramatic transformation in the eligible electorate. New-style politics begins with an understanding of campaign context. Political consultants talk about the "the landscape," "the environment," or "the political terrain." What office is in play? What do the demographics look like? Who else will be on the ballot? A discussion of strategy and tactics is meaningless until the context is understood—until the tractable elements are distinguished from the intractable.

The first part of this book deals specifically with campaign context. These are the things that, for the most part, cannot be changed. This chapter lists many of the basic features of a political terrain—the office being sought, incumbency status, multiplayer scenarios, election-year type, national trends, and candidates for other offices, geography, and other contextual issues. The next two chapters offer a detailed discussion of demographic and candidate profiles; this chapter begins with an elementary problem, understanding the electoral nature of the office sought.

THE OFFICE BEING SOUGHT

Successful mayors sometimes fail miserably when they run for Congress. Successful congressional representatives sometimes endure embarrassing defeats when they attempt to move over to the Senate. One reason for this phenomenon is simple: the large constituency may be different from the smaller districts inside it. The electorate of a city will not be the same as the congressional district in which it is situated. True enough. Another possibility is that voters have different expectations for a mayor, a member of Congress, and a senator. A loud tie and bombastic personality may be loved in local politicians and loathed in higher officials. The formality of an executive might seem pompous in a legislator. Many candidates have learned the hard way that the nature of the office sought affects the fundamentals of the campaign.

What the Voters Expect

In matters as basic as tone, body language, and personal style, distinctions make a difference. Voters might expect a Senate candidate to wear a dark suit but might regard prospective county commissioners in business attire as haughty. A judicial candidate will usually want to sound nonpartisan. Candidates for mayor will be required to know the details of local zoning laws and sewer problems; a candidate for the U.S. House of Representatives, standing before the very same audience, will be forgiven if he or she does not know the nuances of recent tax levies but will likely be expected to speak intelligently on issues of national importance—the federal budget, for example.

How does one discern what types of issues are best addressed in House, Senate, judicial, or mayoral campaigns? There are no clear guidelines. Campaigns look at the political history of the district, paying close attention to the themes of prior successful and unsuccessful candidates. They look at the issues that the current officeholder manages. Well-funded campaigns may commission surveys. When people say education is important, they might mean (1) that the state and local government, not federal bureaucrats, should invest more in schools; (2) that the federal government should offer better education funding; or (3) that there is enough money, but parents need to get involved. Matching the right issues to the wrong office can prove costly, as the campaign gets involved in matters that the electorate thinks inappropriate.

Voters seem to match issues to offices and offices to candidate qualities. Research in this area is not well developed, but, roughly speaking, candidates for executive posts are expected to have leadership skills and the ability to implement programs. Stephen Wayne, a distinguished scholar of presidential elections, conducted a survey to determine what voters most admired in presidents. The chief executive was expected to be "strong" and "decisive" and have the "ability to get things done" (1982, 192–95). Given the way both George W. Bush and John Kerry portrayed themselves during the 2004 election, it seems clear that this has not changed over the past two decades. One would expect to find similar attributes admired in gubernatorial and mayoral candidates, which also involve executive leadership. On the other hand, legislative candidates might need to form a close connection with the average voter. Different candidates have different styles (Fenno 1978), but legislative representation is generally expected to be constituent focused. Asked whether members of Congress should look after the needs of "their own district" or the "interest of the nation," a recent Harris survey found that respondents favored the former, 67 to 29 percent (Harris Interactive 2005).

A final element of voter expectation relates to formality of tone. In some districts, voters expect executive and judicial candidates to run serious, issue-based campaigns but allow legislative candidates free play to go on the attack. In other jurisdictions, all candidates, even prospective judges, can take the partisan offensive. Such expectations change over time. Traditional wisdom holds that candidates for the U.S. Senate should remain stately, but during his successful 1992 bid for the Senate, Russ Feingold ran a television spot featuring Elvis—or perhaps an Elvis impersonator—who had come out of hiding to lend his endorsement. Wisconsin voters gave Feingold a comfortable victory. Gubernatorial candidates should have executive stature, but in 1998 Minnesotans elected former professional wrestler Jesse "The Body" Ventura, whose television ads featured a seemingly naked Ventura as the model for Auguste Rodin's sculpture *The Thinker.*

Ventura used a body double—nudity is still taboo—but the conventions of candidate apparel have been changing. Not long ago, it was believed that candidates should wear business attire in public. They might doff their jackets at barbecues and ice-cream socials, but they should arrive wearing a suit. In some areas this advice still holds true, but in a time when even corporate executives endorse "casual Fridays," business attire tends to connote self-importance. Campaign ads and brochures today often show the candidate talking to citizens with a jacket casually draped over the shoulder. As more and more women have joined the ranks of the elected, bright colors have become acceptable, and during the 2000 presidential primary season much was made of Vice President Al Gore's decision to switch from dark blue pinstripes to friendlier earth tones. Of course, when a candidate—any candidate, mayoral or presidential—is photographed with sleeves rolled up, the intended meaning is obvious: it's time to get to work.

Media Relations

The office being sought affects not just voter expectations but also the candidate's relationship with the media. Successfully obtaining news coverage is one of a campaign's most important goals. In order to gain positive press, a strategist must understand what reporters expect from a candidate. To many voters, the line between local, state, and national problems are hazy, but to good reporters, they are fairly clear: federal candidates will be expected to have a grasp of national issues, state contestants should know about state issues, and local office seekers should understand community concerns.

Generally speaking, the higher the office, the greater the scrutiny. Candidates for top-tier offices are often surprised by the rigorous grilling that they receive from the news media. Candidates caught unprepared are tagged as incompetent or naive. In 2002, Democratic gubernatorial nominee Bill McBride, the challenger to Governor Jeb Bush in Florida, came close to pulling even during the last few weeks of the campaign. During a crucial debate late in the campaign, however, McBride could not provide an answer to moderator Tim Russert's repeated inquiries as to how he would fund his plan to reduce class size in Florida's public schools. With his vague response to the question, McBride suggested to voters his inexperience in dealing with such issues—issues, that, as governor, he would need to deal with regularly. Florida voters would retain Jeb Bush as their governor on Election Day (Semiatin 2005, 221). Incumbents are not immune. Some incumbents have been unlucky enough to be listed among *The Progressive* magazine's "Dimmest Bulbs in Congress." Local papers pick up such stories and run them in their political columns.

Scrutiny of professional and personal shortcomings also varies according to office, with the importance of an infraction increasing with power of an official. A reporter who finds dirt on a state legislative candidate might never report the discovery. Congressional candidates are held to a higher standard. The media hammered Wes Cooley, an Oregon congressman, in 1996 for making false statements on a voter guide. He had claimed to be a veteran of the Korean War when he never actually served in Korea. Cooley later explained, "I shouldn't even have said Korea. . . . I was in the Army. I was in the Special Forces. At that period of time, the Korean conflict was going on" (Egan 1996). The congressman was forced to step down. Previously, when running for a seat in the state senate, Cooley had apparently "moved a trailer into the district so he could qualify as a resident," although "neighbors said he never lived in the district" (Egan 1996). Cooley got away with a seeming untruth at one level of government—he served as a state senator until his election to Congress—but once in Washington, his past became news.

Ironically, the lesser scrutiny to which lower-level offices are held may allow for a greater number of unfair charges. Whereas attacks on House and Senate candidates are often checked for accuracy, charges against state and local candidates are rarely investigated. Reporters are overworked, underpaid, and have a great many demands on their time. They suggest that their job is to report the news, not to referee political fights (Dunn 1995, 117). Rather than track down every charge that a candidate makes against another, journalists concentrate on higher-level races. Since 1992, "ad watch" journalism—emphasizing the disclosure of inaccuracies (Ansolabehere and Iyengar 1995)—has come into its own. Presidential, Senate, and in many instances congressional candidates can expect to see their commercials, speeches, and debate remarks reviewed for content while many state and local candidates are effectively held to a lower standard of accuracy (see, for example, "Ad Watch" at Washington Post OnLine). The task of keeping politicians honest is left to the candidates and their campaigns.

Finally, incumbents generally receive newspaper endorsements and new research suggests these endorsements have an impact on the election outcome. As noted by Paul Herrnson, "In 2002 roughly 85 percent of all incumbents in major-party contested races benefited from [newspaper endorsements]. It improved their electoral performance by roughly 5 points over incumbents who did not enjoy such positive relations with the fourth estate" (2004, 244).

Overall Interest in the Campaign

Political novices sometimes become frustrated that their campaigns rarely make the news—and, in fact, that it may be of little interest to most voters. This is a natural phenomenon. Candidates, party activists, volunteers, and even some professional consultants become deeply involved in their campaigns and start to believe that others should be as well, yet most voters prefer to think about their spouses, children, bills, vacations, hobbies, cars, and jobs. Elections are of marginal concern.

The National Election Studies survey questions roughly 1,600 people about their overall interest in campaigns. A few things stand out. First, the number of truly concerned, interested citizens is low—about 25 percent. But the number is likely much lower because of a "social desirability bias." That is, many respondents probably exaggerate their interest in campaigns because "good citizens" are *engaged* citizens, and they want to seen as informed about public affairs. Even so, the numbers of those ranked as very concerned is rather low. Second, it seems that those "very interested" has declined throughout the years. Finally, the peaks and valleys suggest significantly greater interest in presidential election years than during off-year elections.

Not all offices are ignored equally. There is a hierarchy of interest, starting at the top of the ballot with presidential races and dropping to Senate and House races—with the rest falling a distance below, right down to judicial posts and other offices (e.g., coroner) that few voters care about. One former elected appellate judge dismisses television as a means of communicating with voters: "You can . . . forget about any broadcast coverage of your campaign as a news event. . . . News divisions are operated as entertainment enterprises, and serious news is often not entertaining" (Grey 1999, 170). Statewide and large-city mayoral races receive a good deal of coverage, but most congressional campaigns are given short shrift. Absent a controversy, a colorful candidate, or a cliff-hanger, the general rule is that city council, county legislative, state legislative, and judicial races will be ignored. There are opportunities for coverage—creativity counts—but no guarantees.

The problem of voter inattention for lower-level candidates can be seen in both the number of votes and the amount of money that go to "down-ballot" races. Voters at the polls almost always select a candidate for president, governor, and congressional representative, but many leave the ballot blank for county commissioner. Lower-level offices can suffer more than a 40 percent drop-off from the top of the ballot. The same is true in political fund-raising. Individuals and organizations give money to candidates partly because they are aware of the campaign, maybe even excited by it. Presidents raise millions of dollars; county commissioners raise thousands. If few people are familiar with the race, few contribute. Candidates sometimes feel that they are caught in a vicious cycle: without attention, they cannot get money, and without money, they cannot get attention—and as a result, many voters fail to take the time to look for the candidate's name at the bottom of the ballot.

INCUMBENCY STATUS

No other contextual element has a greater bearing on the outcome of the election than incumbency status. There are three basic types of election: uncontested, contested incumbency, and open seat. An uncontested race in which the incumbent has no challenger is obviously the most predictable since there is literally no opposition and the winner is a forgone conclusion. Races in which the incumbent *is* contested usually go to the current officeholder because, as much as people say they want to "throw the bums out," they usually return their own representatives to office. Most uncertain is an open-seat election. Two well-qualified newcomers running against one another can make for exciting political drama. In rare instances, incumbents are pitted against one another after their districts are merged. In 2002, Democratic incumbent congressman Tom Sawyer was faced with a difficult primary battle when his Akron-area district was merged with another district that included Youngstown, Ohio. While the two areas were similar in that both were industrial cities located in the rust belt, the political environment of each district differed greatly. Sawyer discovered that his main competition would be a young state senator from the Youngstown area, Tim Ryan. Ryan built a large and effective grassroots network, and with his knowledge of Youngstown area politics, he was able to connect with voters in a way that Sawyer could neither appreciate nor accomplish. As a result, Sawyer, the incumbent, lost his hold on the district to challenger Tim Ryan (Beiler 2002).

Despite occasional twists of fate, incumbency offers candidates a tremendously valuable resource. Officeholders enjoy higher early name recognition than challengers, deeper relations with the news media, more experienced staff, better finances, a broader base of volunteers, and stronger connections with parties and interest groups. Incumbents have usually cultivated their relationship with the electorate through publicly financed mailings, town hall meetings, and scores of receptions and dinners. Furthermore, incumbents, by definition, have at least minimal appeal—they were already elected at least once. Even in the Republican sweep of 1994, renowned for the number of sitting members it pushed out of office, fully 90 percent of incumbents were retained. Since 1998, an average of 97 percent of House incumbents running for reelection have won (Opensecrets.org 2005). These percentages are lower for executive posts, but they remain above the two-thirds mark for mayors and governors.

If an incumbent is scandal free and makes no great mistake, the challenger's odds are slim. Most nonincumbents have comparatively little name recognition. Political action committees and major donors are hesitant to back a challenger for fear of antagonizing the incumbent—the person most likely to be making policy after the election. According to congressional election scholar Paul Herrnson, "The typical House incumbent involved in a two-party contested race raised just under $977,000 in cash and party coordinated expenditures in 2002, which is 3.75 times more than the sum raised by the typical House challenger" (2004, 160). An incumbent, whose official position carries intrinsic power, can get news releases printed by local papers, while challengers might not get any reporter to cover their announcement speeches. Incumbents nearly always attract more attention and a bigger crowd.

There are exceptions to the rule. Generally speaking, the higher the profile of the race, the weaker the advantage for the incumbent. Presidents, governors, and U.S. senators benefit from better media coverage, especially in the early periods of the race, but these carefully watched races offer significant media coverage to the challenger as well. Often the challenger is a significant player in his or her own right. When Republican John Thune challenged the well-known Senate minority leader Tom Daschle in 2004, Thune was already a big name in South Dakota politics. A former three-term member of the U.S. House of Representatives, Thune narrowly lost a bid for Senate in 2002 against Democrat Tim Johnson. Given the high profile of the 2004 race, the campaign was closely followed by the national media, and given Thune's career in the House and his 2002 Senate campaign, coverage proved roughly equal for each. Thune narrowly defeated Daschle, stunning the political establishment in North Dakota and in Washington, D.C.

Challengers have a few unique tools at their disposal. Many incumbents run the same campaign time after time—a warning sign, according to polling consultant Neil Newhouse, of "incumbentitis," whereby incumbents look on a past successful campaign as the model for all future campaigns (Shea and Brooks 1995, 24). Moreover, incumbents have a record to defend, while a political novice might have a clean slate—sometimes an enviable possession. Says one columnist, "The most difficult opponent is somebody who's never run for anything" (Persinos 1994, 22). Likewise, although it has traditionally been perceived as undignified for an elected official to go hard on the offensive, challengers have rarely never had much to lose. This rule may be changing—incumbents are going on the attack much more often than they did in the 1980s—but the problem of early attacks can still be dicey. To ignore challengers is to refuse them recognition; to attack challengers is to add credence to their candidacy. As noted by campaign commentator Ronald Faucheux, "An incumbent under attack. . .but still running ahead in the polls, may not have the luxury of being able to ignore the substance of the attacks" (2002, 26). Few political stories get more coverage than an underdog's catching up to an incumbent who everyone thought would win. In fact, a challenger who persuades reporters of the campaign's viability is laying the basis for a media-ready Horatio Alger story.

Although open-seat elections tend to offer a more even footing than those in which the incumbent wins, they present their own unique challenges. In the recent past, many open seats were considered noncompetitive; the partisan predisposition of the districts was lopsided, giving the candidate of the dominant party a distinct advantage. Today, however, with the decline of party identification (at least from 1950 levels), many open seats are considered toss-ups. Ohio's Second Congressional District, located in the southern region of the state, powerfully illustrated this point in 2005. Republican Jean Schmidt faced an unexpectedly strong challenge from Democrat Paul L. Hackett in an August special election—even though the district was considered solidly Republican. Schmidt hung on for a victory, but the race proved exceedingly close, surprising many in Ohio and operatives across the nation.

MULTIPLAYER SCENARIOS

Elections are commonly imagined as head-to-head battles, but many races involve more than two major players. Many elections have multicandidate fields, and some even have outside interests playing a large role.

Generally speaking, there are two types of multicandidate fields: (1) party primaries and (2) general elections containing third-party, independent, and write-in candidates. Both are difficult to strategize. In primaries, party members are running against one another, and it is common to see rancorous family infighting. Three, four, five, or more candidates might run in a primary, and figuring out how the vote will swing often becomes a matter of speculation and argumentation. Some primaries, particularly in the South, have a two-step process. If a candidate garners more than 50 percent, the election is won; if, however, no candidate crosses the 50 percent mark, then the top vote getters are forced into a two-way runoff. In Louisiana all candidates run in one election regardless of party. And in some jurisdictions, a handful of "at-large" seats will go to the top vote getters: five candidates might vie for three seats, and the three candidates with the largest number of votes win. At-large races, like runoffs and all other types of contested elections, require a good deal of planning and forethought in order to win.

The strategic problems of primaries are creeping into general election campaigns. With the decline in party identification, voters are beginning to see greater numbers of multicandidate general elections. Billionaire Ross Perot, a populist fiscal conservative, added strategic complexity to the campaigns of Bill Clinton and George Bush, which were forced to determine which aspect of the Perot candidacy had greater pull: (1) Perot's folksy call for reform, which would appeal to Clinton voters, or (2) his demand for deficit reduction, which would appeal to Bush voters. Neither campaign knew for sure. Perhaps the most dramatic example of a third-party candidacy was Jesse Ventura's Reform Party triumph in Minnesota. The Democratic candidate had suffered through a bitter primary campaign; the Republican candidate was a former Democrat who had yet to establish a firm GOP base. With the major-party candidates busy attacking one another, Ventura ran up the middle and won the election.

Ventura's victory was anomalous. Third-party candidates rarely win, but they often make a difference. They can erode a major-party candidate's base of support, undercut the intended message, and siphon off volunteers. Third-party candidates do not affect incumbents and challengers equally. According to Herrnson, "House members who must defeat both a major-party opponent and significant additional opposition average almost 10 percent fewer votes than those who did not" (2004, 242). One reason for this disparity is that minor-party candidates often join the race because they are dissatisfied with the incumbent. It is no accident that Ventura's win came at the expense of two well-known Minnesota officeholders. That was precisely the point of his campaign.

An ongoing challenge to major-party campaigns in the first decade of the new millennium has been the introduction of interest groups as outside forces. Federal campaign law permits noncandidate organizations to run ads promoting or criticizing candidates for most but not all of the campaign season (see Chapter Nine). One study notes that in the 2002 midterm election, about 42 percent of incumbent-versus-challenger races saw significant money from outside groups (Herrnson 2004, 245). A prominent campaign finance watchdog organization warned, "In advance of the 2004 elections, an untold number of advocacy groups will be spending millions of dollars in a way that will influence the vote on Election Day. They will be running ads on TV and radio stations in your area, sending glossy flyers and pamphlets to your mailbox, calling you at home, and more." It was a solid prediction. In that election, these organizations spent a whopping $607 million (Center for Responsive Politics, 2005).

Outside help, though, is not always helpful. The battle over Utah's Second Congressional District in 1998 saw heavy spending by a group interested in term limits. Incumbent Merrill Cook, an independent turned Republican, faced Democrat Lily Eskelsen, considered by many a strong contender for Cook's seat. Eskelsen wanted to make the election a referendum on Cook's record, touting education and other issues where Eskelsen seemed to have the advantage. The difficulty, however, was that Americans for Limited Terms put $380,000 into a broad-based, anti-Cook ad campaign (Goodliffe 2000, 171). One observer noted that "while the efforts of the parties largely neutralized each other, the term-limits campaign significantly increased the negativity of the campaign, which ultimately reflected poorly on Lily Eskelsen, whom they were supporting" (Goodliffe 2000, 171).

THE ELECTION YEAR

Campaign professionals talk about three different kinds of campaign year: on, off, and odd. An on-year election occurs when there are presidential candidates on the ballot (e.g., 2004, 2008, and 2012). Off-year elections also occur every four years, but the off years are so called because there is no presidential contest (e.g., 2002, 2006, and 2010). Finally, odd-year elections occur in odd-numbered years (e.g., 2003, 2005, and 2007). There are neither presidential nor congressional elections in odd years except for occasional "special" elections held to fill a prematurely vacated House or Senate seat.

The type of election year is important to campaign planning because the number of people going to the polls varies significantly. Turnout is almost always highest during on years because of the attention given presidential campaigns. In addition, the entire House of Representatives, one-third of the Senate, most state legislators, and many governors are elected during on years. Generally speaking, off years will have the next highest turnout. Although the president is not on the ballot, House, Senate, and statewide races boost public interest and send people to the polls. Almost all states reserve odd years for municipal and judicial offices. Without high-profile campaigns, few people go to the polls.

Special elections also suffer diminished turnout. They are often held on short notice when an office suddenly becomes vacant, usually because of a resignation or death. In March 2005, Doris Matsui, a California Democrat, succeeded her late husband in Congress by winning his vacant House seat. Often, as in Matsui's case, there is less interest in politics during these times, and turnout is generally low. Propelled to the winner's circle by her name recognition and her husband's political connections, she won the low-turnout election handily with 71 percent of the vote (Yamamura 2005).

Political scientists have noted a phenomenon they call "surge and decline." In most midterm congressional elections in the past 100 years, the president's party has lost seats. The election of 1990 provides a clear illustration. It took place just two years after George Bush Sr.'s impressive victory in the 1988 presidential election. The months leading up to the 1990 midterm, however, had public opinion surveys indicating that voters were fed up with "business as usual" in Washington. Because Democrats controlled both houses of Congress, one might have expected the Republicans to take over or, at the very least, to pick up a few seats. As it happened, Democrats gained 17 districts in the House and a state in the Senate. While idiosyncratic factors clearly contributed to the electoral outcome, 1990 was consistent with a long-standing trend. On average, the president's party will lose almost 19 seats in the first midterm election of the president's term (Abramson, Aldrich, and Rohde 1999, 228). In 1994, two years after the election of President Bill Clinton, Democrats braced for the worst—and the results were catastrophic. Losing 52 seats in the House and eight in the Senate, Democrats surrendered legislative control to the Republican victors.

Social scholars have struggled to find the causes of the surge-and-decline phenomenon, but no complete answer has emerged. One possibility is that on-year and off-year elections attract different groups of voters. Many people who vote in presidential elections do not cast ballots in the off year. These people, generally less partisan and less ideological, are responsible for a president's success as well as an influx of congressional officeholders of the president's party. During off-year elections, however, the pool of voters shrinks as casual voters drop out. Another possibility is that voters lose their initial excitement for the president. As time goes by, voters become increasingly disillusioned and then cast a ballot for congressional candidates of the other party. A third conjecture is that the type of candidate changes between the two elections. Aggressive candidates, angry with the president, run with steadfast determination, along with money from interest groups opposed to the new administration's policies.

A complete understanding of this phenomenon is elusive, and aberrations make prediction difficult. In 1998, for example, Democrats faced a perilous situation. Historically, the third midterm after a president is elected is especially risky for members of the president's party. In 1986, six years after President Ronald

Reagan's election, the GOP had suffered a net loss of eight Senate seats and consequently ceded control of the Senate to insurgent Democrats. In 1974, in the months approaching what would have been President Richard Nixon's sixth year (had he remained in office), the Republican Party had suffered dramatic losses in the House, losing 43 seats. Prior to the 1998 elections, the president's party could expect to lose an average of nearly 38 House seats (Abramson et al. 1999, 228). Six years after Clinton won the presidency, in the middle of Clinton's impeachment crisis, one might have thought the Democrats would lose badly. Yet the outcome was quite different: House Democrats actually picked up five seats, putting the party within striking distance of majority rule. Another anomaly came in 2002, when the Republicans picked up a several seats. Many speculate that the aftermath of the terrorist attacks on September 11, 2001, disrupted the surge-and-decline process. That is, the party in power was not likely to lose seats in this difficult time, as voters find stability comforting: "The pro-Republican atmosphere in 2002 helped the GOP buck the trend in which the president's party loses seats in mid-term elections" (Herrnson 2004, 245).

NATIONAL TRENDS

Saying that "all politics is local," Tip O'Neill drew attention to the fact that Americans care little about national and international concerns on Election Day, yet even local politics cannot escape national trends, moods, and obsessions. Each year, the national media highlight some concerns and downplay others, as popular perceptions of the "crime issue" show. One legal historian has noted, "Throughout the country, newspapers, movies, and TV spread the word about crime and violence—a misleading word, perhaps, but a powerful one. Even people who live in quiet suburban enclaves, or rural backwaters, are aware of what they consider the crime problem" (Friedman 1993, 452). From a crass, strategic point of view, many candidates find that the difference between perception and reality has little meaning. People believe that crime is rampant, so the discussion of lawless behavior has a definite starting point. Hence, in 1994, Republican George Pataki defeated New York's three-term governor, Mario Cuomo, who had repeatedly vetoed the death penalty, by stressing a tough-on-crime platform. In the 2000 campaign, even as candidates claimed support for better safeguards in capital punishment cases, most still supported the death penalty, mirroring the nation as a whole.

Like crime, economic trends and presidential popularity are powerful political tides. In the early 1970s, election scholar Edward Tufte found that 98 percent of the variability of congressional elections could be explained by these two factors (1975). Although the argument was found to be a bit overstated and although scholars have continued to refine the variables, Tufte's point is well taken: voters reward or punish candidates for events that are largely beyond their control.

But events are subject to interpretation. A Republican may believe that an economic recovery is a product of George W. Bush's tax cut policies, or a Democrat may conclude that crime is on the decline and therefore should not be featured so prominently on the national agenda. Campaign professionals understand that public perceptions can be altered—for better or worse—but only if prior beliefs are taken into account. Whoever might be responsible for economic recovery and whatever may be the statistical reality of criminal behavior in America, crime and the economy are things that voters can feel in their bones. A campaign that wants to bring people closer to the "truth" must begin with what voters believe, not what they ought to believe.

Some of the most significant national trends are set into motion by tragic events, crisis situations, and wars. Strength, foreign policy experience, and military prowess were key candidate qualifications following September 11, 2001, as one might expect. The Democrats attempted to combat long-standing perceptions that the GOP is tougher on security issues by nominating a Vietnam War hero, John Kerry, for president. In the wake of a series of natural disasters in the fall of 2005, namely, Hurricanes Katrina and Rita, which devastated New Orleans and much of the Gulf coast, the mood of the electorate seemed to shift to simple administrative competence. Rebuilding that part of the country would prove expensive, and voters were not eager to have their tax money wasted. The national trend seemed to be that big spending was out, and competent management was in.

CANDIDATES FOR OTHER OFFICES

Most people believe that presidents can help elect their friends down the ballot. The belief in "coattails" is deeply ingrained in American electoral politics. Most observers assume that down-ballot candidates can benefit from the popularity of other candidates of the same party higher up the ticket. The popularity of one candidate, it is assumed, will trickle down to others. In 1980, for example, a large class of Republicans was swept into office with Ronald Reagan. Many argue that Republicans won thanks to Reagan's mass appeal.

As logical as the coattails theory may appear, it is hard to find direct supporting evidence. Leading election scholar Gary Jacobson suggests that "national issues such as the state of the economy or the performance of the president may influence some voters some of the time . . . but for the most part the congressional choice is determined by evaluations of candidates as individuals" (2004, 164). Jacobson's "strategic politician" theory assumes that aspiring politicians want to win; defeat is anathema. As such, smart candidates pay close attention to early polling data, particularly as the information relates to fellow party members. When no member of their party is popular, strategic politicians decide to sit the race out. The party nomination is left to lesser candidates, who, with poor qualifications, scant finances, and minimal name recognition, lose the election. Years later, when it appears that others in the party are once again popular, strategic politicians enter the race. Because they are well qualified and adequately financed, they win. Under this theory, coattails have little effect.

The strategic candidate process was at work in the fall of 2005. Because of lingering difficulties in Iraq, perceived incompetence in the response to Hurricane Katrina, sky-high gas prices, and the indictment of a top White House aide, George

Bush's popularity plummeted to the lowest point of his presidency—well below 40 percent. Some mighty qualified Democrats, waiting on the sidelines until this point, started gearing up for 2006. Said the Campaign Finance Institute, "Our analysis . . . suggests that the Democrats are starting more rapidly than two years ago, and that all major party challengers—but especially Democrats—are doing particularly well" (2005).

A point of clarification: to say that coattails have no direct effect is not to argue that they are inconsequential. The mere perception that coattails exist may bring strong down-ballot contenders into the race when more prominent candidates lead the way. Better candidates bring increased financial support and media coverage. If others believe that a candidate will get a significant boost from higher-ups on the ticket, they will be more likely to lend a hand. Thus, in some ways, the coattails theory may be self-fulfilling: because people believe that a candidate will win, they jump on board; and the more who jump on board, the greater the likelihood of success.

Campaigns can affect one another without a top-down relationship. As the 2000 campaign got under way, many speculated that Vice President Al Gore, who was running for president, and First Lady Hillary Rodham Clinton, who was running for Senate in New York, would draw from the same group of donors. Fund-raising can be a zero-sum game. At the local level, consultants might find that a particularly "hot" race in a nearby county is siphoning off financial supporters and filling up scarce newspaper space. Ballot initiatives can also affect candidates. In 2004, a network of conservative organizations and activists led by President George W. Bush's chief political strategist Karl Rove placed initiatives in front of voters in 11 states that sought to make gay marriage unconstitutional. In putting the highly charged issue in front of voters, Rove hoped to increase turnout among the white evangelical conservative bloc of the Republican Party and thus corral more votes for his boss, George Bush. The plan appears to have worked, as states approved the anti-gay marriage initiatives and conservative evangelicals turned out in large numbers.

GEOGRAPHY

The geography of a district is important for several reasons. Campaign activities are molded by the physical characteristics of the district. Door-to-door projects are possible for the state senate seats encompassing San Francisco's east side, and they are more cost efficient than radio and television advertising. Yet in some downtown areas, a campaign may find problems with this type of electioneering because high-rise apartments often forbid entry to nonresidents. Geography helps determine campaign tactics.

Among the most important matters are a district's size, density, and location. While a candidate for Senate in Rhode Island has about 1 million people compacted into a 1,000-square-mile area, a candidate in North Dakota has about 640,000 people spread across nearly 71,000 square miles. Each state demands its own sort of campaign. Some regions are particularly difficult to work.

In a 2000 Illinois congressional race, Mark Kirk was running for an open seat representing the Tenth District, which encapsulates a chunk of suburban Chicago. Because of the geography of the district, Kirk's campaign knew that ads on broadcast television stations would be less effective than ads on cable and radio coordinated with direct mail. Kirk's campaign used the latter and kept the plan to advertise on broadcast television low on the priority list until late in the campaign so that spots would be purchased only with campaign funds that had not been earmarked for anything else (Blakely 2001).

The geographic distribution of the district may dictate a candidate's activities. The layout of the district might define travel patterns, which may, in turn, dictate the range of viable campaign activities. Some districts allow a candidate to drive from one side to the other with ease, but other districts may demand hours on the road or even frequent plane trips. High mountains, thick forests, or wide bodies of water split some districts. Some have urban density at their center, making the placement of campaign headquarters an obvious decision; others are so spread out that careful calculations must be made, and perhaps two or three headquarters are needed to cover the district adequately.

OTHER CONTEXTUAL ISSUES

Any attempt to detail all the things that a campaign must accept as given would fill volumes. In the following chapters, additional elements are carefully examined: district demographics along with candidate and opposition profiles. For now, a few miscellaneous contextual features are briefly touched on.

Community Organizations

Many districts have strong organizational traditions, boasting a local union, a chamber of commerce, a Rotary Club, and other such organizations. Politically active groups might provide endorsements and contributions, but the importance of an organization should not be measured solely on its explicitly political nature. Nonpolitical groups are often the center of word-of-mouth communication. In some areas, for example, volunteer fire departments loom large, both in size and in stature, and while these organizations are officially nonpartisan, campaigns and elections are a constant topic of conversation.

Elected Officials

Local elected officials can help a campaign attract media attention, contributors, and volunteers, and they can make endorsements as well as introductions to other prominent members of the community. In most states, elected officials can transfer campaign funds to other candidates. That said, rivalries often divide political communities from within, and a candidate who inadvertently lines up on the wrong side of a feud can cause irreparable damage to his or her campaign.

Political Heroes and Villains

Past and present politicians linger in the minds of voters. A political hero can be a powerful electoral force, offering endorsements, organizational assistance, and perhaps a shaving of advice. Not all past politicians are viewed favorably, however. Some depart public life on a bad note. Endorsements and pictures associating a candidate with a political villain can prove harmful. Complicating matters, endorsers do not always share their checkered pasts willingly. Many campaigns have been lured into believing that an endorsement will help, only to discover the full extent of the public's wrath.

Social and Political Customs

Communities often have unique social and political customs. In some districts, yard signs are welcome. In others, they are considered a form of litter. A city might accept the use of mild profanity on the stump, while neighboring suburbs do not. Are political discussions allowed in church? It depends on the community. Is it polite to call people by their first name? Perhaps, but it is best to find out ahead of time. The rules can get complicated. In some locales, there are Democratic taverns and Republican cocktail lounges—and out-of-town guests are often expected to stay at hotels with a traditional connection to the appropriate party.

Parties and Bosses

Local parties vary in the degree of assistance that they give candidates. In some areas aggressive party organizations are eager to assist aspirants to public office, perhaps offering endorsements during the primary season, while in others they are no help at all. Where party organizations are strong, it is common to find a powerful leader at the helm. Often it is the chair, though sometimes an influential veteran is really in charge—and sometimes it is an operative from the neighboring county machine. In a sense, helpful parties and powerful leaders are inextricably linked. Candidates at all levels view local party bosses as a mixed blessing. On the one hand, they can be pivotal players, leveraging money and volunteers as no one else can; on the other hand, the party gatekeepers can become difficult to work with. In New Hampshire, a Republican presidential candidate who wants to call on experienced volunteers must first "enlist a poobah, a warlord, a New Hampshire potentate," with accompanying political machinations reminiscent of "the old Kremlin and the Soviet politburo" (Ferguson 1996, 44). This sort of power structure can be found, in varying degrees, across the United States.

Local History

Communities are proud of their heritage. Understanding what a population has endured, recently or in the distant past, can yield valuable insight to an electorate. Natural disasters, social and political turmoil, and even high school sporting events can be seen in hindsight as momentous occasions. Team songs, former mascots, and great players of the past are critical bits of knowledge. Again, for most people, politics is only a small part of life. A congressional district encompasses a wide variety of communities, and their traditions form a complex mosaic. In many ways, to know this heritage is to know the district.

Tourism and Recreation

Tourism and recreation are important. At one level, ski resorts and stadiums are often large employers, but also knowing what voters do in their spare time helps a candidate develop a connection with voters. A candidate in northwestern Pennsylvania who knows little about waterfowl might want to go on a hunting trip. A consultant arriving in Houston who cannot name a few Clint Black songs should tune into a country station. In campaigns, little things can make a big difference.

CONCLUSION

This chapter suggests the importance of contextual information in new-style campaigning. Campaigns are about strategy, but they are also about the terrain on which the strategy operates: a party boss who will not budge, a district so large that the candidate has trouble keeping to a schedule, a national economic trend over which the campaign has no control but under which the campaign must labor, poor candidates at the top of the ticket, third-party spoilers, and an opponent who enjoys the benefits of incumbency. Strategists who cannot accept "the things that cannot be changed" find themselves at a disadvantage. In many ways, the difference between amateurs and professionals in the world of campaigns is measured by the degree to which they come to a realistic understanding of the district and then find a way to work within intractable circumstances.

Chapter Four

Demographic Research: The Theory of Aggregate Inference

Every election is full of twists and turns, and no election can be mapped out perfectly—but a smart campaign does its research ahead of time. For the Bush 2004 campaign team, the marketing plan began two years before the polls opened. And Bush's campaign manager, Ken Mehlman, was rightly proud of his accomplishment:

> "We did what Visa did," Mr. Mehlman said. "We acquired a lot of consumer data. What magazine do you subscribe to? Do you own a gun? How often do the folks go to church? Where do you send your kids to school? Are you married?
>
> Based on that, we were able to develop an exact kind of consumer model that corporate America does every day to predict how people vote—not based on where they live but how they live," he said. "That was critically important to our success." (Nagourney 2004, A23)

Prospective Bush voters were different from their counterparts on the Kerry side, not just in ideology but in lifestyle. Mehlman notes that "supporters of Mr. Kerry had a preference for Volvos over Lincolns, and yoga over guns" (Nagourney 2004, A23). "Because our demographic studies and analysis showed us that a lot of young families get information not at the 7 o'clock news but at the 7 o'clock workout before they got home," the Bush campaign began running ads, not only on broadcast television, but also on the in-house networks broadcasting in physical fitness centers (2004, A23).

Mehlman's strategy was the logical extension of new-style demographics. To formulate a winning strategy, consultants must know what makes a district tick, and part of the process is understanding a district's demographic profile—its mix of race, ethnicity, consumer preferences, and a range of other defining attributes. Political demographers seek to understand a vast array of characteristics that might affect the electoral outcome. This chapter is designed to acquaint the reader with the importance of demographic understanding, the logic of demographic inference, the basics of demographic profiling, and the process by which campaigns pull the data together into a stable hub for strategic planning and implementation. The Bush campaign relied heavily on demographics; this chapter shows why.

DEMOGRAPHICS AS A CAMPAIGN TOOL

Demographic research is different from opinion polling. With a districtwide poll, for example, reasonably accurate assessments can be made about the overall population. Polling is expensive, so perhaps a sample of only 550 people in a 125,000-person district will be contacted—meaning that the poll will miss some of the nuances of the district. Consultant Wayne Johnson learned early in his career that polling is not enough:

> From the first surveys we learned things like: 62 percent of voters favor taxing the wealthy. So we would send mailings to all voters telling them that the wealthy need to pay more taxes. The problem was that the positive data (the majority position) was as likely to be a lukewarm opinion as a strongly held opinion. In this case, the wealthy mail recipient was far more likely to react than the middle income person receiving the same mailing. We soon found it was possible to mail on a 70 percent plus issue and still lose by a landslide. (1992, 51)

Voter-by-voter income assessments might have identified the people who would be offended by a class-based message, and a smart campaign would remove wealthy households from the mailing. But there are more efficient ways to reach approximately the same result.

Campaign organizations often combine voter opinion data with demographic research. Instead of simply using the issue of greatest concern for the greatest number, survey results are compared with demographic information to refine the analysis. No longer does the campaign try to determine what all the voters want; rather, it focuses on what particular neighborhoods or constituency groups desire, enabling a campaign to target its message much more precisely.

The approach is time-tested. When Mario Cuomo ran his first campaign for governor of New York in 1982, early surveys found him especially popular among voters of Italian descent. Operatives throughout the state were instructed to spur turnout in Italian American communities. On Election Day, they were told to call Democrats; and when this list was exhausted, they simply called voters with Italian surnames. Cuomo won. Likewise, Loretta Sanchez, running a congressional campaign in Orange County, California, took advantage of the ethnic transformation of this once-conservative, once-Anglo district, which over the years had become 50 percent Hispanic. The winning campaign team has written, "Orange County's changing demographics worked in favor of Loretta Sanchez' candidacy. In the spring of 1996, voter registration favored the Democratic Party by 46% to 40%. The appeal of a Latina businesswoman whose platform addressed the needs of working families struck a resonant chord with voters" (Wachob and Kennedy 2000, 102; see also Burton and Shea 2003, 89–111).

Attention to the Hispanic vote, a fast-growing segment of the U.S. population, is greatly increasing. As one measure of this phenomenon, both major party nominees in the 2000 presidential race used Spanish in their campaigns. Al Gore proclaimed, "Si se puede!" (Yes, we can!),'' and George W. Bush ran a television ad touting the governor as "un hombre de familia" (a family man) (Milbank 2000). The reason for growing attention to the Hispanic community lay in the changing demographics of the United States. While the Hispanic population makes up only 14 percent of the electorate, in the early years of the new millennium they constituted half the nation's population growth, much of it in key political states such as California, Texas, New York, Illinois, and Florida.

THE LOGIC OF DEMOGRAPHIC RESEARCH

The goal of new-style campaigning is to target the right voters. In districts the size of a neighborhood, some candidates recognize each voter and know whom to target by sheer instinct. A larger district presents a more onerous task. Getting to know the interests of persuadable voters in a spreading district requires networks of operatives and activists who know the voters personally. This is how the old urban machines worked. A candidate who did not know every single voter went through the party boss, and the party boss, in turn, used his connections to reach out to neighborhoods in need of conversion. But in the digital age, long after the day when political parties and neighborhood clubs were central to American life, candidates cannot rely on personal relationships alone. Especially in districts holding tens or even hundreds of thousands of constituents, political professionals must use demographic research.

"Demography" is the study of populations. Demographers attempt to quantify a population's size, growth, education, gender, race, ethnicity, income, and other such features. "Demographics" are the results of research on these features of a population. "Political demography," therefore, is the study of a population's defining characteristics with an eye to their political significance. It begins with a few basic assumptions.

First, populations are heterogeneous. Districts that appear at first blush to be uniform might actually contain a wide variety of voter concerns. A young, white, middle-class neighborhood in which all the houses look alike gives the impression of Milquetoast consistency. The residents probably share a large number of interests, concerns, goals, and outlooks. But under the surface might dwell a fair amount of diversity. Some people would be pro-life, and others would be pro-choice. Some would be pro-gun, and others would be pro-gun control. All communities, no matter how similar in appearance, are made up of dissimilar elements.

Second, heterogeneity can be used to divide voters into separate analytic groups. The Census Bureau asks people to list their gender, race, age, marital status, and educational attainment, among other things. Because individuals can be categorized by race, populations can be measured in terms of that characteristic.

While there are some ambiguities—people of multiracial heritage are not easily categorized—a political demographer commonly looks for voting differences
between various racial groups. Some categories are not politically significant, and
sometimes the significance of a variable will change. Before 1980, gender was not
a strong variable in presidential elections, but in subsequent years it would become
a powerful predictor of voter preference. Women are now much more likely to
vote Democratic than are men. One trick to demographic research is figuring out
which demographic categories will be politically significant in a given election.

Third, membership in a demographic group suggests shared concerns. Americans
like to think of themselves as individuals, acting from their own interests and not
those of a larger group. A good demographer, however, can make powerful predictions about individuals on the basis of characteristic groups. In the white, middle-
class neighborhood mentioned earlier, there might live a 32-year-old married white
male of English descent employed as a well-paid accountant. Chances are very good
that this person would be a dependable Republican. Of course, not *every* member
of his group has identical interests, nor does *everyone* agree on any one item—
demographic inference is a business of probabilities, not certainties—but there is
a clear correlation between party preference and wealth, geography, marital status,
race, and occupation.

For political campaigns, these three assumptions are translated into powerful
statistical tools. Demographic research helps a political professional discover
electorally relevant groups and target them with the right message. Traditional
demographic research is a process of aggregating data and then drawing reasoned
inferences from it (Robbin 1989, 107–8). The watchword is efficiency. Instead
of compiling information on each *individual* voter, the researcher tries to learn
about large *groups* of voters. Married white males tend to vote differently than
do unmarried black females. The very act of voting seems to be related to demographic characteristics. Older people vote more regularly than younger people.
Wealthier people tend to vote more regularly than poorer people. A new-style
campaign aims its message at those whom it can persuade. Good demographic
research builds a general understanding of an electorate—its differences as well
as its similarities.

DEMOGRAPHIC RESEARCH

In the golden age of parties, what passed for demographic research came from
direct contact. Local bosses knew their constituents. George Washington Plunkitt
could say, "I know every man, woman, and child in the Fifteenth District, except
them that's been born this summer—and I know some of them, too" (Riordon
1995, 25)—an exaggeration, probably, but with a core of truth. Operating in
a world where new immigrants joined social clubs and political parties, at a time
when travel was a luxury that few could afford, neighborhood organizers could
know their voters and send political information up the chain of command. By the
1950s, urban flight and the decline of tightly knit communities rendered neigh-
borhood-based assessments problematic. The flow of information and depth of

commitment that allowed for Plunkitt-style political knowledge were disintegrating. At the same time, primitive data handling was coming into its own. Demographic information could be punched into cards and run through computers. Whereas Plunkitt drew his district from his knowledge of individuals, new-style consultants start with a macrolevel view and then parse the data into microlevel understandings.

Finding U.S. Census Data

Researchers can examine general demographics by looking at the *Statistical Abstract of the United States*. It is among the government's most useful publications, but its mission is to summarize the nation as a whole—not to specify the makeup of a small electoral district.

For most campaigns, the basic source of American demographic data is the U.S. Census. Every 10 years, the federal government undertakes a massive, constitutionally mandated effort to gauge the country's population. Unlike surveys that rely on sampling techniques, the Census Bureau attempts to enumerate every person living in the United States. All residents are legally obliged to fill out a questionnaire. There are two versions of the census form: short and long. For Census 2000, the short form asked people about the type of housing they lived in; about their age, sex, ethnicity, and race; and about their relationship to others in the home. The long form, given to roughly one in six people, asked a series of questions relating to ancestry, household composition, home value, education, family language, veteran status, work experience, religion, transportation, and so on. Those who fail to submit their response receive a visit from a census worker, and the questions are asked face-to-face.

Census data are not perfect. Some people are missed altogether, some forms are not accurately completed, and some people do not want to divulge personal information. More important, researchers cannot study individual unit data—a source of frustration for political demographers. But neither shortcoming renders census information useless. As noted by political communication professor Gary Selnow, "statistical averages often are accurate enough for campaign activities, and they may be a lot better than no information at all" (1994, 95).

A wide variety of demographic characteristics is available to researchers. While local politicos in Plunkitt's day might have been able to say which area is predominantly Polish or Italian or which neighborhood is upper income and which is lower income, new-style consultants can go deeper than direct observation. Demographics can show how many people in the area own their homes, how many are headed by a single parent, how many are blue-collar workers, how many are farmers, and how many are over the age of 65. Census data give a researcher a wide array of options. A demographer can look at the entire nation or a city block. The ability to perform multivariate analyses on a large number of geographic units makes census data far superior to casual estimates.

The Census Bureau continually refines its data collection techniques, adds and subtracts questions, and generally tries to improve its forecasting—but on the whole, the structure of the data has remained fairly constant. Data delivery, however, has changed dramatically over the past few years. In the 1980s, campaigns referenced hard-copy volumes. Research libraries furnished racks of census publications, while local public libraries carried selected titles. Accessing this information was a formidable task, requiring legwork and a great deal of cross-referencing. Information from the 1990 census was available on computer tape reels, tape cartridges, and CD-ROM disks. Not only were the data more accessible, but they were vastly more manageable. Campaign strategists could carry an impressive quantity of searchable data fully loaded into a laptop computer.

For the new millennium, census information moved to the Web. A few clicks from the Census Bureau's home page (http://www.census.gov) tells a researcher that, within the city limits of Wilmington, North Carolina, there were 75,542 people living in 34,268 households. There were 53,058 Caucasian Americans and 19,487 African Americans. The median gross rent in the white population was $641. Among black residents, approximately 467 took public transportation to work, and roughly 38 took a bicycle. All these data can be requested in HTML format for browsing, but they can also be downloaded into commercial database management software. The quantity of information offered by the Census Bureau is mind-boggling, and the bureau collects and sells more than just the data collected in the decennial survey. It produces information on business, agriculture, building permits, federal fund transfers, and other sorts of demographic knowledge.

Census data are provided in two basic formats: "summary data" and "microdata." Summary data sets are based on specific geographic units—states, cities, townships, census tracts, or units that the Census Bureau calls "blocks." Based on the city block, the concept is extended to rural communities by selecting geographically defined areas (using, e.g., roads and railroad tracks) encompassing about 70 people each. At the block level, only the condensed short-form data are available. Up the hierarchy from blocks are census tracts and block numbering areas (the rural version of a tract), towns, cities, counties, Metropolitan Statistical Areas, congressional districts, states, and the nation as a whole. For areas larger than the block level, researchers can obtain preformatted data segmented in a variety of ways. In addition, the Census Bureau and some states have been trying to conform their internal geographic boundaries. Microdata sets are a completely different type of resource. Like summary data, they begin with the answers to census questionnaires, but unlike summary data, microdata can be restructured by the researcher. Census data can show the number of married women and the number of people who commuted to work between 7:00 A.M. and 8:00 A.M. If a consultant wants to aim radio advertisements at women on their way to work, it would be useful to reconfigure the data to see not just the number of *people* commuting between 7:00 A.M. and 8:00 A.M. but also the number of *women* on their way to work at that time. Summary data do not allow this kind of manipulation.

Reconfiguring the data would require that researchers access the raw data from individual census forms. The problem is obvious: even if identifiers such as name and address were removed from the data set, a clever researcher could divide and cross-cut the data into geographically tiny pieces and eventually figure out which household is attached to which census questionnaire, raising serious privacy concerns.

A partial answer to the problem is large-scale sampling. The Census Bureau has created data sets called Public Use Microdata Samples (PUMS). PUMS data sets are not offered for geographic populations smaller than 100,000 residents, and, even then, only a sample of the census form results is provided. Still, microdata sets can be extremely useful, allowing the researcher to perform custom queries on individual-level survey results.

Using Census Data

Raw data sets are only the beginning. The key to using census data is the search for correspondence and specificity. First, census data do not always correspond to the political district in question. If the district is a state, county, city, or congressional district, then researchers can start with predefined summary data. If, however, the district is only a portion of a city or if it snakes across municiple lines, then research-ers will have to piece together the voting district from small units of analysis—government jurisdictions and census blocks—building the district from scratch.

Whether a district as a whole comes ready-made or has to be assembled by hand, intelligent demographers learn how to disaggregate the whole into the smallest unit of analysis. The second key to demographics—building specificity—relies on a researcher's ability to refine macro districts into micro units, from the nation down to the block. This is a good thing because modern political campaigns are judged by the precision of their targeting. Campaigns have become data driven, but there is a cost. In addition to the money spent developing a database, a cam-paign that uses sophisticated database management systems must train its staff accordingly. Furthermore, with each new variable introduced to the database, the number of theoretical groups is multiplied accordingly, and the complexity of the database can become overwhelming.

One answer to the complexity problem emerged in the early 1970s, when the Claritas Corporation pioneered the use of geodemographic clusters. Claritas assumed that people gather into "areas where the resources—physical, economic, and social—will be compatible with their needs" (Robbin 1989, 109). In other words, people create or choose neighborhoods on the basis of personal lifestyle choices. These neighborhoods, in turn, have identifiable demographic charac-teristics. By systematically examining 535 variables for the entire U.S. popu-lation, Claritas established 40 distinct groupings, which combined to account for 87 percent of American diversity. Each cluster was given a nickname. One was tagged "Share Croppers" because it contained low-income, rural, poorly edu-cated southern whites. Other groups were "God's Country," "Blue Blood Estates," "Archie Bunker's Neighbors," and "Bohemian Mix." Each unique cluster was thought to comprise like-minded individuals. In a sense, geodemographic clus-tering moved casual perceptions of neighborhoods toward a more sophisticated understanding of shared geography.

Pundits found fault with the new approach. Was it a magic bullet or just smoke and mirrors? Was geodemographic clustering simply an advertising ploy to build a market for Claritas? Consultant Mark Atlas argued that geodemographics did not live up to its billing. First, there did not appear to be any statistical documentation to support claims of improved targeting. In fact, before-and-after evidence provided by the company, when reexamined, showed that the system did little to change the electoral outcomes. The problem might have been simple methodology. Atlas wrote, "Clusters derived from the entire nation's Census data may be very different from clusters that would be generated if each state's data had been clustered individually" (1989, 134). "The allocation of campaign resources," argued Atlas, "is too critical a task to be undertaken when there is substantial uncertainty about the targeting procedure's validity" (135).

Nevertheless, lifestyle clustering has endured as a form of demographic shorthand. Even though many consultants now believe that clusters derived from a national data set are imprecise and unnecessarily expensive, the lasting impact of geodemographic profiling is the very idea of efficiently identifying targeted groups on the basis of broad sets of characteristics. The GOP longs to capture "soccer moms." In 2000, some Gore operatives scoffed at Bill Bradley's supporters, calling them a bunch of "Volvo drivers." Even if such categories reduce whole populations to a caricature, Claritas-style groupings offer a richer understanding of an electorate than the traditional left–right continuum. As one consultant has noted, "Seasoned political operatives generally concede that the geodemographic approach has some merit" (Beiler 1990, 34).

BRINGING THE PIECES TOGETHER

Because most campaigns cannot afford professionally drawn demographic profiles, the task is often left to candidates, consultants, and volunteer research teams. Much of the raw census data can be downloaded from the Web. Professional reference librarians can be invaluable to novice researchers sorting through census terminology (e.g., the differences between "ethnicity" and "race") and the variety of available data packages (e.g., ZIP codes and block groups). Guides to census data such as Congressional Quarterly's *Encyclopedia of the U.S. Census* (Anderson 2000) also help demystify the statistics.

Once the raw data are gathered, they can be imported into a database as simple as a spreadsheet or as complex as a relational database management system. Relational databasing allows researchers to link data sets. For example, a campaign may have census data for a county, along with a raft of economic data points. With a relational database, the name of the county can be used to link the table containing census information with the table containing economic information. Using basic demographics as a starting point, a campaign can add raw voter files and other "enhancements." Here, public information data, such as state motor vehicle department information, data from the state fish and game commission, and records provided by the county assessor's office, might be combined into a deep profile of the district (Beiler 1990, 33). A list of people with hunting licenses can display high concentrations of hunters, and the appropriate inferences can be drawn from there. Adventurous campaigns will link their relational database to a Geographic Information System—in other words, computer mapping software.

One interesting enhancement is name-based ethnicity. Campaigns have been encouraged to pay close attention to an "ethnic targeting program" in which a researcher will "identify what ethnic group an individual or family belongs to primarily by looking at and analyzing the last name" (Dawidziak 1991, 52). A table of surnames is created, and, by using the last name, each voter's ethnicity is recorded: "A last name beginning with O' might be Irish [and a] last name ending with 'ski' would more than likely be Polish" (52). As the campaign moves forward to voter contact, ethnic-based mailings can be sent on the basis of each ethnic group's presumed interests. The method is not foolproof: "Park" is very commonly a Korean name, but many people with the last name "Park" have no Korean heritage. Some campaigns may look for services that refine the technique by adding first-name matches.

Another source of information is a campaign's "in-house" data set. Nearly every campaign maintains lists of voters, contributors, and volunteers. Data might also be compiled from newspaper clippings, letters sent to the candidate, attendance at candidate forums and fund-raising events, and rosters of prior campaign staff (Selnow 1994, 75). In-house lists might also be garnered from parties, interest groups, and other campaigns. Furthermore, most elected officials have a list of voters who have expressed an interest in one topic or another. Many jurisdictions forbid the use of lists acquired during official hours or in the conduct of official business. Furthermore, election laws and privacy statutes regulate the collection and use of some lists. As with all other aspects of a campaign, compliance with legal and ethical codes must be the top priority.

List production is a lucrative industry. Vendors offer data sets ranging from ZIP code sorts to club membership data to magazine subscription lists. Such lists can be rented directly from the owner or through a list broker. Entrepreneurs help campaigns search the market for lists that suit the campaign's needs. The brokers acquire the lists, handle the billing, and test the data (Selnow 1994, 80–84). The high cost of brokered lists means that most campaigns restrict their use to fund-raising activities, but some campaigns may want to use their lists for narrowly targeted grassroots efforts.

Many demographic databases are dual-use. Aristotle International maintains a nationwide voter database based on party registration, probable ethnicity, gender, and so forth. A client can build customized data sets online: "If you need high-income homeowners who have given to a religious charity, for example, no problem. We maintain a vote history record going back nearly twenty years in some places." These data can be combined with other demographic information and then mapped onto district boundaries.

Such a database provides both general demographic understanding and the opportunity for direct voter contact: the campaign talks to the voter, and the voter talks to the campaign. Precinct walkers and telephone callers gain voter-specific data. Information on specific voters can be returned to headquarters and entered into the larger data set (Johnson 1992). Voter identification is different from polling in that the goal is not statistical inference but, rather, precise information on specific voters.

Attention to demographic detail is time consuming and resource intensive. Only affluent campaigns with a lot of volunteers can gather information on more than a fraction of the electorate. Nevertheless, a list of voters and their specific concerns is a powerful targeting device. Campaigns are won and lost at the margins, and, as one consultant notes, "We are already making direct contact with actual voters. Why shouldn't we be collecting data in the process?" (Johnson 1992, 52). By combining individual-level data with demographic information, campaigns can discern the interests of subgroups. With the increasing use of database technology in political campaigns, demographics have become a routine part of campaign operations.

The looming problem is information overload—and information obsession. If a database is "sliced and diced" too much, it loses meaning. A few census questions, each having a few possible answers, quickly multiply into thousands of theoretical groupings with only a handful individuals occupying each one. The utility of such a narrow cut is suspect from the outset.

Still, there is value in sorting through the numbers. A researcher can get a feel for the district. What is the percentage of blue- versus white-collar workers? How many African Americans live in the district? How many crimes occur each year? Where are they occurring? After looking at the overall statistics, the next step is to examine the data progressively, moving to smaller and smaller geographic divisions. What is the districtwide unemployment rate? What is the unemployment rate for each of the district's counties and townships? This sort of investigation might be open ended, intuitive, and based principally on the political goals of the campaign team, but it has a long-established place in American electioneering.

An obvious component of this analysis is the electoral history of the district along with poll results. Where are the Democrats? Where are the Republicans? Perhaps more important, where are the Independents? Do they live in precincts with high rates of split-ticket voting? Do most of them live in the same media market? All these characteristics can be summarized in a demographic profile. Together, demographic research, survey data, and prior electoral data merge to form a powerful implement of political combat.

Some consultants pay to have the work done for them. The campaign team simply provides researchers with a voter list, and names are matched with a master file. Database companies provide speed and accuracy, and campaign managers can request mailing labels, preprinted envelopes, and even entire mailing packages, transforming the once-onerous voter contact process, which relied on volunteer labor, into an outsourced operation that can be handled via e-mail. The disadvantage of outsourcing is primarily cost, but also the loss of hands-on control. The very act of compiling and configuring the data is a learning experience. Creating a database from scratch helps a campaign come to grips with the electorate by familiarizing team members with the details of the district.

CONCLUSION

Aggregate data improve a campaign's ability to convey an appropriate message to each voter. Understanding that a district's "bedroom community" is where all the Independents live tells a campaign that it should pay attention to train stops, bus depots, and other places where commuters assemble, perhaps suggesting that the campaign should use billboards visible from the main commuter lines. Demographics add wisdom. While imperfect and sometimes difficult to manage, the value of demographic research lies in the way that it helps a campaign reach informed decisions at a relatively low cost, adding to a campaign's strategic vision.

Chapter Five

Candidate and Opposition Profiles: Looking at the Record

Democrat William MaGee's 1990 campaign for New York's heavily Republican 111th State Assembly District paid careful attention to demographics. MaGee operatives knew their voters, and their adversary. MaGee had painstakingly compiled large stacks of information on Republican Jack McCann. Having served 25 years in public life, McCann had amassed a long public record. MaGee's campaign team used that record to assemble a damaging profile of their opposition.

MaGee's line of attack would take advantage of the upstate–downstate split in New York politics. In many ways, New York is two states in one: the greater New York City area is "downstate," and everything north of Westchester County is "upstate." Downstate is heavily Democratic, as are most members of the assembly from the area. Conversely, most elected officials from upstate are Republican. Political and cultural animosity between the two regions is sharp, stretching back to early American history. Among the worst insults that one can hurl at upstate politicians is to call them pawns of downstate interests and vice versa.

In the state assembly, the Democratic Party had held the majority for decades. Accordingly, Democrats controlled the flow of legislation, budget appropriations, committee assignments, office space, and pork-barrel allocations. Republicans were left to nip at the edges and stall the process. Parliamentary games were played out during each legislative term when both sides posture, harass, and embarrass each other. While the Democrats had nearly complete control over the budget process, the Republicans could stonewall by offering amendments. Many tactical measures were intended to embarrass the Democrats. For example, Republicans would suggest adding money for law enforcement, leaving Democrats to vote against the amendment because a budget agreement had already been struck with the state senate and the governor. Republicans would then claim that Democrats were "soft on crime." Republican candidates could tell voters, "You see, we tried to get more money to put criminals behind bars—because we know you're concerned about it—but the Democrats voted us down!"

One year, the Republicans made a pledge to vote as a team. A few of the Republicans were from downstate—Long Island, mostly. These members, like the rest of the minority, offered amendments seeking funds for roads, bridges, rail stations, parking lots, ferry ports, and other projects helpful to downstate residents. McCann was a team player, so he voted for these amendments, even though his district was 200 miles to the north. Here the MaGee campaign found a silver bullet. Why was McCann voting for downstate projects?

The campaign assembled a direct-mail piece with a large picture of then–New York City mayor Ed Koch on the outside and a caption asking, "What Do Ed Koch and Jack McCann Have in Common?" Upon opening the mailer, the reader saw, "They Both Work for New York City!" Below was a list of downstate projects for which McCann had voted, including some staggering legislative price tags. At the bottom, the costs were summed up, and a final caption read, "At a time when *our* roads, bridges, and schools are falling apart, Jack McCann is pushing for over $1 billion for New York City. Who is he working for, Ed Koch or us?" The mailing caused an uproar. Newspapers throughout the district picked up the story, as did many television and radio news programs. The notion that McCann was a "pawn of downstate interests" quickly spread. McCann was forced to defend his tactical votes, distracting attention from his accomplishments. This one mailing, sent early in the campaign, turned a long-shot venture into a neck-and-neck race that MaGee eventually won.

MaGee's victory was made possible by meticulous research. Only 20 years ago, aggressive opposition research—termed "oppo" in the trade, or simply, "O-R"—was a political novelty. Few knew how to compile and organize this information, and even fewer knew how to use it well. Today, new-style campaigners agree that O-R plays a leading role in nearly every campaign. This chapter is designed to acquaint the reader with opposition research. It discusses some of the ethical considerations surrounding oppo, the reasons for its effectiveness, the need for researching one's own candidate, several different types of profile data, where the information can be found, and the efficient management of opposition and counteropposition research data.

ETHICAL ISSUES IN OPPOSITION RESEARCH

Aggressive O-R is a mainstay of American politics. During the presidential election of 1800, Federalist operatives learned that Thomas Jefferson might have had several slave mistresses and may have fathered a child with one of them. (Scientific research performed in the 1990s suggested that the Federalists were right.) Years later, in the election of 1884, Grover Cleveland was said to have fathered a child out of wedlock with a woman named Maria Halpin. Supporters of James G. Blaine chanted, "Ma, Ma, where's my Pa? Gone to the White House, ha, ha, ha." The Cleveland team retaliated by disclosing that Blaine had used his congressional office for financial gain. Democrats returned fire: "Blaine, Blaine, Jay Gould Blaine! The Contentional Liar from the state of Maine." Cleveland won the election. On election night, Cleveland supporters shouted, "Hurrah for Maria, Hurrah for the Kid. I voted for Cleveland, and I'm damned glad I did!" (Johnson-Cartee and Copeland 1991, 6–7).

In the recent past, oppo was conducted by college students or by the candidate's spouse; paid professionals were considered an extravagance. Today, many consulting firms specialize in this field, and the resources available to opposition researchers have increased immeasurably. New-style campaigns have incorporated opposition research into their operations for a variety of reasons.

First, the digital revolution has drastically altered the means of collecting, organizing, and distributing campaign-related data. One consultant writes, "Prior to the popularization of the Internet, [a campaign's] examination of the public record had to be done on-site, by hand." A public record spanning 25 years "took five people six months to complete. In addition to being slow and time-consuming, the cost to the client was staggering" (Bovee 1998, 48). In the digital age, opposition research is typified by "someone sitting in front of a computer examining everything from newspaper articles, to property records, to civil and criminal court records" (48). Online services, such as Lexis-Nexis, Facts.com, and NewsBank, allow for swift candidate research. The Federal Election Commission has posted most of its raw data on the Web. With local papers joining the online community, it seems as though every published word, every vote, and every financial transaction can be located in moments. Furthermore, with the digital storage of oppo, rapid response has become its own art form. Fact sheets correcting the record after the Clinton–Dole debates were issued at about the same moment that the two candidates left the stage. What was extraordinary in 1996 is commonplace in the new millennium. There is simply nowhere left for a candidate to hide.

Second, it has been suggested that the demand for O-R stems from the laziness of some reporters. One consultant notes that policy issues are complex and that politicians are therefore able to spoon-feed reporters with the results of campaign research (Persinos 1994, 21). Some suggest that Watergate brought the rise of investigative journalism and that the news media have thereafter become fixated on "character" (Sabato, Stencel, and Lichter 2000, 37–38)—feeding into the hands of campaigns that are ready and willing to push these sorts of stories. At the same time, campaigns must be wary of oppo overload and must use detrimental data with discretion. "There appears to be a public suspicion that the press . . . has intruded into private territory," wrote Kathleen Hall Jamieson at the height of the Lewinsky scandal. "What some in the press regard as investigative journalism seems to many to be simple voyeurism" (1998).

Finally, even if lurid details cross the line of decency, the increasing use of opposition research may be a function of its unmistakable effectiveness. Oppo is used because new-style consultants understand how to employ it effectively. As media consultant Bob Squier once noted, "I love to do negatives. It is one of those opportunities in a campaign where you can take the truth and use it like a knife to slice right through the opponent" (Luntz 1988, 72). O-R has become a fundamental piece of modern campaigning because it works.

But is it appropriate? One researcher has said frankly, "If [candidates] are not willing to have their backgrounds checked out—particularly their financial backgrounds—they shouldn't be running for public office in the first place" (Robberson 1996). Still, there are broad gray areas. Is it right, for example, to tell the voters about something that happened 10, 20, or 30 years ago? George W. Bush's 1975 drunk-driving arrest offers a case in point. Is all public information fair game? What about the private lives of candidates? After the release of President Clinton's deposition in the Lewinsky case, does any zone of privacy remain?

Many professionals argue that opposition research is good for the democratic process. It moves campaigns away from style and imagery and pushes them toward political issues. Elected officials and candidates are accountable for their actions. In other words, it keeps politicians in line. From this point of view, oppo ultimately leads to a cleaner, more responsible system. When Squier, working for Bill Clinton's 1996 campaign, saw video footage of Bob Dole boasting that he had voted against Medicare, Squier shared this fact with the electorate. He suffered no pang of conscience. Comparative campaigning serves a watchdog function. "This is particularly true," writes scholar Linda Fowler, "when one considers how difficult it is to monitor and evaluate the performance of politicians in office" (1995, 203). So long as the public demands this sort of information, campaigns will supply it.

Others say that aggressive O-R creates mean-spirited politics (Persinos 1994, 20). While there is certainly nothing wrong with disclosing factual information about an opponent's official duties, it is quite another issue to resurrect decades-old personal issues with little relevance to the responsibilities of office. By making *everything* fair game, sometimes even family problems, modern campaigning might drive good people from any thought of seeking public office. Ethics charges, even if trumped up—even if proven wrong—can permanently damage a person's reputation. Moreover, personal attacks and misrepresentations of policy commitments might alienate voters. Opponents of oppo argue that the steady decline of voting is linked to the malicious nature of modern politics.

At least one observer believes that oppo should be allowed whenever it is "honest, legal and relevant to the race" (Persinos 1994, 22). At the end of the day, however, it matters little when scholars, pundits, consultants, or candidates mark the ethical boundaries of opposition research. The real question is how the findings of O-R will affect the campaign. If the press declines to run with negative information, it has little or no value. If the campaign does an end run around reporters and airs its charges through paid advertising, the campaign risks backlash. The 1992 Bush campaign deliberately avoided talking to reporters about allegations of marital infidelity by Governor Clinton out of fear that Bush would pay a price for raising the issue. During the 1996 campaign, many established news outlets made a conscious decision not to run salacious rumors about Bob Dole. According to a close analysis of recent political scandals, "Major national publications initially refrained from publishing stories about an extramarital affair in the candidate's past. Yet the eventual coverage of Dole's long-ago affair also shows how competitive forces can effectively override good editorial decisions" (Sabato et al. 2000, 101). The rise of amateur reporting on the Internet

further threatens to undermine professional journalistic standards, as the blogo-
spheric wars over George W. Bush's military records attest.

Scandal is a powerful persuader. One of the biggest upsets in New Jersey's
1992 state senate election was the defeat of the Republican majority leader, John
Dorsey, who had held the post for 18 years. The news media uncovered, among
other things, the fact that "Dorsey had been retained as an attorney by four local
governments, and that his billings to them had totaled more than a million dollars
in the previous year—fully 6,000 hours of claimed work" (Beiler 1994, 45). An
editorial in a lead paper noted,

> While Dorsey gets rich off his political friends, he uses his position to ruin politi-
> cal enemies. After 18 years in the Senate, Dorsey acts like he owns the place. He
> is a walking argument for term limits. (Beiler 1994, 61, citing *The Daily Record,*
> October 24, 1992)

Dorsey lost because the problems went to his own record, but scandal sometimes
paints candidates with a broad brush. The 1991 "check-bouncing" scandal in the
House of Representatives centered on a long-standing privilege allowing members to write penalty-free overdrafts on a huge, Congress-wide joint checking
account. Taxpayers' money was not used to cover the checks, but many people
were enraged over the "abuse." When a list of overdrafts was published, members had to explain themselves. Some retired voluntarily; others were forced into
retirement. The affair helped foment the anti-incumbent sentiment prevalent in the
early 1990s. The exact effect of the check-bouncing affair is difficult to discern;
there are conflicting arguments among social scientists (Ahuja et al. 1993; Alford
et al. 1994; Dimock and Jacobson 1995), especially since a large number of members who had bounced checks were reelected. In any event, the issue made 1994 a
much more difficult year for incumbent campaigns.

While the standards set by the press and public are sometimes cryptic, there
are a few reasonably clear guidelines in political news that wise campaigns must
follow.

Truthfulness

Professional reporters are concerned that their stories are both newsworthy and
accurate. Rumors are rampant in the political community and on the Web, but
most are not reported because the hearsay cannot be verified. Without verification, a reporter who runs a rumor-based story violates a key tenet of the profession. Worse, elections sometimes turn on false information. There are few filters
when reporters are cut out of the process. In Georgia, Republican nominee Guy
Millner ran television ads accusing his opponent, Roy Barnes, of voting to allow
parole for murderers and rapists. "The only problem," according to the *Atlanta
Constitution,* which tamped the story down, was that "Barnes actually voted for
the only amendment put before the House [in 1998] that specifically named those
crimes and 10 other violent offenses as ineligible for parole" (Helton and Pruitt

1998). The ad was soon pulled from the air. But journalists are not perfect. One analyst suggests that erroneous opposition research, passed to journalists, may have changed the course of the 1991 mayoral race in Houston (Frantz 1999).

Two subsets of the truthfulness criterion are that the information must have been gained from a legitimate source—one that is both legal and appropriate—and that the information must be independently verifiable. Examples of stories being spiked because the sources were illegitimate are scarce for an obvious reason: they were never run. Those few that have gotten out have made news, though not always in the way that the campaign would have liked. When reports emerged in 1992 that Bush administration officials had pulled Bill Clinton's passport file, the result was short-lived anger in the Clinton campaign and a federal investigation of State Department employees that led to serious legal proceedings. In addition, some lawful and ethical information is withheld because it cannot be confirmed through independent sources. At about the same time as the passport file incident, the Clinton campaign was given a foreign news report that Bush campaign materials were being produced in Brazil, but the Clinton campaign was unable to get the U.S. media to air the story because no one could find independent verification that the Bush campaign actually knew that its materials were being manufactured abroad. The story could not be authenticated, and therefore it could not be run.

Relevance

A candidate's official actions are automatically considered relevant. Negative information is newsworthy. The difficulty comes in the sometimes vague distinction between official conduct and personal behavior. Larry Sabato et al. have offered a standard that draws a line between reportable and unreportable news according to relevance (2000). A candidate's personal life becomes news only when it affects public business, and thus, for example, extramarital affairs are usually out of bounds, but if the relationship is with a lobbyist, the news is reportable because in that case "there is a clear intersection between an official's public and private roles" (8). In general terms, the public has a right to know when it might be affected by otherwise private behavior.

Fairness

Fairness is closely related to truthfulness and relevance, but it has a unique quality that campaigns sometimes misunderstand. The guiding question will be, Is it fair to single out one candidate for criticism when all are guilty of the same misdeed? More to the point, campaigns that level a charge must be sure that their own candidate is clean. In 1998, Senator Al D'Amato's campaign accused opponent Chuck Schumer with having missed critical votes while he was out campaigning. Unfortunately, D'Amato himself had missed a number of votes when he was running for Senate in 1980. Although D'Amato originally gained a lot of traction against Schumer, the missed-votes argument turned into an embarrassment for the D'Amato campaign. Not only did D'Amato lose whatever advantage he once had with the issue, but lethal questions of hypocrisy and incompetence were added to the mix.

Opposition research is largely unregulated. A consultant might suffer the scorn of associates, but there are few ways of officially condemning a consultant's misuse of opposition data. In January 1994, the American Association of Political Consultants (AAPC) passed a "Code of Ethics." Members pledge, among other things, to "document accurately and fully any criticism of an opponent or his or her record." Still, there is no strong disciplinary mechanism enforcing the code, and those running campaigns need not belong to the AAPC, as there exist no licensing requirements for campaign consultants.

THE FUNCTION OF OPPOSITION DATA

Students of the political arts talk about *prospective* and *retrospective* evaluation. Prospective evaluations are based on anticipatory assumptions. The voter looks at the candidate—qualifications, party label, personality, and campaign promises—and then guesses what kind of job the candidate will do in office. When Bill Clinton promised a "bridge to the twenty-first century," he was asking voters to view his campaign prospectively. Retrospective evaluations look in the opposite direction. Past actions are weighed in order to judge a candidate's future behavior. When Ronald Reagan asked, "Are you better off now than you were four years ago?" he was inviting citizens to think about the problems of the Carter administration. The consensus is that retrospective evaluations are the dominant mode of decision making because (1) prospective evaluations require voters to study campaign plans, and (2) all else being equal, the past seems to be a strong predictor of the future.

Opposition research taps into the process of retrospective evaluation. It is an attempt to convey the perils of selecting the opponent by pointing out the shortcomings of past behavior (see Fiorina 1981). In a sense, voters are confronted with a choice: either look at each candidate's plans for the future (a speculative, time-consuming chore) or examine what the candidates have done in the past (a quick, "factual" process). If the backward-looking clues are unflattering, the evaluation of the candidate will be likewise. The power of this process carries an obvious appeal to candidates. As more and more contenders use the technique, voters become accustomed to it, and they may be starting to depend on it even while they decry negative campaigns. Hence, opposition research has become an important specialization in the campaign profession.

COUNTEROPPOSITION RESEARCH

Opposition research cannot focus exclusively on the opponent. It is a nearly universal philosophical principle—from existentialism, to Christianity, to military theory—that one must look at one's self before attacking others. To the extent that O-R is a search for comparative advantage, both sides of the equation have to be known. After all, opponents conduct research, too. The only way to be prepared for negative attacks is to know what the opposition might have. Missed votes need to be accounted for, along with defaulted loans, off-color comments, and difficult votes. As D'Amato learned, campaigns must avoid charging the opposition with misdeeds that the candidate has also committed.

Just as any job seeker must assemble a résumé, prospective candidates must develop a scrupulous account of their past work experience, political affiliations, memberships, outside activities, and the like. This sort of information is generally distributed in the form of a one-page biography, but files are kept to back up any question—positive or negative—about the candidate's background. Particularly since the 1970s, when journalists began writing investigative profiles of public officials, political campaigns have kept records on even the most trivial bits of information. A documented fact can stop a rumor before it starts, but exculpatory information that cannot be authenticated might just as well not exist. Politics can be a rough game.

A good campaign team will not assume that its candidate has perfect memory and candor. Problems can be painful; memories can be selective. The only way to understand a candidate's strengths and weaknesses is via thorough research. Even private information leaks into electoral campaigns. All the candidate's writings, tax records, school transcripts, court cases, tax forms, investment documents, vehicle registrations, medical histories, and so forth should be retrievable at a moment's notice. It can be a difficult chore. Most people dislike taking stock of themselves. Layers of pride, shame, and forgetfulness tend to make self-portraits difficult to render. Listing simple biographical information can be difficult enough. Given the scrutiny that attaches to contemporary candidates, it is important to record exact titles and job descriptions, but determining whether a candidate upholds the highest ethical standards can become an uncomfortable journey. Some consultants may begin to think that lying to oneself really *is* more deeply ingrained than lying to others.

TYPES OF PROFILE DATA

The point of counteropposition research is to help a candidate know him- or herself better than anyone else ever could because only then can the campaign respond to attacks. As campaigning becomes more and more aggressive, opposition research will continue to be an integral part of new-style campaigns. It is therefore important to know how oppo works. In this sense, the information involved in opposition research can be separated into four different types of information: (1) political, (2) campaign finance, (3) career, and (4) personal.

Political Information

Political information is that which pertains to activities undertaken by a candidate while in an elected or appointed public position or to statements the candidate has made while seeking public office. Many of these activities will have been overt—made for public consumption—and others will have been made behind closed doors.

No matter how thoughtful, careful, and attentive to the public's needs an official might be, a candidate's record always seems to hold something damaging. The task of the opposition researcher is to find words, deeds, and works that will disappoint swing voters.

Voting Record. The 1994 midterm election was a disaster for Democrats. Myriad gubernatorial, state legislative, and U.S. Senate and congressional candidates went down to defeat. Bob Barr knocked off 10-year incumbent Buddy Darden of Georgia because Darden was perceived to be out of touch with the district (Burton and Shea 2003; Shea 1996b). Among the votes highlighted by Barr was his support of the 1994 crime bill. Even though the bill sought to increase funding for prisons and police protection, one section banned the sale of assault rifles. This part of the bill became the rallying call for gun advocates throughout the district. Darden had also voted for Clinton's budget bill in 1993, which raised taxes on gasoline and upper-income taxpayers. In the end, Darden found himself dubbed a "liberal" in conservative Georgia. His defeat shocked political observers around the country. Ironically, had Darden voted against the 1994 crime bill, he might have been labeled "soft on crime."

Congress, as well as most city councils, county legislatures, and state legislatures, confronts literally thousands of measures each session. Many of these bills are technical and may be of little importance to the voters, but a few are hotly debated. Research teams find it imperative to record all these votes, no matter how insignificant some might seem, spanning the opposition official's entire career—including both floor votes and committee votes. Which votes matter? Campaigns often consult lobbyists and legislative staffers familiar with the legislation as well as the best ways to word the significance of "bad votes" in plain language. Surveys and focus groups can also be helpful.

One readily understood "bad vote" is the "flip-flop," in which an official's position changes from one time to another. The 2004 Bush campaign charged that John Kerry had changed his position on a whole range of issues, particularly his support for the war in Iraq. It did not help Kerry that he had a passion for windsurfing. An anti-Kerry ad cheerfully showed the senator tacking back and forth in the wind. Highlighting a flip-flop is effective. First, the switch might offend people on both sides of the issue. If a candidate is shown to have changed positions on abortion from pro-life to pro-choice, the pro-choice voters may doubt the candidate's sincerity and pro-life voters are reminded of the candidate's present views. Second, a flip-flop goes to the question of trust. Politicians who changed their votes in the past may well do so in the future. Indeed, some will ask whether newfound convictions were planted for no other reason than electoral politics.

Absenteeism. Missed votes suggest dereliction of duty. Some absences are understandable, of course. Family and health concerns will be excused, but a sure way to intimate that an official is not "working for the people" is to point out chronic absenteeism. In the 1984 Kentucky U.S. Senate race, Republican challenger Mitch McConnell was able to unseat incumbent Democrat Dee Huddleston by highlighting the senator's missed votes. In a legendary television spot, a man led by four bloodhounds frantically searched for signs of Huddleston—in his

Washington office, back home in Kentucky—but Huddleston was nowhere to be found. According to the ad, Huddleston missed important votes while collecting money for speeches in California and Puerto Rico. Sometimes, a single vote can make a difference. Democrat Harley O. Staggers was defeated in 1992 in part because he missed a key vote funding a new FBI center in his West Virginia district. Voters expect their representatives to be there for *every* vote—even every committee vote—a point that opposition researchers stand ready to exploit.

Bill Sponsorship. Another aspect of an official's record is an incumbent's bill sponsorships. Some bills have only a single sponsor, others have two or three, and a few popular measures see dozens of members "sign on." Members are not always careful in screening their colleagues' bills, and there are several methods of using this information. First, if the legislator fails to sponsor legislation important to the voters, he or she can be attacked for this neglect. Second, if the legislator sponsored a bill that did not become law, he or she can be charged with ineffectiveness. Third, when the member has a tendency to cosponsor many bills, it might be fruitful to ask whether their combined weight would have busted the budget. (The National Taxpayers Union scores members of Congress in just this way.) Finally, campaigns examine the relationship between bill sponsorship and voting records. Occasionally, legislators vote against measures similar to ones that they are sponsoring—an act that can be portrayed by a skillful campaign as a legislative flip-flop.

Committee and Leadership Assignments. Committees and subcommittees have jurisdiction over only a limited set of issues. An official's committee assignments, therefore, tend to reflect on the legislator's priorities. Some committees are more prestigious than others, some tackle problems relevant to the candidate's district, and some are neither prestigious nor helpful to the people back home. Leadership responsibilities also speak to an official's status and effectiveness. A failure to move up the leadership ladder might indicate a host of problems, ineffectiveness, or simple apathy.

Pork. A mainstay of incumbency reelection is the procurement of "pork barrel." Each year, city, county, state, and federal budgets are carved up for specific projects—military contracts, environmental remediation, highways, and the like. These projects, called "particularized benefits" by one scholar (Mayhew 1974a), allow public officials to get credit for actions performed in the Capitol, the courthouse, or city hall. Officials report their success in the media and the mail, leading voters to believe that they are being represented by effective legislators. But the issue can cut either way. The quest for high-grade pork can be viewed as a propensity toward profligate spending—a possible problem for a fiscal conservative—and yet sometimes a legislator will be punished for failing to take care of the district, as Harley Staggers's problem with the FBI center makes clear.

Official Mailings. Many public officials have the ability to use official mailings to keep the voters informed. The privilege is called "franking," and it originated with congressmen and senators being allowed to substitute stamps with handwritten signatures. Later, printed signatures were deemed acceptable. The upside for incumbents is that they can stay in touch with the district. The downside is that an overly ambitious mail program can lead to charges of misusing public funds. In the 1990 Indiana U.S. Senate race, Democrat Barron Hill gained ground against incumbent Republican Dan Coats by highlighting Coats's ambitious franking. In a television spot, a home owner stood in front of his open roadside mailbox watching a gusher of letters spray out. The flow continued as the announcer said, "Dan Coats has dumped 13.1 million pieces of junk mail on Indiana." The message: Coats was wasting taxpayer money.

There are legal and ethical issues as well. In the House of Representatives, for example, the words that go into franked mass mailings are tightly regulated. No express call for votes can be made, for example, and references to oneself and one's party cannot be excessive. Mailings contrary to the rules are rejected. In the current political environment, however, even an approved mass mailing can be used against a candidate. In May 2000, Nebraska Republican Lee Terry was accused by the Nebraska Democratic Party of sending out a franked message that looked more political than informational. The legality of the mailing—a case strongly argued by Terry's senior staff—seemed a weak defense.

Office Staffing and Expenses. Perhaps the only thing that voters despise more than a public official wasting money on unnecessary projects is a public official wasting taxpayer money on him- or herself. Democratic Ways and Means Committee chairman Dan Rostenkowski's fall in 1994 can be attributed, in part, to allegations that he had kept ghost employees on the payroll, had converted office stamps into cash, and had used taxpayer money to buy a variety of expensive chairs and other "gifts." Opposition researchers look at an opponent's office expenses and compare them to those of the opponent's colleagues. Incumbents who seem to waste taxpayer money can find themselves in trouble with the voters.

Travel Information. Wise campaigns pay special attention to the opponent's travel records. Elected officials often conduct business on the road. These trips, often called "junkets" by political opponents, are a rich source of embarrassing information. Members can often be found to have traveled with their spouses to conferences, seminars, study sessions, and the like—sometimes held in exotic, sunny places. Any travel can be made to look bad, particularly if the press fallout is not handled well. In 1999, Congressman Brian Bilbray of San Diego, California, traveled to Australia, where he attended a conference on U.S.–Australian relations, saw the Chargers and Broncos play an exhibition game, and took a couple weeks of personal time. The costs were borne by an Australian province. Playing defense, the congressman's chief of staff responded to press inquiries by saying that Bilbray "only missed one week of votes for this, none of which were determined by one vote" (Braun 1999). The *San Diego Union-Tribune* reported, "Bilbray, who has not returned from Australia, could not be reached for comment" (Braun 1999). A trip to Scotland helped draw Ohio congressman Bob Ney into a national Scandal over improper labbying.

Gaffes. Everyone makes mistakes, but candidates live among reporters and opponents who are eager to point out any blunder for the world to see. In the 2005 race for New York mayor, Democrat Freddy Ferrer told a group of police officers that he thought the death of African immigrant Amadou Diallo, which had become a cause célèbre among liberals concerned with police brutality, was not a crime. The remark may or may not have pleased some in the law enforcement community, but it forced Ferrer to offer a quasi apology, and when Ferrer's numbers dropped, *New York Newsday* wondered if political suicide itself might be a crime (Duggan 2005). The previous year, a congressional challenger in Indiana, Maria Parra, began her opening statement, froze, then walked off the stage. "I'm not used to being in front of the camera. . . . I couldn't get my words out. I was just overwhelmed," she later said. No additional research was required by the incumbent's team.

Contradictions. In addition to verbal gaffes, a campaign can compare the words of an opposition candidate with his or her deeds. In many instances, candidates and elected officials make remarks that contradict a prior speech, vote, or bill sponsorship. Often, holders of lower-level posts pledge to serve the full term, only to find opportunities for higher office before the term ends. Others are dogged by term-limits pledges made in earlier years. Taxes are another problematic area. In 1988, George Bush, in a dramatic display of resolve, pledged, "Read my lips: No new taxes." After the president joined with Democrats in raising taxes to lower the deficit, the 1992 Clinton campaign had a ready-made campaign issue.

CAMPAIGN FINANCE INFORMATION

A second type of oppo looks at campaign finances. Federal candidates make detailed reports to the Federal Election Commission listing, among other things, all the individuals and political action committees that contributed more than $100 to their campaign. Nearly all states have similar disclosure requirements. Opposition researchers scour these data for irregularities. For example, if four people with the same last name and address give the maximum allowable contribution and two of the contributors list their occupation as "student," then some might wonder if the head of the household was actually augmenting a personal donation by funneling disallowed contributions through family members. Additionally, extremist groups or very unpopular individuals can sometimes be found backing the opponent. Martin Luther King III was hurt in his race for the Fulton County, Georgia, Commission chair by the discovery that one of his contributors was suspected in a murder case. Money is always needed, and in the hurry to fill war chests, many candidates pay inadequate attention to who is giving it.

Moreover, well-funded campaigns can be accused of "buying" the election. In California, exorbitant personal spending is an emerging tradition. Michael Huffington spent $27 million of his own money in 1994 on a Senate seat. He lost. Darrell Issa spent $11 million of his own money for the other Senate seat in the 1998 GOP primary. He lost, too. Al Checchi, who spent $40 million in the 1998 gubernatorial primary, lost with an embarrassing 13 percent of the vote. According to one analysis, "Despite all the popularity in recent years of anti-establishment, 'outsider' candidates such as Perot, voters ultimately have chosen candidates who paid their dues by serving first on school boards or city councils, volunteering in community organizations, or attending countless political meetings and conventions to help other candidates or the party" (Westneat and Brown 1998). If that is what voters ultimately choose, then charges of excessive candidate spending would seem to cut deeply.

Career Information

Public service is not the only way that a candidate can amass a record. Prior business activities and other career information can provide a powerful stockpile of inauspicious material. This information can be grouped into three broad areas: résumé inflation, questionable practices, and dubious associates.

Résumé Inflation. Many voters stretch the bounds of honesty when they write their résumés, but this sort of behavior is not tolerated in candidates for public office. Wes Cooley paid a price for puffing up his credentials, as noted earlier. Democrat Ken Bentsen's 1994 upset victory over Republican Eugene Fontenot in Texas' Twenty-Fifth Congressional District also illustrates the perils of résumé inflation. Fontenot had billed himself as a physician and a lawyer, but he was forced to admit that he had not practiced medicine in a decade and had never practiced law. The candidate's collapse did not end there. As consultant Craig Varoga notes,

> Prompted by Bentsen's TV and mail showing $3 million in IRS tax liens against Fontenot's hospital, Fontenot said he hadn't run the hospital during the years in question—contradicting his official biography. (1995, 35)

Bentsen successfully defined his opponent, essentially stripping Fontenot of his ability to stress professionalism and character.

Questionable Practices. A candidate's professional years can be important. In the race for the 1994 Ohio state attorney general's office, Betty Montgomery continually reminded voters that her opponent had never prosecuted a criminal case—even though he was the incumbent attorney general. She argued that he lacked courtroom experience. The voters gave his seat to Montgomery. Financial investments can become particularly problematic. Republican presidential hopeful Phil Gramm of Texas found that some of his investment money had gone to the production of pornographic films. Even though Gramm had no knowledge of, or role in, inappropriate activities, the investment was deemed by many conservative voters to be a serious misjudgment.

Dubious Associates. Guilt by association may be considered unsporting in many arenas, but it remains fair game in politics. Former senator Carol Moseley-Braun's boyfriend, who also served as her campaign manager, was accused of sexually harassing female campaign workers, leading to charges that the senator was ignoring the situation. In recent years, membership in clubs that exclude people on the basis of gender, race, creed, color, or religion has been considered a violation of public ethics. Sometimes the matter is a mix of personal and political association, as in Moseley-Braun's case, and sometimes the association in question is expressly political, going straight to ideology. In 1996, Senator Max Baucus of Montana endured claims that he "votes like Ted Kennedy." Likewise,

a strong record of support for the National Rifle Association's agenda is sometimes seen as an electoral liability among moderate swing voters.

Personal Information

A last broad classification of O-R is personal information. It is widely deemed
unethical to find or use information that is either (1) untruthful or (2) not readily
available to everyone. In other words, it is generally considered unscrupulous
to hide in the bushes with a camera or to present gossip as if it were fact—or to
hire a private investigator to do the dirty work on the campaign's behalf. Indeed,
an investigator is rarely needed. A good deal of personal information can be
obtained from the media; court records; the local recorder of deeds, liens, and
taxes; professional associations; the board of elections; and the candidate him-
or herself. Still, even if the information is available to the public, a campaign
must proceed carefully with personal information, as the news media are wary
of low-blow attacks.

The current news environment can be traced to an episode of drunk driving
by Chairman Wilbur Mills of Arkansas, who led the powerful House Committee
on Ways and Means. In the 1960s, the private lives of politicians were largely
considered out of bounds. Reporters would overlook personal indiscretions so
long as there was no gross interference with a candidate's public duties. But
with the onset of journalistic distrust of government that accompanied Vietnam
and Watergate, a more skeptical approach came into vogue. In 1974, Mills was
pulled over for speeding at night without headlights, at which point a stripper
jumped out of his car and into Washington's Tidal Basin. While reporters had
known about Mills's problems with alcohol for some time—one even engaged
in a detective-style stakeout (Sabato 1991, 47)—the chairman's drinking did not
become an issue until his run-in with the police. After Mills, the floodgates were
opened. Ohio Democrat Wayne Hays, chairman of the House Administration
Committee, employed a secretary, Elizabeth Ray, a former beauty pageant con-
testant who admitted, "I can't type." After that, Utah Democrat Alan Howe was
arrested for soliciting police officers who were posing as prostitutes and was
thereafter disavowed by his own party. (The party launched a write-in campaign
for an alternative candidate.) Mills, Hays, and Howe all saw their congressional
careers cut short.

While a candidate's extramarital affair may become a campaign issue, a simple
divorce raises few eyebrows—but slow child support payments draws interest.
Bill Yellowtail Jr., a Montana Democrat vying for the state's at-large congressional seat in 1996, was reported to have been long delinquent in this regard. The
story hit the papers on Mother's Day. Yellowtail lost the election by five points.

A good deal of research suggests that, as party identification becomes less meaningful, voters look to personalities. As they do, candidates will be more inclined to
use character-based attacks, painting their opponents as morally corrupt. Playing
the character card can be effective—but risky. Even though voters use personality-
based information to help make up their minds, they are also sensitive to overly

hostile or clearly undocumented charges. Wise campaigns proceed thoughtfully before using this type of O-R.

LOCATING PROFILE DATA

With the onset of digital capabilities, opposition research has come to be divided between old information and new information. Generally speaking, newer information from national and regional sources can be retrieved in data form; older, more local information is still on hard copy. Even though some research must still be done on-site, more and more data are available on the Web.

Public Records

There is a method to researching public records. The *Guide to Background Investigations* (1998) gives detailed instructions for searching state, federal, and educational records. Some of the procedures are suited only to a researcher's own candidate—educational institutions require permission before a transcript can be released—but public records are, by definition, available to everyone. Companies like knowx.com, a fee-based public records researcher, put many of these tools on the researcher's desktop. Writes one consultant, "If there is something you are looking for—Social Security numbers, DMV [Department of Motor Vehicles] records, credit reports—chances are there is some data company that sells it" (Bovee 1998, 52). But at this point the question starts getting into legal and ethical issues—of which there are many—as well as matters of political wisdom. The very fact that a campaign sought an opponent's Social Security number can become a campaign issue in itself. Inappropriate opposition research reflects poorly on a candidate.

That said, almost every government agency, branch, or office provides public information about its members. Government "blue books" and "red books" are official reference manuals providing everything from government structure and process to office telephone numbers to official biographies for sitting government officials. Commercial "yellow books" offer much the same information, often in a more useful format. All these are available at good libraries.

In the past few years, however, a great deal of this information has been made available on the Internet. Web sites for legislators and executive officers are now online. Agencies and legislative bodies offer data on budget actions, vetoes, measures signed into law, agency orders, staffing, and so on. Offline, nearly all legislatures have some sort of public information office. These offices archive the actions of the entire legislature and of each member. They provide information on bill sponsorship, amendment referrals, voting records, committee assignments, and committee actions. Many incumbents and senior government officials are required to submit financial disclosure forms. In Congress and in several states, records of each member's mail account are kept by the secretary of the Senate and the House clerk, allowing for public inspection. For state and local candidates, these records are kept by secretaries of state and a variety of local governmental offices. Research may require sending letters, paying for copies, and waiting, but vigilance and patience should prevail.

Thorough research demands legwork. Local libraries often maintain files devoted to the city, county, and state governments. Privately operated data services that monitor the actions of the executive or legislature can also be used. StateNet, for example, provides a comprehensive database of state legislative actions nationwide, including bills, sponsors' memos, members' voting records, campaign contribution reports, and a host of additional information on state legislative actions. Many states have put legislative data online, and those that have not can provide the information for a fee. In fact, many online resources might not go as far back as an opposition researcher would hope. Hard-copy reports are still part of the process. At the congressional level, virtually all the information that a researcher would desire can be retrieved from the Congressional Universe of Lexis-Nexis, and recent actions are searchable on the official Web sites of the House and Senate. To learn what a bill in the U.S. Senate was all about, a campaign can turn to official reports of the Congressional Research Service (a branch of the Library of Congress) available online at major libraries and through private vendors. Many states have similar legislative study agencies.

Surprising as it might seem, another source of information is the opponent's office. By simply requesting information on bill sponsorships or committee assignments, for example, detailed information can sometimes be obtained. The same is true for local projects—pork, that is. If a researcher is interested in the amount of money that an official secured for various projects, the incumbent's office might be helpful. Public officials realize the importance of keeping in touch with concerned citizens, and those requesting information are given prompt consideration. But opposition researchers should understand the ethical problems with contacting an incumbent's office under any sort of false pretense.

For campaign-related information, the best place to start is the local media outlets and online databases. The library may keep past campaign literature. Local parties collect radio and television spots. It is unlikely that the stations themselves will have saved the ads and even more doubtful that broadcasters would provide tapes or transcripts. Another resource for campaigns ads might be a friendly political science professor at the local college or university. Contribution and expenditure information on federal candidates is provided by the Federal Election Commission (FEC). Official records are located in Washington, D.C., but FEC data are posted on the Web at the commission's own Web site as well as the Web sites of "good government" groups. The Center for Responsive Politics maintains a comprehensive online database of campaign finance information.

Data on property liens, which can show whether a business failed to pay its taxes on time, can be useful. The researcher may have to check a variety of sources for this information, including the local recorder of deeds, the district courts, or the county or city courthouse. If the candidate has run a business regulated by a state or county agency, the agency likely has public information related to licensing and enforcement activities. Likewise, states have employment offices, chambers of commerce, and professional organizations that track industries, companies, and professions. Legal proceedings are available from civil courts, criminal courts, family courts, and appellate courts. Each has its own defendant index. Local boards of election are usually checked to see whether the opponent has voted in past elections. This information can also suggest how long he or she has lived in the area prior to the campaign.

News Media

With ever-narrowing profit margins, newspapers have become far less accommodating to requests for old articles, but new restrictions are accompanied by a great increase in the availability of news on the Web. The old ways of research had campaign operatives leafing through yellowed clippings at the library, in the offices of interest groups, or at party headquarters. Political professionals might still take advantage of these resources, partly because the strategy brings one in contact with knowledgeable librarians, lobbyists, and party chairs. Increasingly, however, the research is done on desktop computers, where an abundance of information can be retrieved in short order.

Rapid news delivery is one of the great, if imperfect, boons of the digital age. Databases such as Lexis-Nexis and NewsBank offer a great deal of assistance. Lexis-Nexis offers national, regional, and major-city papers, along with news wires, news releases, magazines, newsletters, statistics, and legislative data. NewsBank is particularly helpful for researching local papers. A researcher using NewsBank to look at a candidate from Elkton, Maryland, can search old copies of both the *Cecil Business Ledger* and the *Cecil Whig*. For an extensive listing of press outlets from major daily newspapers to weekly shoppers and niche publications, a researcher will look to industry reference materials such as Editor & Publisher's *International Yearbook* and the *Gale Directory of Publications and Broadcast Media*. Lexis-Nexis and NewsBank carry the full text of many articles, but for research that goes back more than a decade, particularly where small-circulation publications are involved, operatives may need to make a personal library visit. Publications can be located by searching WorldCat at a college or research library. The *Cecil Whig*, it seems, is carried by a dozen libraries, including the General Libraries at the University of Texas, Austin. For many obscure sources, a researcher may be disappointed to find that the publication is not searchable and not indexed. Still, local libraries and historical societies commonly maintain clip files on public officials, so all is not yet lost.

There are a growing number of options for collecting business-related opposition data. A starting point would again be an online service. Instead of just searching under the opponent's name, the candidate's business or organizational affiliations would be scanned. A search might begin with Lexis-Nexis and Business NewsBank, but a number of other publications can also prove helpful, including trade journals, regional business publications, chamber of commerce reports, biographical directories, and corporate annual reports. Local newspapers and community libraries may have files on the opponent's business.

Researchers pay particular attention to the partisan press. In Washington, D.C., for example, the *Washington Times* serves as a conservative national newspaper. It keeps a close eye on scandals involving liberal officials. Also in Washington is the *City Paper,* an urban alternative weekly that, like many such papers, tends to run scandal stories. Researchers will want to bear in mind that the mainstream press tends to be suspicious of partisan and alternative news sources, but campaigns should also note the increasing speed with which nonmainstream stories, including amateur pundits with popular blogs, are making their way into the dominant media.

DATA STORAGE AND RETRIEVAL

Once a mountain of information has been compiled, the next step is to organize it for rapid response. In the 1970s, filing cabinets were filled with folders. There might be, for instance, one thick file of news clippings and another of campaign finance reports. As questions arose during the course of the campaign, files would be pulled for the counterattack. Carefully segmented hard-copy information was seen as the cutting edge—the best new thing. Once again, computer technology has changed all.

Like many other new-style campaign technologies, computerized opposition research was pioneered by the Republicans during a presidential contest. In 1984, the Republican National Committee spent $1.1 million to create its Opposition Research Group. The group's first task was to collect detailed information about each of the eight Democratic candidates running for president. The group pulled together a mountain of facts, using more than 2,000 sources and 400,000 documents. Next, a staff of readers sifted through the material looking for direct quotes, statements attributed to the candidates, and comments about the candidates by others. The information was coded and entered into a massive computerized database. In the end, the system contained approximately 75,000 items and 45,000 quotes (Bayer and Rodota 1989).

When Democrats nominated Walter Mondale, the Republicans were ready. They produced "Vice President Malaise," a 200-page analysis of the Mondale record, and sent it to every party official in the nation. Each time Mondale spoke, Republicans were ready to highlight problematic actions or comments. As Mondale campaigned from location to location, Republicans told voters about his past positions.. The database was later instrumental in preparing Ronald Reagan for debates. When all was said and done, the project was viewed as the "secret weapon" of the race (Bayer and Rodota 1989, 25).

But even with new-millennium digitalization, one of the most important resources that a campaign can tap is the knowledge of experienced operatives. There may be someone in the community who collects political mailings and past party chairs who can recall the details of ancient races. Aspiring candidates are advised to call on an "old hand" who has been through the process before (Grey 1999, 53). It helps with strategy, and it helps with candidate profiles as well. Those who have seen candidates come and go remember old scandals and how they played out. A new-style campaign listens to war stories, first to get information about the foibles of past candidates but also to learn the sensibilities of the district. In some areas, a certain amount of scandal is written off as a cost of doing business, while in others, absolute adherence to moral and ethical codes is paramount—and even opposition research is considered unscrupulous.

CONCLUSION

The collection and organization of opposition research have come a long way since Grover Cleveland was accused of fathering a child out of wedlock. At the Republican National Committee, a year and a half before the 2004 election, the pro-Bush oppo operation was moving ahead full force, "in a basement room constantly record[ing] C-Span and television news programs, preserving almost everything said in public by the Democratic candidates for president." One floor up, "15 people—many of them baby-faced computer whizzes—sit in cubicles, scanning newspapers, magazines, the Internet, and online databases" (Johnson 2003).

In a sense, however, Bush's research team shows that opposition research is the same as it ever was. Opposition research is a way to learn the strengths and weaknesses of an opponent. If properly used, O-R can change the course of a race, and with the increasing depth and variety of online data, there is little reason to expect that oppo will fade away. Whether the movement toward fast-paced O-R helps political accountability or decreases campaign civility, new-style consultants pay close attention to these new information resources—and opposition research will continue to grow in importance.

Part Two

STRATEGIC THINKING

Chapter Six

Prior Electoral Targeting

Ed Baum, a Republican challenger for a seat on the city council in Athens, Ohio, faced a difficult challenge. His town was heavily Democratic, he had never held office before, and he was running in one of the most difficult strategic scenarios that a candidate might confront—a multicandidate, multiwinner, at-large election. There were six contenders for three seats. The top three vote getters would take office; the rest would get nothing. Such an election can be won only through smart targeting.

Baum was a college professor and Athens is a college town. The campus area—the student wards—were heavily Democratic, as were many of the suburbs. To win, Baum had to maintain the traditional Republican vote and pick up some portion of the swing vote to put him over the top. He also had to make sure people knew *how* to vote. Of the six candidates, there were only two Republicans, but voters had the chance to vote for three individuals. If GOP-leaning voters cast all their ballots, it was likely that one of the Democrats would have enough votes to go over the top. Baum wanted to deprive the Democrats of any chance to pick up extra votes. Voters should cast only two votes, one each for the two Republicans on the ballot.

Much of Baum's targeting was geographic. Students are concentrated near the university, and, generally speaking, distance from campus was a fair measure of a suburb's GOP lean. But a better way to determine the partisan makeup of the electorate was to examine history. Baum looked at the way each precinct had voted for president in the previous three elections and ranked them as "Democratic," "Republican," or "mixed." There was little reason to campaign hard in the solidly Democratic areas or even in the areas that had a strong Republican lean. But the mixed areas, which could swing either way—this is where Baum could spend his time most efficiently, where a knock on the door to say "hello" and to drop off some literature might have the greatest payoff. While the strategy did not prove perfect—Baum lost a couple targeted neighborhoods—victory on Election Day suggested the value of strategically choosing voter precincts.

Baum's method could be reproduced on the back of an envelope. Elaborate polling and computer mapping are expensive—beyond the reach of most local organizations—but the same general theory of electioneering that works in a technologically sophisticated general election campaign applies to campaigns at lower levels: one must visualize the district strategically. Political professionals seek a lucid understanding of any district. The most important information can be gleaned from electoral history—inexpensive, publicly available information that says a lot about a district. A precinct that voted two-thirds Republican in 2000 will probably vote two-thirds Republican in 2004. Simple arithmetic can readily estimate the number of votes needed to win and even where those votes can be found.

Electoral data offer critical information to help a campaign allocate resources efficiently. This chapter reviews the logic behind electoral targeting, the elementary calculations needed to understand historical data, and the manner in which electoral analysis helps campaign professionals develop precinct-by-precinct campaign strategies.

UNDERSTANDING THE DISTRICT

In the study of campaigns and elections, one finds an important distinction between *individual-level behavior* and *aggregate-level behavior.* Individual-level behavior is encrypted in the habits of daily life. Scholars have long struggled with the question, What makes a person vote for a particular candidate? Party politics, of course, but there are other forces—ideology, economics, candidate imagery, a sense of belonging, and so forth. Some voters surely base judgments on the cleverness of a candidate's campaign commercials, others may cast their lot this way or that in order to impress a friend, and still others simply assume that short people cannot lead the country. Students of politics will always be frustrated by the eccentricities of individual decision making, but aggregate-level campaign statistics look at the big picture, examining the behavior of large blocs of voters.

At the aggregate level, myriad individual actions combine into voting districts, states, and the nation as a whole. Eccentricities are dampened by the sheer weight of numbers. Some districts go Republican by roughly the same percentage every single year. Some states are more favorable than others to third-party candidates. In fact, while Americans are constantly moving from house to house—one in five people moves to a new address each year—the predisposition of voters in any given neighborhood remains roughly constant. A city with a high turnout in one year will show a high turnout again eight years later, even though many of the earlier residents have long since moved out of town. The individuals change, but the community remains the same.

A common voting configuration is illustrated in Figure 6.1, which represents a district that generally splits its vote 50–50 between Democrats and Republicans (the average party performance). About 16 percent of the vote (the toss-up) is up for grabs, and another 17 percent on each side (the soft-partisan vote) can usually be depended on by each party, though not always. Finally, some 25 percent of the electorate (the base-partisan vote) goes with even the worst Democratic candidates, and the same is true on the Republican side.

Figure 6.1
Diagramming an Electorate

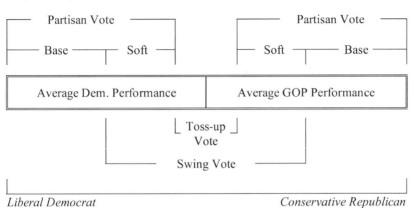

This model illustrates an important political truth: competitive elections are usually decided by small groups of people. If 25 percent of the electorate always votes Democratic and another 25 percent always votes Republican, the remaining 50 percent will decide the winner. Only half the electorate is persuadable. If another 17 percent votes for barely acceptable Democratic candidates and yet another 17 percent votes the same way for Republicans, then 84 percent of the electorate is off the table in a competitive race. Only 16 percent—the "toss-up" vote—remains in play. Winning requires a bare majority of the toss-up, just over 8 percent. And because turnout is commonly less than 50 percent of those qualified, the key to victory is held by little more than 4 percent of the eligible electorate! Of course, the problem facing campaign professionals is finding the (sometimes elusive) middle ground. Electoral targeting is the quest for the deciding vote.

Running the Numbers

Targeting begins with an understanding of the most important single characteristic of a district: the number of potential voters it holds. It is easy to determine the overall population of a district—census data offer a close approximation—but a campaign professional is not interested in *total* population nearly so much as *voting* population. How many people are registered? Perhaps up to 70 percent, but not much more. How many of the eligible voters actually vote on Election Day? This figure generally ranges between 35 and 65 percent, depending on the district, election year, and the kind of offices on the ballot. A county that boasts 130,000 voting-age people may have only 100,000 registered voters, of whom only 75,000 might actually vote in a presidential election year. Moreover, while almost everyone who enters the voting booth selects a candidate for president, people tend to suffer "voter fatigue" as they work their way down the ballot toward judges and county officials. Often constituents choose not to vote for "down-ballot" offices (see Figure 6.2). This

Figure 6.2
Turnout and Roll-Off

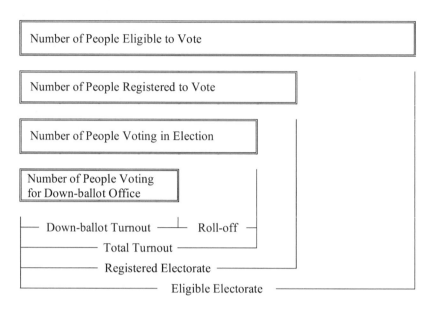

phenomenon, whereby voters cast their ballots for candidates at the top of the ballot but not at the bottom, is called "roll-off." To figure out how many people will actually vote in an election, a researcher preparing for a county-level campaign should look not at the county's whole population or even its registered voting population but at the way that the electorate has traditionally voted for the office in question.

The most obvious source of aggregate statistics is local newspapers and general reference works. Municipal libraries normally have files on recent elections, and many newspapers make back issues available online. Lexis-Nexis and NewsBank give access to a wide variety of journalistic sources. For congressional and state-wide races, most libraries carry *America Votes* (Congressional Quarterly Press), *The Election Data Book* (Brenan Press), *America at the Polls* (Congressional Quarterly Press), *Congressional Quarterly's Guide to U.S. Elections* (Congressional Quarterly Press), and other reference works. These books focus on presidential, U.S. Senate, U.S. House, and gubernatorial election outcomes. While such volumes can be helpful—some, for instance, provide maps and election overlays with demographic data—they do not supply much information on smaller geographic units.

More refined electoral data are available from the government agencies responsible for compiling them. In some jurisdictions, one goes to the local board of elections; in others, one goes to the office of the secretary of state or the county or town clerk. Data can be requested over the telephone or by mail, but often these requests are put at the bottom of a pile. Many researchers find it more useful to go to the office and ask for the data personally, partly because the agency might offer a number of data options that cannot be easily described in a brief telephone conversation.

The board of elections might offer several precompiled tabular reports (e.g., "2004 Congressional Election Results by Ward"), or it might offer the raw data in a variety of database formats. It may offer to include percentage results in addition to the raw numbers, party registration, turnout scores, and other valuable information. Ohio, Texas, and Illinois were early providers of computer-accessible data, and many states followed suit, posting much of these data on the Web—and yet older races often remain on hard copy only. Party organizations often keep this information on file. Well-heeled campaigns have yet another option. Professional voter contact services compile data sets and provide them in database format, often with the added value of cross-referenced census, voter, and party registration as well as general demographic information—even home phone numbers. While government agencies charge little or nothing, professional service providers tend to be expensive.

Smith County, USA

Whatever the source, a campaign amasses these data to gain a general sense of the district and the ways in which past elections have been won and lost and, more critically, to figure out what must be done the next time. Although politics goes beyond simple numbers—researchers need to know about the social, economic, and political cultures of the district that they are mapping—statistical analysis helps manage large quantities of data in an efficient, often thought-provoking manner. The knowledge one gains in crunching the numbers from past elections helps the researcher develop a strategic understanding of the district; a strategic understanding of the district, in turn, helps a researcher determine how the data should be examined. Calculations might be adjusted to fit the local landscape, recent history, and the tactics under formulation. No single statistic can describe any district. Political wisdom is needed not just under the hot lights of a press conference or television debate but also in the cold calculation of electoral statistics.

To illustrate the calculation of historical performance, it is useful to look at a hypothetical district, Smith County, examining six electoral contests in preparation for a year 2006 run for the auditor's seat. The balance of this chapter is devoted to campaign mathematics, showing how a Republican consultant might dissect a heavily Democratic county in order to strategize a GOP triumph in the auditor's race.

First, the basics. Assume that the election is a competitive two-way, open-seat, general election race between a Republican and a Democrat where the retiring GOP incumbent has endorsed her successor (thereby avoiding intraparty struggles). The fact that this is a two-way general election simplifies matters. Three-way races are far more complicated to project. Not only does the researcher have to figure out the number of votes the third candidate will take (and which major party will suffer the greatest loss), but the calculation must often be made without benefit of electoral precedent. Relatedly, third-party candidates tend to attract people who do not usually vote, and their voting behavior is therefore not well known. The same problems crop up in party primaries. Sometimes primaries catapult three, four, five, or more candidates into the field. In the 2003 governor's race in California, voters first chose whether they wanted to recall incumbent Gray Davis, and then those who believed the governor should be replaced went on to choose their favorite of 135 candidates, including the eventual winner, Arnold Schwarzenegger. In an election like this, it becomes difficult to figure out from electoral history alone where the voters will turn. A wise student of campaigns will spend a good deal of time learning the statistics of two-way elections before trying to evaluate a multicandidate primary race.

Table 6.1 contains raw voting data for the hypothetical Smith County, an older, heavily unionized electorate in the Midwest. Assume that the county has a rusting city at the core of several residential neighborhoods, all of which is surrounded by farms and agriculture-related industry. The numbers offer a preliminary understanding of the county's voting behavior. Turnout is generally greatest in presidential election years. No surprise there. Democrats do much better than Republicans, but Republicans can still win. More people vote for president than vote for auditor; Roll-off is a real issue. Perhaps just as important, the consistency of the numbers across time suggests that elections in Smith County are somewhat predictable.

Strategizing a Republican's bid for auditor in the year 2006 is a daunting task but one that can be managed by breaking it into small steps. The first job is to project the number of votes that will be cast. Year type is important. The race will occur during an off year: voters will not choose a president, so many on-year voters will stay home. The appropriate points of departure might be the two most recent off-year elections, 1998 and 2002. An elementary procedure for finding the size of the electorate is to take the number of votes cast for the office in separate elections, add them together, and divide the sum by the number of elections under consideration. In this case, 68,234 votes were cast for auditor in 1998, and 63,694 were cast in 2002. Add the two figures together for a sum of 131,928. Divide the sum by 2, the number of elections considered, and the result is an average vote total of 65,964. This last figure is a good prediction of the number of votes that will be cast in 2006.

Note that projections for 2004 would have been problematic using this method because recent on-year elections have had idiosyncratic features. The 1996 election seems to have had a three-way race for auditor, and 2000 had a Republican running without opposition. These quirks distort the calculation. The elections could render a mathematical "average" but not a good prediction. One way to make up for these idiosyncrasies is to use surrogate races. Swapping a state senate race for a problematic state house race might work. Trading a gubernatorial election for a U.S. Senate race would help even out the calculations. For auditor, a county commissioner's seat might have been used as the point of reference. Even this approach is not without hazard, however. In 1996, there seemed to have been a great deal of excitement among voters in this county, perhaps because one of the candidates came to town. The year 2000, by contrast, was fairly dull, as illustrated by low voter turnout across the board. A review of past auditor's elections might reveal that at various times the auditor's race was subject to intraparty conflicts, hapless candidates, and brilliant campaign tactics. Taking a simple average downplays the variations, but it does so ham-handedly.

Table 6.1
Smith County, General Elections, 1990–2000

	1994	1996	1998	2000	2002	2004
Eligible Voters	142,651	138,455	127,984	128,301	130,682	130,512
Registered Voters	106,762	103,132	99,678	101,874	101,904	101,803
Democratic	25,658	26,674	24,865	24,659	24,568	24,468
Republican	20,586	19,458	20,485	20,467	19,437	19,734
Actual Voters	75,512	87,085	75,490	75,250	68,080	77,692
Votes for Candidate (by Party)						
President	87,034	—	75,234	—	77,608	—
Democratic	38,453	—	36,647	—	36,505	—
Republican	35,379	—	32,576	—	32,959	—
Other	13,202	—	6,011	—	8,144	—
U.S. Senate	75,478	86,823	—	75,042	68,046	—
Democratic	56,582	44,509	—	51,524	35,709	—
Republican	18,528	41,444	—	23,069	32,137	—
Other	368	870	—	449	200	—
Governor	75,489	—	75,457	—	69,354	—
Democratic	38,674	—	40,967	—	38,549	—
Republican	36,495	—	34,282	—	30,615	—
Other	320	—	208	—	190	—
U.S. House	75,204	86,579	75,452	74,893	67,843	72,415
Democratic	44,854	46,935	23,582	42,783	40,012	47,043
Republican	30,111	38,844	51,626	31,705	27,643	25,273
Other	239	800	244	405	188	99
Auditor	72,372	86,001	68,234	60,053	63,694	67,285
Democratic	37,675	42,785	32,411	0	28,701	29,503
Republican	34,515	28,574	35,596	58,785	34,823	37,573
Other	182	14,642	227	1,268	170	209

A second method of prediction tries to compensate for such problems by look-ing at the place of the auditor's race in the larger scheme of things—average turnout, roll-off, and registration (see Figure 6.3). Political judgment is involved at each step. For example, what exactly is meant by "turnout"? Is it the share of *eligible* voters? Or is it the share of *registered* voters? This distinction is critical. A district with high voter registration and only a few people moving in or out prob-ably merits the use of registered voters because that number may not change over the course of an election. A district with low voter registration and a lot of people on the move might require analysts to anticipate preelection registration drives. For the purposes of understanding Smith County, assume a stable district with reasonably high registration. In such a case, registration, not eligibility, should be the baseline.

The turnouts for 1998 and 2002 are gauged by dividing the number of people who actually voted by the number of people registered to vote. Once again, off-year elections are used because turnout varies drastically between on-year and off-year elections. Smith County shows a significant drop between 2000 and 2002. Municipal elections in odd-numbered years can render exceptionally low turnout scores. Choosing similar years is important because the sorts of people who turn out for an on-year election might be very different from the sorts of people who show up in an off-year election. Those who take the trouble to vote

Figure 6.3
Projecting the Size of the Electorate

Method 1: Averaging Two Similar Years

| Votes for Office
in Similar Election Year #1 |

| Votes for Office
in Similar Election Year #2 |

| Projected Electorate |

Proj. electorate = ((votes in year #1) + (votes in year #2)) / 2

Method 2: Multiplying Registration, Turnout, and Down-ballot Vote

| Expected Registration |

| Average Turnout |

| Average Down-ballot Vote |

| Projected Electorate |

Proj. electorate = (exp. registration) x (avg. turnout score) x (avg. down-ballot turnout score)

in an odd-year primary are probably die-hard partisans, not casual voters who go to the polls once every four years to vote for president—hence, the use of 1998 and 2002.

In Smith County in 1998, a total of 75,490 people voted in the election out of 99,678 people registered. Dividing 75,490 by 99,678 gives a rounded turnout score of 0.757, which is 75.7 percent. (Turnout calculated as a percentage of the 127,984 *eligible* voters is a weaker 59 percent—still quite strong by national standards.) Repeating the process for 2002 yields a turnout score for registered voters of 0.668. Next, the average is found by adding the individual turnout scores together and dividing the sum by the number of elections considered, which in this case was two. The sum of the 1998 and 2002 scores is 1.425, which, divided by 2, leaves 0.7125. Rounding to 0.713, the average turnout in off-year elections is 71.3 percent.

Knowing the percentage of the electorate that will show up to vote is important, but not all voters cast a vote for auditor. It becomes necessary to calculate roll-off or, better yet, the portion of the electorate that does *not* roll off—in other words, the remaining share that will vote in down-ballot races. The equation for calculating this down-ballot share of the total vote is similar to the one used for determining turnout, except that it looks at *all* the years during which the office in question was on the ballot. (The conjecture is that roll-off remains stable regardless of year type.) In this case, the years under consideration would be all the elections, on and off year, 1994 through 2004. Again, political judgment should guide the analysis. If a data set shows one pattern for on-year elections and another for off-year elections, it is unwise to combine the two types of years into a single score.

Calculating the down-ballot share of the vote for any single given year is a simple matter of finding the portion of the total vote that wound up going to candidates for the lower office. For example, in 1994, 75,512 voters went to the polls, of whom 72,372 voted for candidates in the auditor's race. The number of votes cast for auditor divided by the total number of votes cast gives a rounded score of 0.958. Roll-off is often expressed as a percentage—here it would be 4.2 percent—but more important is the number of people who persevered. A score of 0.958 means that 95.8 percent of those who voted in the 1994 election voted in the auditor's race. Down-ballot vote scores can be determined for each subsequent election year, 1996 through 2004, and then calculated as an average for all years. The average down-ballot vote score for the auditor's office is 0.908, or 90.8 percent. (Average roll-off is 9.2 percent.)

With this finding in hand, the expected number of voters can be determined. It is found by multiplying the average down-ballot vote share by the average turnout and then multiplying the product of that calculation by the number of voters who will be registered on Election Day. The first step (multiplying the average down-ballot vote share by the average turnout) figures the portion of the registered voter population that will actually vote for auditor. In this case, the rounded score is 0.647, or 64.7 percent. The second step (factoring in the registered voters) produces the predicted down-ballot vote count for auditor.

As easy as it may sound, the second step can be the most difficult in the process. Registration rolls change constantly. Generally speaking, more people are registered in October than in the previous March. Voter registration drives increase the totals. In college towns and areas with seasonal employment, the swings can be substantial. Additionally, because election registrars sometimes purge outdated registrations—all the better to prevent the deceased from voting—researchers try to find out whether they are looking at statistics from before or after a purge, a voter registration drive, or a large-scale population shift.

One way to account for change is to revise strategic estimates as new registration figures become available. The obvious problem with this approach is that it does not allow for much forward planning. Each month would bring a new strategic reality. Another option is to examine past registration trends. For example, assume that the latest available numbers are from March 1, when the registration was 101,409. Assume also that past registration trends for similar election years suggested an average increase of 5 percent between March and November. The next step is to multiply the March registration by 1.05 (the existing registration plus 5 percent), thereby yielding a projected registration of 106,479 on Election Day. Multiplying this projected registration by the predicted down-ballot vote score, which was 0.647, one gets a projected electorate of 68,892 for the auditor's race.

To project the number of votes necessary to win, divide the expected number of votes by 2 and then add 1. Again, slightly easier said than done because two figures have been offered as the expected number of votes: the first projection, from method 1, averaged the total number of votes from 1998 and 2002; the second, from method 2, took a big-picture approach by averaging turnout and down-ballot vote over six electoral cycles and then factoring in the projected registration. Which figure should be adopted? Campaign professionals should err on the side of caution and use the higher of the two figures. "Close" will not count on Election Day. In this example, method 2, which calculated turnout, down-ballot vote, and registration, gave the greater figure at 68,892. Dividing this higher figure by 2 leaves 34,446 votes. Adding the tiebreaker makes it 34,447.

This last number is a slightly fictitious estimate. The break point seldom cuts at 50 percent exactly. Some people vote for third-party candidates, while others vote for independent candidates, and a few people write in their own names just to see if they show up in the newspaper. Races can usually be won just under the 50 percent mark, yet few campaign researchers would average the "other" votes and subtract them from the total. Better safe than sorry.

The calculation for two-candidate race is reasonably straightforward. Multi-candidate elections, however, demand more creative thinking. The formula has to be altered to accommodate the number of candidates in the race; the total number of votes cannot simply be divided in half. If a third-party candidate is at issue in a general election, the best approach is to determine the percentage of votes that similar third-party candidates have received in the past. If no precedent exists, the researcher is left to make an educated guess. In primaries, which routinely have three or four candidates, past elections might show competition between two

rival machines, leading to a rough idea of how much of the vote each operation's candidate can expect. Campaigns can sometimes set their sights low.
Bill Clinton beat George Bush Sr. and Ross Perot with only a 43 percent vote
share. In a strong four-way primary, the win might be calculated at 33 percent.
Although researchers would prefer a magic formula to project the number of
votes needed to win, political judgment must be combined with past electoral
data—including imperfect comparisons.

Base Vote and Party Performance

Once the total number of people needed to win the election is determined, distinctions must be drawn between the portions of the electorate that are in play and
those that are not. Professionals talk about "average party performance," "swing
vote," "split-ticket factor," "base vote," and so forth. Each measure is designed to
carve the electorate into useful categories. Understanding how to calculate these
figures is important. Even more useful is understanding how they build on each
other. Because such formulas must be picked apart, refined, and reassembled to
meet the particular needs of individual electoral contests, it is crucial that campaign professionals see how each component operates.

A few thoughts and caveats are in order. First, although these analyses require
time, campaign operatives find that the rewards far exceed the cost. The point of
electoral statistics is to simplify a complicated data set. The time invested in a few
tables pays for itself in ease of management down the road. Second, all campaign
statistics must be tailored to the district and race in which they will be used. Statistics like "average party performance" and "swing factor" were developed to
handle real-world problems. A campaign professional who remains fastened to
prescribed statistical formulas without asking whether they offer the best practical guidance for a given race is courting disaster. At each step, the questions
should be asked, "What is this statistic telling me?," and "Is there a better way
to approach the problem?" Finally, on a technical matter, all decimals in the following discussion (as with the preceding discussion of electoral size) are rounded
to the third place (e.g., 0.002). Rounding is done for the sake of simplicity, but
simplicity comes at the expense of accuracy. Rounding errors are compounded
with each mathematical iteration. True professionals carry the decimals out as far
as their software allows.

Aggregate Base-Partisan Vote. In politics, a "yellow dog Democrat" is someone
who would vote Democratic even if the candidate was a yellow dog. Some Republicans are "true-blue" or "rock-ribbed." Although many voters tend to reject party
labels, some ostensibly nonpartisan voters consistently vote for candidates of the
same party in one election after the next. In this sense, both parties have "base-
partisan voters" who, though they might need to be energized now and again, can
be counted on in tough times.

Base-partisan voters are critical to campaigns—they are particularly important
as volunteers—but to understand a district, it is important to suspend the desire
to find them. Aggregate statistics focus on the historic performance of entire

precincts, districts, and states. Individuals are all but irrelevant. A precinct where 31 percent of the population is absolutely committed to the party will look no different from one that contains only 11 percent party stalwarts but always seems to gather another 20 percent to vote for the party's candidates. The reason that the calculation is the same is rooted in the overarching purpose of aggregate campaign statistics: charting a winning path regardless of individuals. The aggregate base-partisan vote calculation is simply intended to figure out how many votes can be taken for granted, not who those people are.

The conceptual issue here is critical. When discussing "base-partisan vote," "swing vote," and other such categories, it is important to remember that the terms denote statistical aggregates. They are mere abstractions. They refer not to specific groups of individuals but to recurring electoral phenomena. The distinction is important because the number of true base-partisan voters (i.e., party loyalists who always vote straight ticket) is probably far smaller than the size of the base-partisan vote (i.e., the number of individuals on whom the party can always count). Even the most die-hard Republican occasionally votes Democratic, and vice versa. Thus, a base-partisan vote of 12,000 does not mean that there are 12,000 base-partisan voters in the district. A district could conceivably be populated with nothing but swing *voters*—everyone splitting his or her vote between the parties, maintaining no loyalty year to year—and still have a strong base-partisan *vote* if the two parties could always count on receiving 30 percent of these fickle voters. In a situation where there is absolutely no partisan loyalty but each of two parties always receives half the vote, it can be said that the district is made up entirely of swing voters but has no swing vote to speak of. Again, "base-partisan vote" is a mathematical abstraction that can be manipulated to produce useful projections.

"Aggregate base-partisan vote" represents the worst that a party's candidate will do, indicating the number of votes that will go to a dud candidate wearing the party label. An easy statistic to figure—just find the worst-performing candidate—but a researcher still has to be careful. In Smith County, Democrats did worst in the auditor's race of 2000, getting no votes—zero—but there is a problem with using that election as the starting point for the base-partisan vote. The Democratic Party hit bottom because no Democrat filed for the race. Such elections are not useful; they say little about the district. The next worst election for Democrats was the House race two years earlier, in 1998, when the Democrats had an exceptionally poor showing. On the Republican side, the worst race was for Senate in 1994. Like the 1998 House race, the 1994 Senate race offers a workable benchmark.

Calculating the aggregate base-partisan vote score is a simple matter of finding the share of the electorate that cast their lot with the worst candidate (see Figure 6.4). The Democrat in the 1998 House race received 23,582 votes out of 75,452. Divide the first number by the second, and the result is an aggregate base-partisan vote score of 0.313, or 31.3 percent. For the Republicans, the Senate candidate in 1994 received a mere 18,528 votes out of 75,478, giving the party an aggregate base-partisan vote score of 0.245, or 24.5 percent. Of the 68,892 voters expected to play a part in the auditor's race, approximately 21,563 can be expected to vote for the Democrat, and 16,879 can be expected to vote for the

Figure 6.4
Calculating the Base-Partisan Vote

```
┌─────────────────┐                              ┌─────────────────┐
┊  Base-Partisan  ┊                              ┊  Base-Partisan  ┊
┌─┊      Vote      ┊─┐                          ┌─┊      Vote      ┊─┐
│ └─────────────────┘ │                          │ └─────────────────┘ │
├─────────────────────────────────────────────────────────────────────┤
│                        Projected Electorate                         │
└─────────────────────────────────────────────────────────────────────┘

├─────────────────────────────────────────────────────────────────────┤

Liberal Democrat                                  Conservative Republican
```

Base-partisan vote = lowest score received by candidate of the party

Republican *no matter how bad the candidates might be.* (There will be a cruel irony in this: the very loyalty of the base-partisan voters will remove them from strategic consideration.)

Average Party Performance. How well can each party expect to do, on average? A party's aggregate base-partisan vote shows the portion of the district vote that the parties can count on through thick and thin. "Average party performance" (APP), on the other hand, reflects the portion of the total vote that candidates of each party generally receive and is used to determine the normal percentages of party strength in a precinct (Beaudry and Schaeffer 1986, 30). Functionally speaking, it is the vote that the party can expect when evenly matched candidates go head-to-head.

Average party performance is calculated by first selecting three typical, competitive races in which two quality candidates ran strong campaigns against one another without becoming ensnared in a scandal or falling victim to a disproportionate campaign-spending differential. Presidential races are often used, but the 1996 presidential contest included Ross Perot as a third-party candidate, 2000 saw Green Party candidate Ralph Nader and a pair of Reform Party candidates, and 2004 saw the return of Nader. One-to-one comparisons are slightly problematic. Once again, political judgment is called for. What are the right races to use? Which candidates are "quality" candidates? Which campaigns were truly strong? Calculating electoral statistics demands that researchers be familiar with the trends of electoral politics and view the district through the lens of history to determine what is meant by "typical." No easy task. It may require extensive discussions with party leaders, a fair amount of time looking through old newspaper clippings, and some educated guesswork. Once the typical races are chosen, the researcher takes the average of the three, finding the vote percentage for each party (see Figure 6.5).

In Smith County, an analysis of the past three electoral cycles might show that the best-paired campaigns were the House races in 2000 and 2002 and the gubernatorial race in 2002. For the 2000 House race, the number of votes for the Democrat, which was 42,783, divided by 74,893, the total number of votes cast for auditor, gives the result, 0.571, the score for the race. For the 2002 House and gubernatorial races, the results are 0.590 and 0.556, respectively. Adding these

Figure 6.5
Calculating the Average Party Performance (APP)

Average Democratic Performance	*Average Republican Performance*

Liberal Democrat   *Conservative Republican*

APP = ((performance #1) x (performance #2) x (performance #3)) / 3

figures together and dividing by 3 yields a Democratic APP score of 0.572. Put differently, 57.2 percent of the electorate generally votes Democratic. The Republican APP score turns out to be 0.424, or 42.4 percent. Note that adding the percentages together often renders a sum that is slightly less than 100 percent. Stray votes for third-party, independent, and write-in candidates cause the discrepancy.

The utility of APP scores quickly becomes obvious. To determine the number of votes that, all else being equal, each party can expect to garner in the Smith County auditor's race, multiply each score by the projected electorate. The Democratic APP is 0.572, and the vote projection is 68,892. Multiply the two figures, and it appears that roughly 39,406 people can be expected to vote for a quality Democratic candidate running a decent campaign. On the Republican side, the APP score is 0.424, which generates an expectation of 29,210 votes for the Republican.

Swing, Soft-Partisan, and Toss-Up Votes

The political contours of the district are coming into view. It is heavily Democratic, with quality Republicans losing by wide margins. Almost 56 percent of the vote qualifies as base partisan—more of it Democratic (31.3 percent) than Republican (24.5 percent). This means, however, that a large portion of the electorate remains in play—the swing vote.

Swing Vote. The measure of persuadable voters—the share outside each party's base—is easy to calculate. The swing vote is the inverse of the combined base-partisan vote (Democrat and Republican) (see Figure 6.6). Smith County Democrats have a base-partisan vote of 21,563 for the auditor's race, and the Republicans have a base-partisan vote of 16,879. Add the two together, and one finds combined party bases of 38,442. This much of the electorate will not budge. The inverse of the combined base-partisan votes—the 68,892-vote electorate less the 38,442-vote combined bases—is 30,450, or 44.2 percent of the electorate. This swing vote—the portion of the electorate that resides outside the base of the two parties—will decide the election.

There are two variations on this approach, each designed to deal with electoral volatility. The "swing factor" is concerned with the extent to which voters move from one party to the other between two different election years. The first step is to find a party's most successful race in a given year and then find its score, dividing

Figure 6.6
Calculating the Swing Vote

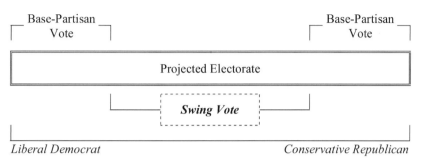

Swing vote = projected electorate – (Democratic base + Republican base)

the votes cast for the candidate by the total votes cast for all candidates in the race. Next, one chooses a race during a *different* election year and takes the score of the party's least successful election. The swing factor is simply the difference between these scores, usually expressed as a percentage. The "split-ticket" factor provides information similar to the swing factor, except that it is founded on intraelection volatility. In other words, it measures the extent that voters switch from party to party within the same election. To calculate the split-ticket factor, the strategist simply finds a recent race in which a candidate of a party did well and a race in which the party's candidate did poorly in the same election. This score becomes particularly important when there is a strong candidate on the ballot.

Soft-Partisan Vote and the Toss-Up Vote. The generalized definition for "swing vote" might be too broad for a refined analysis. It encompasses all the electorate except for the portion that the parties hold through thick and thin. Gradations can be parsed within the swing vote, and they should be. The margin between the party bases might be somewhere in the range of 50 to 60 percent. The point of targeting is to economize—to increase the accuracy of the campaign by eliminating wasteful spending of time and resources. A good political strategist refines the swing vote in ways that ensure strategic utility.

Any effort to carve distinctions within the swing vote is bound to be somewhat arbitrary, but reasoned differentiations can be made. Recall that the base partisan was defined according to the *absolute* worst performance by a party's candidate during a given time period. A "partisan vote" can be defined in accordance with the *average* worst performance in that same time frame. The worst race might keep a quarter of the electorate in a party's fold. An average worst over a five-election period might show a party holding a third of the electorate. There is value in identifying the overlap between the partisan vote and the swing vote. This portion of the electorate votes for less desirable party candidates, even though it might not vote for the worst of the lot. Holding one's own soft-partisan vote is critical; persuading the opposition's soft-partisan vote to defect is difficult but not impossible. Partisans can thus be distinguished between (1) a base-partisan vote, the portion of the electorate that will vote for the absolute worst candidate, and (2) a soft-partisan vote, which can be calculated as the portion of the electorate that will vote for the average worst candidate but not the absolute worst (see Figure 6.7). That is, the soft-partisan vote is the total partisan vote minus the base-partisan vote. One additional category, the toss-up vote, would be the remaining portion of the electorate—everyone not in the partisan vote (either base partisan or soft partisan).

The Democratic partisan vote in Smith County is determined by taking the average of the worst Democratic score for each year, 1994 through 2004. Once again, decisions must be made. In 1996 and 2000, the lowest Democratic score was in the presidential race, both of which had a third-party challenge. The same is true of the GOP in the 1996 auditor's contest. Should races with independent candidates be excluded? It is a judgment call. On one hand, three-way races might depress soft-partisan vote scores, perhaps in ways that distort projections for a two-way race. On the other hand, voters who go for an independent candidate epitomize toss-up voting, so it might be smart to include them in the toss-up category.

For this last reason, three-way presidential races will be used in the analysis of Smith County. For Democrats, take the lowest score for each election, 1994 through 2004. Add the scores together and then take the average, which is 0.441, or 44.1 percent. Multiplying the score by the number of people expected to vote in the auditor's race finds a Democratic partisan vote 30,381 strong. This vote includes both the soft partisans and the base partisans, so the base-partisan vote of 21,563 must be removed from the overall score in order to identify the number of soft partisans. Subtracting this number from 30,381 leaves a soft-partisan vote of 8,818, which is 12.8 percent of the total projected electorate. The same procedure on the Republican side shows a GOP total partisan vote of 24,043 and a soft-partisan vote of 7,164. The GOP soft-partisan vote is 10.4 percent of the overall electorate.

Finally, the toss-up vote. Four distinct groups have already been calculated— a Republican base-partisan vote and a Democratic base-partisan vote along with

Figure 6.7
Calculating the Partisan Vote and the Soft-Partisan Vote

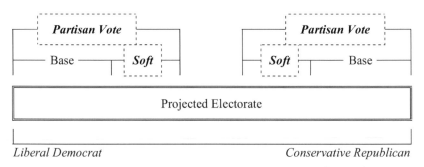

Partisan vote = (vote for average worst candidate)
Soft-partisan vote = (partisan vote) - (base-partisan vote)

a Democratic soft-partisan vote and a Republican soft-partisan vote; combined, these votes represent the partisanship of the district. The toss-up vote is the left-over portion of the electorate. Because the partisan vote is nothing more than the sum of the base-partisan vote and the soft-partisan vote, the toss-up vote is nothing less than the vote that remains after the partisan votes are subtracted from the overall vote total (see Figure 6.8). Democrats have 30,381 in the partisan category; Republicans have 24,043. Added together, the partisan vote will come in at 54,424. Subtract the partisan vote from the total electorate, and the toss-up vote is calculated at 14,468, or 21.0 percent.

Target Votes. Just about every candidate will hold the base-partisan vote. The idea is written into the very definition of "base partisan." If a luckless candidate does worse than all of his or her predecessors, then the base-partisan score is promptly revised downward. It is nearly impossible to lose one's own base or to reach into the base of one's opponent. Strategic thinking forces the campaign professional to develop a target. In the Smith County auditor's race, a full 34,447 votes are needed to win. A competitive Republican must hold the APP—the first 29,210 votes (42.4 percent) or simply give up the fight. This leaves a vote deficit of 5,237. There are 21,563 votes (31.3 percent) in the Democratic base-partisan vote, and these are, by definition, out of reach. The remaining 18,119 (26.3 percent) are in play. To win, the Republican must garner 5,237 (28.9 percent) of these remaining 18,119 votes—the target (see Figure 6.9).

The strategic consequences of this last calculation should not be missed. Looking at the average party performance, the Republican appears to be facing a tough fight. An APP of 42.4 percent means that the GOP candidate needs to get 7.6 percent more of the electorate than average—a formidable task, though doable. But looking at the makeup of the target vote, the job looks nearly impossible. These votes are (1) the portion of the toss-up vote that lies outside the Republican APP plus (2) the Democratic soft-partisan vote. The Republican, who starts with the low APP, needs to capture a large share of the vote that would ordinarily go

Figure 6.8
Calculating the Toss-Up Vote

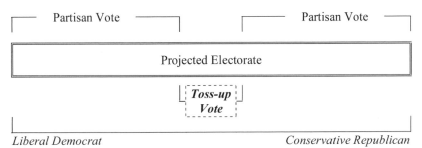

Toss-up vote = proj. electorate − ((Dem. partisan vote) + (GOP partisan vote))

Figure 6.9
Diagramming the Electorate—Smith County, 2002

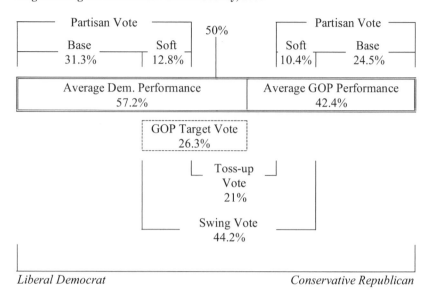

Democratic. Classic strategic theorizing would have the Democrat communicating themes that appeal to the natural Democratic constituency. The Republican, by contrast, must pick up a moderate Democratic message in order to capture the middle ground. Complicating matters, this must be done in a way that still gives the base Republican vote a reason to go to the polls—letting conservatives feel that there is a difference between the Democrat and the Republican.

A Note on Predictions and Aggregate Statistics. The payoff from these calculations is a clean and simple number. In Smith County, it appears that something over 5,000 voters can make a difference. Still, it is important to remember that the quality of the outcome is no better than the quality of the input: "garbage in; garbage out." A great many assumptions were made along the way. It was assumed that past elections are a good guide to future performance, that registration can accurately be projected, that roll-off will remain constant, and that the partisan behavior of the electorate will not change dramatically. Human error creeps into each of these calculations. "Similar" elections were chosen, and "well-matched" candidates were designated. Electoral statistics are not just a product of mathematics; they involve political judgment of the highest order. Without a broad understanding of politics and a deep understanding of the electorate, it is difficult to formulate a strategic awareness of the district.

Judgment is one variable; action is another. Often a campaign team will run the numbers, only to find itself on the short end of the stick. The APP may be only 43 or 44 percent, suggesting that a candidate will lose. The final picture of Smith County suggests difficult terrain for Republicans. Nevertheless, the difficult numbers accrue from aggregate estimates. They do not reflect all possible outcomes. Another way to examine the partisan disposition is to choose a large number of normal races, perhaps 15 to 20 over the past 10 or so years, and see how often candidates of each party have won. A GOP consultant working in Smith County will take heart in the fact that a Republican won the House in 1998 and that a Republican has held the auditor's seat since that year. There *is* a way to win. Quite frequently, the key to success is parsing the aggregate-level statistics by way of careful targeting.

PRECINCT-LEVEL STRATEGY

Bad odds can be beaten. Consider Bill MaGee's New York Assembly district, which by all accounts was a Republican area. Nearly every local elected official in the district was Republican, and voter enrollment was roughly two to one in favor of the Republican Party. Nonetheless, MaGee, a Democrat, was able to win the seat, defeating a 10-year Republican incumbent. It was a victory over the fates. MaGee's 1990 campaign team confronted a variety of difficulties, not the least of which was modest funding. MaGee's operation would have to be run with extreme efficiency. A finely tuned targeting plan had to be devised, combining prior election statistics with polling data.

Rock-ribbed Republican areas were identified. Of the 105 election districts, roughly 25 were deemed solidly Republican. The average Republican Party performance in these areas was more than 60 percent. Few Democrats had ever won them. Despite criticism from both the news media and local politicos for not working these parts of the district, the campaign directed no energy to the heavily Republican sectors. In addition, the strategy team sought out the few solidly Democratic areas. About 20 districts were found. Because resources were tight, little effort was made in these areas. If MaGee could not count on solid Democratic voters, he was sunk anyway. Instead of cultivating base precincts, the campaign team was forced to assume that the Democratic voters in these districts were already in the bag and needed only to be reminded to vote on Election Day.

Remaining were the election districts that might, by some optimistic measure, be labeled "swing." Yet the campaign still did not have enough resources to work the voters in all the remaining 60 election districts. A concerted effort was made to find the districts with the highest propensity toward persuadable voting and to rank order these areas by their relative weight. This information was combined in a series of calculations, using a "votes needed to win" estimate as the guide. Considering his base of support along with that of his opponent, how many swing election districts were needed in a target group if MaGee was able to win them all by 52 percent? By 55 percent? By 57 percent? By 60 percent? In the end, roughly 40 election districts formed the principal target group. If MaGee could win more than one-half of these precincts by at least 55 percent and break even in others, he stood a chance.

The campaign proceeded aggressively to court the voters in these precincts, sticking closely to the issues and themes tested in survey research. The most appropriate way to reach these voters, given their dispersion throughout the district, was finely tuned direct mail, carefully constructed literature drops, and canvasses, augmented by an ambitious telemarketing operation. MaGee won the election by fewer than 500 votes. MaGee's base-partisan vote came through, and, more important, he captured more than 55 percent in most of the targeted election districts. The campaign had successfully tackled a serious deficit in resources and voter support and had done so with prior election statistics. The campaign had targeted the right group of voters.

Ranking Precincts

A Republican candidate for auditor in Smith County is in MaGee's starting position. From the Democratic perspective, all is well. True, a Republican has taken and held the seat in the past, as simetimes happens. Many Republicans are elected in Democratic districts, and the same goes for Democrats in Republican districts. Some people are good campaigners. With the GOP incumbent gone, the statistics heavily favor a Democrat to win. From the Republican perspective, matters are dire—but not impossible. MaGee offers a model for success. The question is how to tailor an underdog strategy to this particular district.

After the numbers are drawn for the district as a whole, the research moves to smaller units of analysis. A statewide race might be separated into counties, a county race might be separated into townships, or a city race might be separated into wards and precincts. The guiding principle is that election data should be taken down to the smallest manageable unit of analysis. It is a matter of costs and benefits. Keeping the data at a high level of abstraction means cheaper data management but less elegant targeting. As the unit of analysis is refined, the targeting is more exact, but the increased number of electoral units raises the data management costs. The individual segments should be small enough to render precise estimates but not so small that compilation and analysis become arduous. There may be 250 precincts in a citywide race or 175 in a state senate district. (Generally speaking, a campaign will find several hundred voters per precinct.) Sorting through the data becomes a chore, particularly if the job is done by hand. The benefits of increased tactical clarity must be weighed against escalating costs of administration.

To allow for the use of smaller units of analysis, new-style campaigns computerize their operations. Small campaigns can probably get by with index cards and spreadsheets. Large operations might want to employ the services of professional data management firms that can maintain, search, merge, and purge enormous data sets. One reason that databasing is now a major part of new-style electioneering is the sheer number of calculations necessary for refined targeting. The statistical measures noted earlier are the tip of the iceberg. There are scores of other statistics that one might uncover, conveying new subtleties and findings. Moreover, the calculations are performed not just on the district as a whole but also on each unit of analysis. The size, turnout, roll-off, total expected votes, APP, base-partisan vote, soft-partisan vote, and toss-up vote might be calculated for a hundred or more precincts. Each geographic unit must be ranked against the others. After the calculations are completed, precincts are classified by size, performance, and persuadability. Strategists want the ability to call up the precincts, counties, or towns with the greatest number of soft-partisan voters—the ones that candidates from each party can count on—and the ones with voters amenable to the candidate's appeal.

Some operatives establish rank orders according to simple scores. Precinct 73 might be worth 103.34 points, for example, and precinct 85 might be worth only 24.82 points. Other professionals develop graduated rankings broken into stratified categories such as "high," "moderate," and "low" and then project the rankings on a map of the district.

By calculating the relative priority of each precinct, areas with the most target voters come to light. A precinct with a high APP and low turnout is asking to be courted; a precinct with a low APP, high turnout, and large base-partisan vote in the opposing camp need not consume much of a candidate's time. The "art" of new-style campaigning lies in the creative use of more ambiguous information. Smart consultants know how to read the numbers. There is tremendous leeway in a data set, and consultants are limited by little more than their own ingenuity. Statistics from one source are merged with statistics from other sources, reconfigured, recalculated, and enhanced to produce deeper meaning and improved strategy. Each campaign offers a unique set of constraints and opportunities.

Strategic theorizing can make a grim situation manageable. A consultant in Smith County would probably urge a Republican candidate to concentrate resources on the precincts that hold the greatest percentage of target voters. New problems arise. If it is difficult to guess the number of people who would be registered on Election Day, predicting the share of the target vote that can be persuaded to vote Republican is truly daunting. Political judgment is called on, past GOP victories are researched, discussions with knowledgeable partisans are held, and ultimately an educated guess must be offered.

A plausible strategy might run as follows. If the entire Republican APP vote sticks with the candidate, the GOP candidate needs another 5,237 votes to win, and these votes must be gathered from the 18,119 votes between the Republican APP and the Democratic base. If 1,540 votes can be produced via districtwide communications (e.g., radio ads and newspaper endorsements), the remaining 3,697 target votes could be picked up through precinct-by-precinct campaign activities. Assume further that precincts targeted for mailings, phone calls, door-to-door visits, and so forth can yield a full 25 percent of the target vote. For example, a precinct with a 200-vote target zone might offer 50 votes beyond the APP. Calculating the yield for each of the district's precincts and then ranking them accordingly suggests the electoral priority of each precinct (see Table 6.2). An analysis of the data might show that most of the precincts at the top of the list come from suburban precincts with high swing factors. Farther down the list might be found the solidly Republican rural communities and the equally committed Democratic central city.

Evaluating precincts strictly in terms of available targets is a crude way of doing business. Additional weights and measures can be added to create the right mix of the base-partisan and swing votes, to adjust for geographic size, or to favor

Table 6.2
Ranking Precincts

		Targeted Votes Needed to Win		3,697
Rank	Precinct	Target-Zone Votes	Projected Vote Yield	Accumulation
1	56	371	93	93
2	89	359	90	183
3	51	347	87	270
4	81	345	86	356
		(Precincts Ranked 5 through 55 Not Shown)		
56	94	267	67	3,569
57	79	260	67	3,636
58	82	255	64	3,700

precincts contiguous with other targeted precincts and then to take account of demographics, polling, volunteer lists, and other such resources. A wise political consultant will work toward the best combination of criteria to develop a general strategy, as will be discussed in Chapter Eight. For now, it is important to note the possibility of Republican victory. If the GOP candidate can hold the Republican APP and get a large portion of the target vote in half the district's precincts, the Republican Party can actually capture the auditor's seat. Not easy, but at least it seems possible—and plannable—because of a narrowly focused strategic conceptualization.

CONCLUSION

Strategists pride themselves on the accuracy of their predictions (even if their prophecies might be partly self-fulfilling). Early in the 1996 campaign cycle, Clinton operatives developed a list of target states designed to give the president his victory. In the Midwest, the campaign focused on Minnesota, Iowa, Missouri, Wisconsin, Illinois, Michigan, and Ohio. Bill Clinton and Al Gore made frequent trips to the area, ignoring heavily Republican Indiana, Nebraska, North and South Dakota, and Bob Dole's home state of Kansas. The reason for hitting a few states and skipping the rest should be obvious. Some states *had* to be won; others never could be (though there were moments when South Dakota seemed in play.) The result on November 5 was a Clinton victory in all the targeted Midwest states alongside a defeat in all the midwestern states that were not on the original list, exactly as planned.

Chapter Seven

Polling: The Focus of Strategic Vision

George W. Bush's controversial win in 2000 showed how close the next election would be. Political professionals understood that the 2004 contest would be very tight and that the outcome would come down to a handful of states (or perhaps just one). Many candidates have found their way to victory by turning the corner in just a state or two. A razor-thin (and controversial) victory in Illinois propelled John F. Kennedy into the White House, for example. But the urgency of *every* vote in *every* swing state in 2004 was underscored by the previous election. It was not surprising that as the race neared the finish line, the number of targeted states narrowed. Pennsylvania remained "in play" throughout the summer and early fall. Bush and Kerry activists flooded the state. The intensity was profound. Headquarters buzzed, college campuses came alive with student activists, phone banks hummed, money flew in, and canvassers hit the streets with a vengeance. Which side would pull it out in Pennsylvania and win its 21 electoral votes? Poll after poll suggested that things were tight—that is, until the final weekend of the race.

With just a few days to go, the campaign operatives from outside the state were gone—many leaving in the dark of night. "It was incredible," said Bob Concilis, chair of the Crawford County Veterans for Kerry. "One day everything is in full gear, we were all out hitting the streets, and the next day everyone is gone—poof! But we also knew it was a good sign. We had the feeling that we were taking the lead in Pennsylvania, and the departure of the out-of-state folks confirmed it." Indeed, both sides had discerned that while the outcome would be close, John Kerry would win the day. The struggle in the Keystone State was over, and it was time to shift resources to another still-to-be-decided state. In the final days of the campaign, both sides flooded into Ohio, knowing that in all likelihood the overall contest would be decided there. They were right. Bush won Ohio by just 140,000 votes. Somehow both sides knew that Pennsylvania would narrowly go to Kerry and that the true battleground state (at least in the Midwest) would be Ohio. This precision was due to carefully orchestrated survey research.

This chapter discusses modern survey research—the need for polling, basic concepts, types of polls, quality control issues, procedural issues, proper sampling, and data analysis. Polling has become the cornerstone of new-style electioneering. Survey research is a critical factor in decisions about the allocation of resources, candidate positioning, and the vulnerabilities of the opponent as well as the timing of campaign events and paid advertising. Simply put, polling has become one of the most efficient means by which campaigns come to understand the hearts and minds of voters.

THE NEED FOR POLLING

Polls are costly, leading many to argue that polling data are unnecessary. "I've lived in this district all my life," a candidate might proclaim, "and I know what people are thinking—why should I run an expensive poll to find out what we already know?" A "feel for the district" is basic to old-style party activism. Precinct captains and ward leaders would listen to voters and transmit their interpretations up the chain of command. Additional knowledge was garnered from newspaper reporters and civic leaders. Sometimes political assessments were based on the size of rallies or number of letters written to officials on a given issue. The quest for public opinion began long before the science of survey research was developed. New-style campaign operatives, however, cannot rely on these informal measures—if for no other reason than the breakdown of party hierarchies makes this kind of communication impossible. While much of the electorate distrusts polls (Traugott and Kang 2000, 185), comparisons of polling projections and electoral results show that modern survey techniques render accurate information (Visser et al. 2000, 225). Survey research is often the best way to learn about the attitudes and perceptions of the electorate. When political operatives want reliable information about voter attitudes, polling is considered a necessity.

POLLING BASICS

Polls are expensive. A "benchmark poll," used at the beginning of a race, might cost some $15,000 to $20,000. When combined with "tracking" and "brushfire" polls, the expense of monitoring public opinion adds up quickly. An outlay of 10 percent of a campaign's total budget is common. Survey costs are a function of several factors, mostly questionnaire construction, interview length, and depth of data analysis. A complex questionnaire requires time for development and pretesting. Long interviews and large samples consume interviewer and supervisor time and often long-distance telephone charges. Large samples require the purchase of phone numbers. Given the variety of options, many campaigns request several estimates based on a variety of survey configurations. One consultant suggests that poorly funded campaigns look for an academic to help with the survey (Simpson 1996).

Polling begins with assessments of name recognition and candidate preference. Many who run for public office have been members of civic organizations or have held positions that put them in the public eye. They hope that this visibility will help them in a race for elective office. While community service may aid in fund-raising and campaign organization, it does not necessarily translate into fame. Candidates are frequently humbled by low name recognition in the beginning stages of the race. Candidates who believe they are known across the district often find 1 in 10 voters recognizing their name. Consider, for example, that in 1994 only 49 percent of voters in Georgia's Tenth Congressional District could identify their five-term incumbent immediately after a hard-fought election (Shea 1996b, 402). Moreover, some candidates will be disheartened to find out that they are not well liked.

Another major use of polling is the identification of voter concerns. At the beginning of any campaign, candidates often have a large number of issues that they wish to pursue. The list must be pared. Recalling the way that he helped plan a 1991 Senate victory in Pennsylvania, James Carville wrote, "Harris Wofford believes in a lot of things, but our researchers came up with three key issues that the people of Pennsylvania cared about deeply: a middle-class tax cut, more affordable education, and health care. Wofford did too. That's what we ran on" (Matalin and Carville 1995, 74). Resources are always tight, so campaigns have to focus on topics for which there is a receptive audience. Polling helps a campaign organization find the right issues.

Underlying attitudes about various social and political values make up a fourth major area to be investigated. The difference between issue preferences and underlying attitudes is that an issue preference represents a choice among current policy options, while underlying attitudes exist even in the absence of specific proposals. A generalized respect for human life, a belief in individual responsibility, and a sense that the public sector must care for the poor are all examples of underlying attitudes. Campaigns need to understand these beliefs if they are going to frame their policy issues appropriately. A pro-choice policy position might be framed in terms of individual freedom, for example; a flat-tax proposal might go to fundamental fairness. Overarching ideology, strength of religiosity, and partisan preference are all clues to the behavior of an electorate, and each can be tapped by using surveys.

At their best, polls allow campaign managers to gauge the potential effectiveness of strategies and tactics. With an accurate analysis of the electorate's attitudes, a campaign organization can make informed decisions about message, targeting, and the allocation of campaign resources. As potential donors try to place their best bets and as the news media try to decide which candidates deserve coverage, new-style campaigns gain credibility by showing—scientifically—that they have a shot at winning.

TYPES OF SURVEYS

Political polls can be separated into six major categories: "focus group," "benchmark," "follow-up," "tracking," "quick response" and "push." Generic survey research commissioned by a media outlet is usually intended to sell a story—not to strategize a campaign. Thus, although some information might prove useful, media-backed polls cannot be relied on when making critical tactical decisions. One reason is that campaign operatives do not have access to the raw data. With only the surface numbers, they cannot manipulate the information to discover electorally significant information that might lie inside. Victory is often found in the "internals." When the candidate's future and the consultant's fortunes are on the line, polls conducted by a private firm with an understanding of political campaigns are often considered a necessity.

Among the types of research such a firm might offer is the focus group, a type of survey that emerged in the early 1990s. Small groups of respondents "chat" about their opinions, beliefs, and attitudes for up to four hours. A moderator helps "pull" comments from the participants while a survey team records the conversation. Although the sample size is small, the breadth of opinions offered in focus groups often captures the emotion beneath the issues. And although focus groups might appear to be simple affairs, they must be carefully supervised in order to draw out the greatest possible volume of information. Moderators encourage shy members to speak, for example, and prevent outspoken participants from dominating the conversation.

Close cousins of the focus group are "dial groups" and "mall intercepts." In a mall intercept, an interviewer approaches a shopper, asks a few questions, and then takes the respondent behind a closed storefront for additional questions. Intercepts are particularly useful for reviewing direct-mail pieces, checking to see how people unfold and skim enclosures. For television spots, a campaign might use a dial focus group. Here participants turn a control knob back and forth, indicating lower or higher satisfaction with different information. This kind of second-by-second analysis can pinpoint strengths and weaknesses within a campaign's message, even capturing problems with wording and sentence structure.

Focus groups are widely used at the beginning of a campaign, setting the stage for a benchmark poll. A benchmark poll is a major survey designed to provide baseline measures on a variety of factors at the beginning of the race. A large sample is used to assess name recognition, issue preferences, underlying attitudes, and prevailing levels of knowledge regarding campaign issues. Measures of partisanship, ideology, religiosity, and standard demographic data are also gathered. This information is used to design a basic campaign strategy and to choose questions that will be asked in subsequent polls.

A follow-up poll is often conducted around the halfway point of a campaign. The idea is to uncover strategic mistakes and correct them while there is still time. Follow-ups are shorter than benchmarks, and tracking polls are shorter still. They cover a limited range of issues or information, but they are administered on a regular basis—sometimes daily—in order to follow voter trends. Key items are name recognition, candidate support, issue support, and the effectiveness of campaign events and commercials.

A run of surveys allows a campaign to observe changes in the overall distribution of preferences in the electorate, but it cannot say much about decisions at the individual level. One way to get at this problem is to gather an initial sample of voters and then reinterview the same panel of respondents throughout a campaign. This approach is informative but expensive. Moreover, some people quit participating—and indeed repeated interviews may change the attitudes of some respondents. A less burdensome approach is the quick-response poll, intended to identify the effect of a campaign event immediately after the event has occurred. For example, if the opponent launches a series of attack ads, then a quick-response poll determines the effect of the commercials on the candidate's standing.

Some polls attempt to push voters away from the opponent. Usually conducted during the final days of a campaign, push polls disguise voter persuasion as survey research. In fact, the term "poll" is inapt because the calls are not random—usually the caller moves down a list of targeted voters—and the intention is not to collect data but to move support.

Advocates of fair campaign practices, as well as in the polling and survey research industry, have expressed great concern over push polls. Push polls simulate an interview on the telephone, but they often do not involve genuine data collection. A question like "Would you still be inclined to vote for Mr. Smith if you knew that he was once arrested for drunk driving?" is characteristic of this technique. While the practice has caused deep concern among some candidates, consultants, and media commentators, push polls are done for a reason. As an Illinois pollster recently noted,

> The political process is an advocacy process. For those people in the middle of it, push polls are seen in a very different light than they are by the research professionals. In the real life and death struggle of win or lose, no holds are barred. Everyone thinks that everyone else is doing it. It's on the increase as it goes further down the line to the state representative level. It's a difficult genie to put back in the bottle. (Richard Day, cited in Bogart 2000, 317)

In a competitive environment, self-regulation is both necessary and difficult. As noted by one observer, "The push poll is a Godzilla in sheep's clothing. The tragic thing is, the average American knows far more about Godzilla than about push polls" (Morrow 2005).

A disturbing example of push polling occurred in 1996. Independent and Republican voters in Kansas were urged to vote for Representative Sam Brownback over his Democratic challenger, Jill Docking, in a telephone "poll" that reminded listeners that Docking was Jewish (Tapper 2005).

Allegations of push polling were rampant during the 2000 campaign. Prior to dropping out of the race for New York's Senate seat, Rudolph Giuliani accused Hillary Rodham Clinton's campaign staff of using push polls to spread dissatisfaction about his stance on abortion (Bumiller 2000). During the early days of the Republican primary season, presidential hopeful John McCain accused George W. Bush's survey research team of "disillusioning a young boy" with a push poll that portrayed the senator as a "liar and a fraud" (Mitchell and Bruni 2000). (The reason that an interviewer would badger a boy too young to vote remained unexplained.) Later, in South Carolina, voters were asked by anonymous pollsters,

"Would you be more likely or less likely to vote for John McCain for president if you knew he had fathered an illegitimate black child?"

Sometimes the line between legitimate polling and push polling is quite clear, but other times it is ambiguous. Would a Bush poll that tested Gore's vulnerabilities on trust issues fit a broad definition of a push poll? Perhaps, but in general terms the difference is one of intent rather than effect. If the survey is designed to provide feedback from a random sample of voters—that is, if it is intended to gain generalizable information—then it *is not* considered a push poll. If it is designed to persuade voters, then it *is* considered a push poll. The American Association of Political Consultants has condemned the practice. Moreover, allegations of push polling make for damaging news. Some state legislators have even proposed legislation to outlaw it. (First Amendment guarantees of free speech would likely preclude any such law.)

Consultants are well advised that both the public and the media are poised to condemn the use of push polls, and the repercussions from using them might well outweigh potential gains.

QUALITY CONTROL

To maximize the value of polling, political consultants generally outsource their survey work to professional pollsters. Still, consultants must be, at a minimum, good consumers of survey data, being aware of the many pitfalls of polling. Not every used-car buyer is a mechanic, but an informed shopper can look under the hood for oil leaks and broken hoses, minimizing the chance of being defrauded. The same holds true for consumers of polling services. The better is one's understanding of survey techniques and statistical tools, the less likely one is to make a costly mistake.

A "good" poll has minimal error. If 55 percent of the population would vote for a candidate on Election Day, then the poll should represent that fact with little deviation. The difficulty is that a campaign does not know the actual opinions of the population; it just knows the polling data. The only absolute test comes on Election Day itself—too late for correction. The best the a pollster can do is to make sure that its survey procedures minimize error. Three types of error are particularly salient: "instrument error," "measurement error," and "sampling error." The total error in a survey—the difference between the political reality and the survey results—is the product of these three sorts of inaccuracy.

Instrument Error

Questionnaires are difficult to construct. In a classic piece of research, Howard Schuman and Stanley Presser found that attitudes toward freedom of the press changed significantly as the order of questions was altered (1981). If the survey instrument—in this case, the questionnaire—is poorly constructed, the resulting data will be a poor reflection of public attitudes.

Instrument error is the bias created by the wording of a question or the implementation of the survey. A good deal of instrument error comes from "undecided" voters. The classic example is the question, If you were going to vote today, would you vote for candidate Smith or candidate Jones? With only two choices, many respondents would feel that the appropriate thing to do is to choose between the two alternatives. Few individuals volunteer, "Look, I haven't made up my mind." Some pollsters *want* to force an answer. After all, Smith and Jones are the only names on the ballot. For top-of-the-ticket races, such as governor or president, most people will make a choice even if they are not very happy about it. (This is not always the case. From the campaign consultant's point of view, undecided voters may be exactly the audience that it wants to identify.) Another form of this question is, If the election were held today, would you vote for candidate Smith, candidate Jones, or have you not yet made up your mind? The addition of the phrase "have you not yet made up your mind" enables an undecided respondent to reply comfortably, "No, I haven't thought about it yet."

Measurement Error

Measurement error is the bias created by improper recording of a respondent's answer. It is typified by the mistakes made by interviewers asking questions in the wrong sequence or by data-entry personnel prone to typographical blunders. Even if the question has been properly phrased and duly answered, it is possible for an interviewer to record the answer incorrectly. With pencil-and-paper administration, which must be input for analysis, the data can still be corrupted by data-entry personnel. Large survey houses use computer-assisted telephone interviewing (CATI). Interviewers use a personal computer on which the CATI presents questions one at a time. As the polling agent records answers from the respondent, each answer is checked to ensure that it is within the range of acceptable responses. The interview is then branched to the next appropriate question. Controls on input validity and branch sequencing increase data quality.

Sampling Error

The third major type of error in a survey is sampling error, the difference between the characteristics of a sample and the overall population it represents. Only a small portion of the total population is interviewed, from which are drawn inferences about the entire population. Unfortunately, each sample will produce a slightly different mix of people. In one sample, there might be a few more wealthy individuals than expected; in another, there might be too many young males; and in yet another, environmentalists might be underrepresented. If the sample is carefully drawn, the extent of these errors can be calculated. In fact, some degree of sampling error *must be* tolerated. The only way to ensure perfect sampling is to poll the entire population—an unrealistic approach to public opinion research.

Unbiased samples are difficult to gather. Samples picked out of a phone book, for instance, are biased against people without telephones (who may be poorer than average), people with unlisted phone numbers (who may value privacy more than others), and people who rely on cell phones (who may be younger). Among those who have a phone, a growing percentage refuse to give their opinion. As campaign operatives, product advertisers, and the media rely increasingly on survey research, polling agents have saturated the public with calls, and the increase in telephone solicitations for sometimes dubious goods and services has been particularly harmful to pollsters. Many people have stopped answering questions. The problem for pollsters is not simply that they have to make more calls to complete their surveys; rather, the type of person who refrains from answering survey questions is not distributed equally among the population.

Some demographic groups, such as well-educated men, are less likely to entertain questions than are other groups. Real problems arise. "The key to polling accuracy is the principle of 'equal probability of selection,' says columnist Arianna Huffington, "but if larger and larger numbers among those randomly selected refuse to participate, this principle no longer applies" (Daves 2000, 219). Against those who think the Web offers some kind of solution, Roger Mortimore, senior political analyst with the research company MORI, explains that "there is no way of drawing a scientifically representative sample of the population from Internet users. The extremely old and extremely poor are difficult to reach via the net" (Marks 2005, 1).

THE INTERVIEW PROCESS

Reliable surveys come from friendly conversations. Interviewers and questionnaires must put the respondent at ease. Useful information must be sought and collected, but the respondent must never feel interrogated. A good interview ends with the respondent feeling grateful for the opportunity to have an interesting dialogue with the polling agent.

The introduction is crucial. The vast majority of refusals come within the first few seconds. A properly constructed introduction should tell the respondent the purpose of the survey and then identify which member of the household should answer the questions. (Many pollsters fear that, say, too many women answer the phone first.) While polls should always disclose the name of the survey firm, the identity of the candidate is not offered up front because the very mention of his or her name can skew the results.

Question Design

Pollsters talk about "good" and "bad" questions. A good question will be understood by just about every member of the surveyed audience. Clear language and even a bilingual interviewer can aid in the process. The average citizen has little policy expertise, so questions about environmental issues might demand, for example, the use of terms like "the loss of forests" rather than "deforestation." Moreover, the question should not steer respondents toward any particular type of answer: "Do you believe in the constitutional right to keep and bear arms?"

predisposes a respondent toward answering "yes." Finally, as noted earlier, a good question offers a range of appropriate responses.

Professional pollsters spend a great deal of time wording their questionnaires properly. Colloquial phrases can skew results. By definition, colloquialisms mean different things to different people. Slang is particularly difficult to use when its interpretation differs by age, class, or ethnicity. Indefinite terms can also become problematic. What does "frequently" mean? What does "several" mean? Even the word "voter" can represent a complex concept. If the interviewer asks a respondent, "Are you a voter?" and the reply is "yes," does this mean a vote in every election, every general election, every presidential election, or a one-time vote 10 years ago? Clarity and precision minimize this sort of ambiguity.

Types of Questions

To reduce uncertainty, distinctions are made among "information," "knowledge," "opinion," and "self-perception" questions (Backstrom and Hursh-Cesar 1981). An information question goes to facts relating directly to the respondent, such as standard demographic items (e.g., age, sex, race, and income). A knowledge question goes to the wider domain of facts (e.g., the identity of the respondent's congressional representative). An opinion question asks the respondent for a judgment (e.g., the respondent's attitudes toward an issue or candidate). A self-perception question is an opinion question about oneself (e.g., whether the respondent considers him- or herself a Democrat). By understanding the types of questions being asked, pollsters can gain a better understanding of the information they are getting from the public.

Any of these types of questions can be asked in an "open-response" or a "closed-response" format. In an open-response question, respondents answer questions in their own words. In the closed format, the respondent is asked to choose from a predetermined set of answers. Note that open-response formats require interviewers to know a great deal about the topic at hand. Asking, "What do you believe is the most important problem facing America?" might bring a wide array of answers. A part-time interviewer might not understand how to code a complicated answer. Fixed-response items are easier to record, but they may force respondents into judgments that they would not otherwise offer.

One important use of closed-format questions is respondent screening. "Filter questions" control the flow of the interview, ensuring the relevance of the questions that follow. For example, it is inappropriate to ask a widow about the effect of the "marriage tax" on her family. Therefore, a marital-status question, "Are you married, widowed, separated, divorced, or never married?" could be used as a filter question. Individuals reporting that they were currently married would receive an appropriate block of marriage-tax queries. Everyone else would branch out to another set. A common filter question asks whether respondents intend to vote in the coming election. If they say "no" or "probably not," the survey might end. Why spend money gathering information from a nonvoter? Then again, a campaign might want to know what would make the person go out and vote.

Once a respondent gets through the filter, the polling agent might ask a "sleeper" or "probe" question. A probe seeks detail about a previous response. For example, if the questioner asked, "In politics, do you normally think of yourself as a Democrat, an Independent, a Republican, or something else?" and the respondent replied, "Democrat," a probe might ask, "Do you consider yourself a strong or weak Democrat?" Individuals who call themselves "Independent" would be pressed to see if they lean toward one party or the other. In this case, the probe question seeks intensity. Sleeper questions check the veracity of a respondent's answers to other questions. At some point in the questionnaire, the respondent might be asked whether he or she voted in the most recent election; somewhere else in the questionnaire, a sleeper question is asked about the location of the polling place. If the respondent is unable to answer the question about the location, then doubts are raised as to whether the respondent actually voted. Some polling schemes actually check answers against local voting records.

Modes of Administration

Accuracy is paramount but costly, and each of the four general modes of conducting surveys involve trade-offs. Face-to-face administration has an interviewer go to the home of a selected respondent. A mail survey usually takes the form of a short letter. Internet-based surveys are coming of age. Surveys may be e-mailed directly to the respondents or the subjects are redirected to a Web site where they can complete the poll. The fourth and most widely used mode of administration in political polling is via telephone.

Each mode of administration has virtues and drawbacks. Face-to-face interviewing usually gives the best results in terms of data quality and respondent cooperation, but the process is expensive and time consuming. Mail surveys are relatively inexpensive, but they generally offer low response rates—and response time is too slow for campaign work. In addition, since mail surveys depend solely on the respondent's interest in answering, their results tend to be biased. Those who are either very much in favor of or very much opposed to a candidate are more likely to return the survey than those with only marginal interest. The "self-selection problem," sometimes called SLOP, should be sufficient to preclude any serious use of a mail poll, but for political campaigns, the difficulty is particularly acute since unpersuaded voters are usually the campaign's target audience. Telephone interviews dominate political polling by default. They cost about the same as mail polls, but they produce much higher response rates and allow for complex question branching.

In the new millennium, Internet polling is entering the marketplace. Some companies offer complete, Internet-ready software packages. These packages eliminate data entry. Responses are precoded, and on completion of the survey by the respondent, they are entered immediately and directly into the analysis software. Although rapid turnaround is a great advantage, concerns about sample bias remain. As such, Internet polling suffers some of the drawbacks of mail surveys. The types of people who go online are disproportionately well educated, young, and affluent—and those willing to respond to an online survey are probably more engaged in politics than the average voter. These difficulties must be recognized and managed.

Because no database contains every e-mail address on the Internet, random sampling in online polls is impossible. Feld notes that "for the foreseeable future, its use cannot be separated from the telephone or mail research modes" (2001, 4). Another commentator put it this way: "On-line polls results might be nothing more than fool's gold" (Johnson 2001, 100). One solution to the problem of skewed demographics is to weight responses. That is, responses are statistically adjusted to compensate for the demographic differences between respondents and the voting population (Johnson 2001, 101). Given the lower cost and higher speed of online polls, one can imagine that this approach would be attractive, and there is little question that in the years ahead pollsters will make greater use of Internet polling in one form or another.

Occasionally, a "bullet poll" might be used. Here the poll is conducted completely by a computer, with a feel similar to voice-mail systems (Johnson 2001, 95). The respondent is directed to key his or her answers into the phone: "Press 1 for yes, 2 for no, 3 for unsure." The upside to such polls is speed and cost; they can be done quickly and, with little labor cost, at a minimal expense. The downside is that there is no control over who answers the survey. A specific person might be requested, but there is no way to know for sure whether his or her 10-year-old son was the one punching the answers. Great caution should be used when interpreting the results of such polls.

Commercial Polling Firms

Campaign polls are usually performed by commercial polling firms, not in-house volunteer operations. The amount of time spent training volunteers is relatively short—usually they want to "get on with the job"—but even the best-motivated volunteers can be unreliable. Attendance is erratic, and the very enthusiasm of campaign volunteers stands in the way of proper survey administration. The collection of data requires a dispassionate approach. Tone of voice, by itself, conveys the desirability of one's candidate. Campaign operatives can try to impress on volunteers the importance of being neutral, but this is usually an uphill battle. New-style campaigns turn to professionals.

Outsourcing carries its own risks, however. Just as volunteer polling operations suffer from inexperience and overenthusiasm, professional polling firms vary according to the value of their hiring procedures. Recruitment pools, training, and retention rates bear heavily on survey accuracy. While almost anyone can be taught to read a questionnaire out loud, few people are superb conversationalists. Good polling depends, in part, on a firm's ability to recruit good employees. Even the method of payment—hourly wage or piecework—affects data quality. An hourly wage reduces an interviewer's incentive to submit a stack of bogus call reports, but because payment will be received regardless of call completion, there is little motivation to get the job done in a timely manner. Piecework payments, by which a caller is paid according to the number of calls completed, rewards persistent employees for recontacting appointments, working numbers at odd hours in order to contact hard-to-reach respondents, and otherwise completing designated calls, but it also rewards the filing of sham call reports. There is no perfect formula. Many survey shops use a combination of an hourly rate and some kind of incentive for completing interviews.

Smart political consultants ask polling firms about their training procedures—manuals, instruction time, and the sorts of behavior expected of employees. The reason: interviewers are themselves part of the measuring instrument, and a polling-center employee must accurately report all possible information, remaining neutral and unmoved no matter how obnoxious respondents may be.

Many polling firms have their supervisors hook into calls and listen to selected interviews, and some now let the client do so. This type of supervision helps prevent the fabrication of interviews—a form of negligence common among interviewers working from home. A well-run survey firm keeps records of random monitoring sessions. Survey directors adjust pay rates and manage job assignments accordingly. Interviewers who perform well on these random checks are given difficult, highly paid survey projects. Consultants looking for quality research sometimes verify completed interviews, perhaps by having a supervisor call back random interviewees to confirm that an interview was actually conducted.

SAMPLING

One of the most daunting problems in survey research is determining precisely who should be interviewed. A pollster cannot build a list of possible respondents until the campaign decides which population it wants to analyze. Is it the entire district? Registered voters? Likely voters? Democrats? Registered Democrats who rarely vote? Researchers define "population" as the overall group of people that will be analyzed by the survey. A "sample" is any subset of that population—a microcosm of the whole population. From a scientific standpoint, modern survey research works because pollsters draw their samples from the population at random. Data collected from the sample will be representative of the broader population, and standard statistical equations can then be used for analysis. It is a risky business. In a gubernatorial race, 800 individuals might be drawn from a population of 5 million registered voters. The sample in this case represents only 0.00016 percent of the registered population. If the sample has been biased in any way, then the data will not be representative, and the survey's conclusions will likely be inaccurate.

One approach to sampling is to use random digit dialing (RDD). RDD, a technique that generates sample telephone numbers based on area codes and local exchanges. A pollster might be tempted to draw a sample from a telephone book, but high rates of unlisted numbers would render the sample nonrandom. Random dialing overcomes this bias. Specialized sampling firms, which screen out non-working and business numbers to increase the efficiency of an RDD list. Because such a list still includes nonvoters, political pollsters often cross-reference lists with registered voter lists. The problem with voter lists, however, is that they are frequently out of date, and their quality depends on the effort of government agencies to keep the rolls current. Some polling firms rely on "stratification," whereby geographic areas are randomly selected, and then a number of voters within each area are themselves chosen at random.

When deciding on sample size, a consultant must determine how much error can be tolerated. A campaign might be ready to accept a 3 percent margin of error—meaning that a district showing of 46 percent favorability toward a candidate might actually have a population that lies somewhere between 43 and 49 percent favorability. Having decided on the acceptable margin of error, a campaign must decide on an acceptable level of confidence. "Confidence" is the probability that the poll actually falls within the margin of error. At 95 percent confidence, there is a 5 percent chance that a perfectly randomized sampling procedure will produce responses that fall outside the margin of error. The reason: random sampling, by its very nature, is a game of chance, and sometimes even randomly selected groups will be highly unrepresentative. Minimizing the odds of a "fluky" poll requires campaign operatives to seek a large sample. A 5 percent margin at 95 percent confidence demands 384 respondents; a 3 percent margin of error at 99 percent confidence demands 1,843 respondents (see Table 7.1). Because tighter error boundaries and higher levels of confidence increase sample size exponentially, campaigns find themselves choosing between money and accuracy—sometimes a tough decision.

If procedures are not random, even a large sample will not solve the problem. Some polls consciously recalculate the value of certain responses in order to ensure balance. Frequently, samples need to be weighted to account for problems that arise in the interview methods. For example, 600 interviews might be taken over the course of a single afternoon. At that time of the day, the sample will likely be older and more female than the general population because these groups have a greater tendency to be at home and a greater willingness to field

Table 7.1
Margins of Error and Measures of Confidence

	Simple Random Sample Size	
Margin of Error (%)	*Confidence*	
	95%	*99%*
+/− 7	196	339
+/− 6	267	461
+/− 5	384	663
+/− 4	600	1,037
+/− 3	1,067	1,843
+/− 2	2,401	4,147
+/− 1	9,604	16,587

questions. If 250 males are interviewed but the general demographics of the district show that 312 males would have been needed for the sample to be representative, then greater substance will be given to each response from a male. But even this approach is flawed. The males whom one finds at home might have different party or candidate preferences from those of men at work. They might labor at night jobs, be employed part-time, or simply be unemployed. The same goes for female respondents. Thus, the set of individuals whom a pollster is able to interview in the middle of a workday is not necessarily representative of all the individuals in the district, and even demographic weighting can mislead.

DATA ANALYSIS

Consultants inquire about the procedures used in the construction of a poll, but they are most interested in the results. Tables 7.2 through 7.5 display a set of questions asked in a poll regarding the hypothetical Senate race between Democrat Bob Jackson, Republican Mark White, and Independent Joe Jones.

In the item displayed in Table 7.2, respondents were asked how interested they were in the race. In this case, 452 individuals said that they were very interested in the race, representing 42.6 percent of all the individuals polled. This number is called the "frequency distribution." At the bottom of the panel, a value reported as "Don't know." These respondents were unable or unwilling to answer the item. The 13 individuals coded in that category constituted 1.23 percent of the entire sample. For most purposes, individuals who are unable to answer the question are

Table 7.2
Interest-Level Question

In the election for the U.S. Senate, the Democrat Bob Jackson is running against Republican Mark White and the Independent Joe Jones. Would you say that you are very, somewhat, just a little, or not at all interested in this race?

(1) Very (2) Somewhat (3) Little (4) Not at all (9) Don't know

Value Labels	Scale Value	Observed Frequency	Percent of Total	Percent of Non-Missing Cases
Very	1	452	42.60	43.13
Somewhat	2	360	33.93	34.35
Little	3	115	10.84	10.97
Not at all	4	121	11.40	11.55
Don't know	9	13	1.23	—

Valid Cases: 1,048   Missing Cases: 13

removed from further analysis. A lot of "Don't know" responses can suggest a badly written question.

The poll shows a clear White lead. Table 7.3 presents reported vote preference, including the breakdown of responses to that item immediately below the question. The results of the question indicate that White was well ahead in the race with about 43.2 percent of the voters who had a preference as compared to about 33.2 for Jackson and about 3.8 percent for Jones. In Table 7.4, one finds an item that was administered to those individuals who made a choice among the three declared candidates for the race. The computer filled in the question so that the interviewer would have read to Jackson supporters, "How certain are you to vote for Mr. Jackson?" A third reported that they were not very sure that they would vote for their current candidate on Election Day.

Perhaps the most important category in the constituency is the "undecided" voter. Table 7.5 shows preferences for those individuals who indicated that they had not yet made up their minds or were intending to skip the race. Each was asked which way he or she leaned. The uncommitted are apportioned to the respective candidates. More than 80 percent had some preference in the initial vote-choice question and therefore branched around this item. Those who remained leaned toward Jackson, but most were truly undecided.

Cross Tabulations

A "cross tabulation" displays the frequencies of responses to one item within the categories of another item. This type of breakdown helps the campaign visu-

Table 7.3
Candidate Preference Question

If the election were held today would you vote for Mr. Jackson, Mr. White, Mr. Jones, or would you skip the race?

(1) Jackson (2) White (3) Jones (4) Skip (5) Undecided – IF VOLUNTEERED
(9) Don't know

Value Labels	Scale Value	Observed Frequency	Percent of Total	Percent of Non-Missing Cases
Jackson	1	343	32.33	33.17
White	2	447	42.13	43.23
Jones	3	39	3.68	3.77
Skip	4	109	10.27	10.54
Undecided	5	96	9.05	9.28
Don't Know	9	27	2.54	—

Valid Cases: 1,034   Missing Cases: 27

Table 7.4
Certainty Probe

How certain are you that you will vote for Mr. _____?

(1) Very certain (2) Somewhat (3) Not at all (9) Don't know

Value Labels	Scale Value	Observed Frequency	Percent of Total	Percent of Non-Missing Cases
	-1	232	21.87	
Very	1	521	49.10	63.30
Somewhat	2	273	25.73	33.17
Not at all	3	29	2.73	3.52
Don't know	9	6	.57	—

Valid Cases: 823   Missing Cases: 328

Table 7.5
Leaning Question

Are you LEANING toward Mr. Jackson, Mr. White, or Mr. Jones?

(1) Hyatt (2) DeWine (3) Slovenec (4) Skip (5) Undecided (9) Don't know

Value Labels	Scale Value	Observed Frequency	Percent of Total	Percent of Non-Missing Cases
	−1	856	80.68	—
Jackson	1	34	3.20	20.36
White	2	27	2.54	16.17
Jones	3	4	.38	2.40
Undecided	4	102	9.61	61.08
Don't know	9	38	3.58	—

Valid Cases: 167   Missing Cases: 894

alize the effect of the second variable on the first. Table 7.6 shows candidate preferences cross tabulated by their interest in the election. The column headed "Very" shows the number of individuals who said that they were "very interested" in the race. In that column, White led Jackson by about 54 to 35 percent. In the second column are individuals who reported that they were "somewhat" inter-ested in the race. Here Jackson closed the gap to a 41 to 35 percent spread. Among those individuals who said they are only "a little interested," Jackson appears to lead by about 39 to 34 percent. A majority of those who said that they are "not at all interested" in the race reported that they did not intend to vote.

Table 7.6
Cross-Tabulation of Interest by Vote Intention

	Degree to which the respondent is interested in the campaign					
	Very	Somewhat	Little	Not at all	Margin	Percentage
Jackson	158	124	43	17	342	33.3%
	35.35%	35.0%	38.7%	14.9%	—	—
White	242	244	38	21	445	43.4%
	54.1%	40.7%	34.2%	18.4%	—	—
Jones	18	15	3	3	39	3.8%
	4.0%	4.2%	2.7%	2.6%	—	—
Skip	3	35	11	59	108	10.5%
	.7%	9.9%	9.9%	51.8%	—	—
Undecided	26	36	16	14	92	9.0%
	5.8%	10.2%	14.4%	12.3%	—	—
Margin	447	354	111	114	1026	n/a
Percent	43.6%	34.5%	10.8%	11.1%	n/a	n/a

There are, to be sure, scores of analytic techniques that pollsters can use to coax hidden findings from the data. Some polling firms conduct regression models and probability equations. Finally, it is quite common to overlay survey data with demographic and electoral data. Drawing strategic information from survey results is one of the most important skills in modern electioneering.

CONCLUSION

Consultants must think carefully about their choice of pollster. Trust is paramount. Campaigns expect that pollsters will give accurate answers to pressing questions, even when the news is bad. Done well, survey research affords a campaign one of its best opportunities to understand what the electorate thinks—what the voters care about and who they want to put in office. There are other ways to measure voter opinion, but new-style campaigning is about mathematical precision. Few managers go into the field without survey data.

NOTE

A significant portion of this chapter is adapted from Jesse Marquette, "How to Become a Wise Consumer of Campaign Polling," in Daniel M. Shea, *Campaign Craft: The Strategies, Tactics, and Art of Political Campaign Management* (Westport, CT: Praeger), 1996.

Chapter Eight

General Strategy

In 1984, voters had no doubt where Ronald Reagan stood. He sought renewed economic strength and international security. It was "Morning in America." His campaign theme—romantic in its vision and brilliant in its efficient use of political imagery—has become a legend in the world of American political campaigns. Eight years later, the rationale of Bill Clinton's bid for the presidency was captured on a sign that James Carville posted in the campaign War Room: "Change vs. more of the same; The economy, stupid; Don't forget health care." George Stephanopoulos called it a "campaign haiku," and no matter what the issue was, the campaign wrapped its message around one of these "three commandments." "In our world," Stephanopoulos has written, "the only mortal sin was to be 'off-message'" (1999, 88). In retrospect, the winning campaign themes from 1984 and 1992 seem obvious. When times are good, accentuate the positive. When times are bad, call for a change.

But the dilemma facing Bill Clinton in early 1995 was more complex. In late 1994, voters took power away from the Democrats in the House and Senate and gave Congress to the Republicans. "Safe" Democratic candidates went down to defeat. Speaker of the House Tom Foley lost his district to an attorney who had never held elective office. It was a dramatic reversal of fortune widely interpreted as a rejection of the Democratic Party in general and the Democratic president in particular. Many thought Clinton could do little more than bide his time until inevitable defeat in November 1996. Some thought that a challenge would rise from within the Democratic ranks, perhaps defeating the incumbent president in the primaries. It was not clear that any campaign theme could rescue the Clinton White House.

The dire predictions of 1994 never came to pass. Not only did Clinton escape a primary challenge, but he held a consistent double-digit lead over his Republican opponent throughout most of 1996. The press corps found the race dull, so unflagging was the president's popularity.

Clinton's victory can be attributed partly to the failures of his opposition. The GOP was never able to get into campaign mode, and it often seemed as though the candidate, Senator Bob Dole, was having trouble focusing on a single message—perhaps a natural outcome of a heated Republican primary that left no time to reorganize GOP support. Clinton's success has also been attributed to the Democratic National Committee's spending on anti-Republican ads in 1995, to the support of organized labor, and to the improving American economy. Victory has deep roots. But in many ways, Clinton's 1996 triumph arose from wise strategic positioning.

After 1994, there were two schools of thought as to how the president should proceed. The first was liberal. Many of the losing Democrats were moderate or conservative, and the ones who remained after 1994 were more partisan than their predecessors. The liberal take on 1996 strategy was that the president should concentrate on his core Democratic base of support. The idea made sense. Why should the president move to the right? Why should he cast himself as a Republican in Democratic clothing? After all, it was said, given the choice between a Republican and a Republican, the people will choose a Republican every time. The other school sought a moderate approach. The votes that were lost in 1994 fell from the center, not the left. To win in 1996, moderate territory had to be recaptured.

Consultant Dick Morris, who had advised Democrats and Republicans alike, gave the centrist approach his own sly twist: press against the Democratic left and simultaneously against the Republican right, find the center, and then rise above partisan conflict. Morris called the strategy "triangulation." In Morris's words, "The president needed to take a position that not only blended the best of each party's views but also transcended them to constitute a third force in the debate." By taking the prescribed approach, Morris wrote, "either he will be repudiated by the voters and slink back into the orthodox positions or he will attract support and, eventually, bring his party with him" (1999a, 80–81). While the policies engendered by triangulation have been criticized as too moderate or too small, most observers have concluded that the positioning of the Clinton campaign was electorally smart. The reasoning behind triangulation becomes clear if one understands the fundamentals of strategic positioning.

This chapter deals with matters of general strategy. Strategic issues have been touched on in previous chapters, and in many ways a discussion of general strategy is the culmination of campaign planning, demographics, candidate and opposition profiles, prior electoral history, and campaign polling. Without a target, a campaign has no direction; without a theme, it has no rationale. General strategy entails strategic positioning, mapping the target vote, and developing an effective campaign theme.

STRATEGIC POSITIONING

A wise campaign strategy is selective. The size and disposition of the electorate varies from community to community. A sparsely populated section of a district might supply a rich lode of swing votes, while an urbanized area might offer few.

In some precincts, Democrats never stand a chance, while in others, the Republican always suffers. In some areas, the outcome always seems to be in doubt. These areas can be labeled "Democratic," "Republican," or "swing." The strategic approach that a campaign takes—whom it will target and what it will do to gain the target votes—stems largely from the composition of the electorate. A precinct or district with a strong party tradition commands one strategy; an area with a large toss-up vote calls for another. For campaign professionals, there are few immutable rules but a number of reasoned guidelines.

First, some basics. There are three main goals of campaign strategy: "reinforcement," "persuasion," and "conversion." Reinforcement is the task of making sure base voters stick with the candidate, persuasion is the process of bringing swing voters on board, and conversion is the act of getting the opposition's voters to switch sides. In campaign parlance, the precise meaning of these terms is ambiguous—is a Democrat courting nonbase Republicans trying to persuade or convert?—but in general terms, a campaign *reinforces its own partisans, persuades the toss-up, and converts the partisans of the opposition.*

It is easier to reinforce or persuade voters than to convert them. When the candidate is a member of a heavily favored party, the entire focus might be on reinforcement. The objective is to get the party's voters to show up at the polls. In volatile areas, where neither candidate has an edge at the outset, persuasion is the central strategy. If most voters are committed to the opponent's party or a challenger faces a popular incumbent, conversion is called for. One way to approach a district is to draw a continuum, where the extremes of the line represent the most partisan supporters and the center area denotes swing voters (see Bradshaw 1995, 31–33)—basically the approach taken to Smith County in Chapter Six. Electoral research, demographics, and early campaign polling say much about

Figure 8.1
Strategizing a Partisan District—The Democratic Favorite

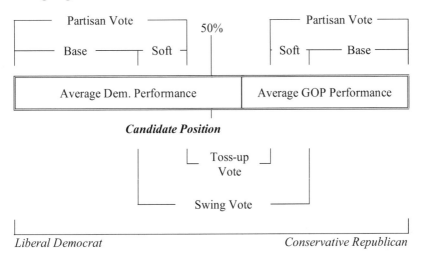

a district, and registration lists offer basic facts about individual voters, including party affiliation. (Party identification is the best single predictor of voting habits.) Combining this information into a larger portrait suggests the partisan loyalty of a district. The same calculations can be made for counties, cities, wards, precincts, parishes, or any other unit of analysis.

Figure 8.1 shows the Democratic candidate in good shape. Democratic partisans make up about 50 percent of the vote, while Republican partisans are only 30 percent. In fact, the Democratic base is about 50 percent larger than the Republican base. As such, the Democratic goal should be the reinforcement of Democratic voters and the persuasion of a small number of swing voters. Winning does not require a single convert. The task should not be difficult because many of the swing voters would be predisposed to vote Democratic. A Democrat's best strategic position is at the center of the pack of Democratic partisans or perhaps a bit to its right.

There was little question as to which portion of the electorate Democrat Jesse Jackson Jr. needed to target in his 1995 special election to fill Illinois' Second Congressional District seat. African Americans made up more than two-thirds of the Second, which extends from Chicago's South Side to the suburbs in the southern part of Cook County (Benenson 1995, 3836). Party enrollment roughly paralleled the demographics, with the inner-city areas overwhelmingly Democratic and the suburbs solidly Republican. The Jackson campaign targeted only the city. On Election Day, Jackson won 98 percent in the inner-city precincts and 51 percent of the suburban vote. This was enough to give him a three-to-one majority overall (Johnson 1995, B17).

Some candidates enjoy the benefits of a partisan district; others suffer. Looking at partisan districts from the other direction, one finds a bleak. In Figure 8.2, a Republican campaign has little choice but to convert a number of Democratic

Figure 8.2
Strategizing a Partisan District—The Republican Underdog

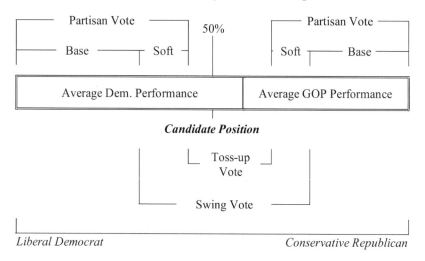

partisans. Because the race is a long shot, it may be necessary to take most of the Republican voters for granted, hoping they will stick with the GOP candidate. Few resources should be spent on reinforcement—except, perhaps, for a last-minute, get-out-the-vote drive. Assuming that some Republican partisans will be lost and a fair number of swing voters will go Democratic, a significant number of Democratic soft partisans must be persuaded. A Republican candidate should take a strategic position at the center of the full electorate, significantly to the left of the GOP base.

This is not to say that Republicans are unelectable in Democratic districts—it just takes creativity. Republican Bill Redmond was able to prevail in the heavily Democratic Third District of New Mexico. In 1996, Democrat Bill Richardson beat Redmond with two-thirds of the vote. When Richardson was later tapped to become U.S. ambassador to the United Nations, the seat opened up for a special election in 1997. Like Jackson, Redmond would benefit from low voter turnout, which makes a motivated base all the more significant, but Redmond had to do more. In addition to energizing the base, the Redmond campaign moved to break up the Democratic partisans by praising a Green Party candidate who was peeling off left-liberal voters. As the third party increased its share of the electorate, the number of Republican votes required to beat the Democrat declined. To rally his own supporters, Redmond raised questions about his opponent's official behavior and made direct appeals to swing voters. According to Redmond's campaign team, the strategy was basic: "By identifying Redmond as a warm, caring person, we were able to blunt . . . textbook Democratic attacks of extremism that hurt so many candidates in 1996" (Wilson and Burita 2000, 98). Having positioned himself as a moderate—not emphasizing his conservative credentials—Redmond won the election with a 43 percent plurality, beating the Democrat by just three points.

Toss-up districts present a different sort of project. Figure 8.3 suggests a district with no clear bias. In one sense, the strategy is the same as it would be for an underdog—the candidate should be positioned toward the center. Unlike the underdog, who has a broad range of voters to persuade, the Republican in an evenly matched district can focus on a narrower target. A basic strategy is to reinforce the partisans, persuade some swing voters, and convert a few of the opponent's supporters.

Few races are more evenly matched than the 1998 Senate fight between Democrat Scotty Baesler and Republican Jim Bunning. The first was known in Kentucky for his college basketball days, the second for a career in professional baseball. Each was a sitting congressman in a state that split its votes between Democrats and Republicans. Both were in the conservative wing of their respective parties. Bunning, however, positioned himself as a moderate, then ran aggressive attack ads. According to a team of political scientists who studied the race, "Bunning . . . lay claim to the traditional Democratic issue of protecting Social Security" (Gross and Miller 2000, 189), and this positioning gave Bunning a strong foundation from which to commence one of the harshest political ad campaigns in recent memory, and it was successful.

Figure 8.3
Strategizing a Toss-Up District

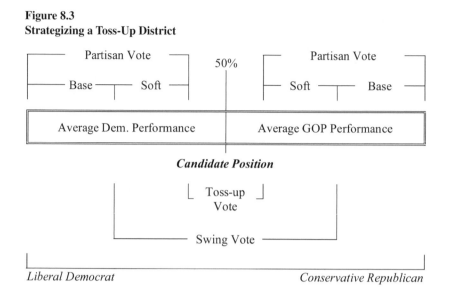

Narrow targeting works. Bunning, Redmond, and Jackson ran hard, but they also ran smart. The folly of reaching broadly is twofold. First, campaigns feed off scarce resources. Time and money should be spent where the expenditures will do the most good. Less obvious is the second problem: campaigning in areas where there is little chance of success can do more harm than good. If voters in precincts predisposed against the candidate start to receive literature, see volunteers on their doorsteps, and hear radio and television advertisements criticizing their party, opposition interest will be piqued, and opponents will be more inclined to vote (the wrong way).

There are exceptions. In 2004, the Bush campaign eked out a win by focusing on its highly motivated base. And a centrist approach sometimes fails. In 1998, Ohio Lieutenant Governor Nancy Hollister, a Republican, tried to draw moderate voters from incumbent Democrat Ted Strickland. The Sixth Congressional District had switched back and forth between the parties since 1992, with 2 percent margins each time. Hollister was a quality candidate, but after a bruising primary with conservative GOP rivals, Hollister was caught on the horns of a dilemma: winning the district meant holding the center, but holding the center meant risking the base. When Hollister's moderate campaign began, the right wing of the GOP had trouble understanding where she stood on conservative issues like abortion. The more centrist she sounded, the more disenchanted the right-wing base voters became (Burton and Shea 2003). In the end, Hollister was soundly defeated, losing the socially conservative district by 14 points.

MAPPING THE WIN

Strategic positioning operates in the abstract, and a general strategy is effective only when it synchronizes its component parts. Electoral targeting fleshes out the high-level theory of the race. A campaign must combine polling, electoral research, and demographic analysis and relate each of these perspectives to individual parts of the district. It is a difficult chore, but technology is making the job easier.

Computer mapping is the new key. "At the onset of any military campaign, decision-makers are constantly reviewing maps to develop strategy, evaluate performance, identify strengths and compensate for weaknesses," writes the president of Spatial Logic, and "campaigns, polling and political analysis are no different. Maps can be used for any size battle, from a local sheriff's race to the U.S. presidency" (Lindauer 1999, 48).

Many political professionals find the ever-growing volume of useful data overwhelming. A number of businesses sell software to help access and refine data, combining census demographics, business statistics, and lifestyle information. It is possible to merge census data with scores of other government-derived data sets, such as crime reports, health statistics, economic information, and precinct-level electoral data, which is increasingly available online. A wide range of Geographic Information System (GIS) consultants work with clients to design and support mapping databases. Some programs are specially designed for campaign work, letting a campaign add in-house lists and field reports. As long as data sets share a common field of information—voter names, for example, or street addresses—they can become part of the unified database.

By the late 1990s, GIS had become an integral part of the campaign environment. Linking relational databases with visual representations of the district, vote-rich pockets can be rapidly displayed. The idea is not new—crayon-colored maps have long hung on the walls of campaign headquarters—but the advent of GIS has brought instantaneous placement of data onto custom maps, with tactics diagrammed street by street, even house by house.

In the hypothetical Smith County race discussed earlier, Republican strategists might rank precinct targets by prior electoral history alone, or they might take into account the demographic favorability of each voting ward, along with the exact location of registered Republicans and unaffiliated voters. From these data, the campaign might distinguish low-priority areas that are solidly partisan (Democrat or Republican) from areas that should be given higher priority. The highest priority can be given to parts of the city that might go one way or the other (see Figure 8.4). GIS software will crunch the numbers and display the result. In one sense, a mapped illustration of the data adds no new information. The numbers have not changed. But the experience of visualizing the numbers, seeing where the average party performance is high and where the swing votes are concentrated as well as the ability to manipulate the maps almost at will, gives campaign researchers a unique set of conceptual tools that invite detailed analysis.

CAMPAIGN THEMES

Campaign targets are mapped, in large part, to help a campaign find pockets of support that will be responsive to a campaign theme. A good theme is a carefully crafted merger of what the voters want, what the candidate has to offer, and what

Figure 8.4
Mapping Target Votes—Smith City, 2002 (by Voting Ward)

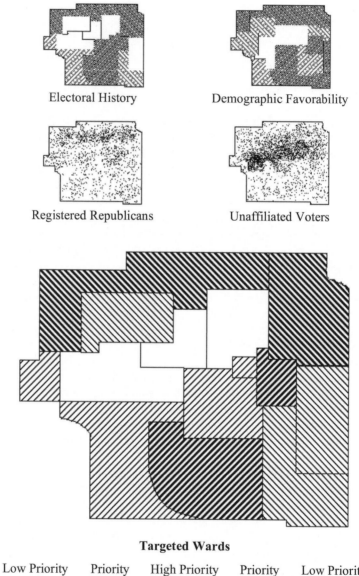

Electoral History

Demographic Favorability

Registered Republicans

Unaffiliated Voters

Targeted Wards

Low Priority (GOP)	Priority (GOP)	High Priority (Swing)	Priority (Dem.)	Low Priority (Dem.)

the opponent brings to the table. Campaign professionals believe it is imperative for voters in the target group to hear the theme repeatedly: "If you stick to it, and say it often enough, you will define the criteria for the voters that they should use to make their choice" (Bradshaw 1995, 44).

A good theme can be powerful. Political novice Peter Hoekstra stunned the Washington establishment by knocking off the chair of the National Republican Congressional Committee, Michigan Republican Guy Vander Jagt, in a 1992 primary contest. On a shoestring budget, Hoekstra pounded home the idea that Vander Jagt was a career politician, more interested in national affairs than in the voters back home. The message was echoed when Hoekstra rode around in a 1966 Nash Rambler, made the year Vander Jagt was first elected. The sign on the car read, "Isn't it time for a change?" (Morris and Gamache 1994, 116). Jesse Jackson Jr. turned his youth—he was just 30 years old—into a powerful message. In a 1995 special election, he said he was "young enough to stay long enough" (Johnson 1995).

Targeted themes are vital to contemporary campaigns. As partisanship became a less meaningful voting cue (see Wattenberg 1998), voters had to find other ways to distinguish among candidates. Scholars who study campaign politics have suggested that incumbency filled the vacuum (Cover 1977; Ferejohn 1977; Mayhew 1974a). David Mayhew writes, "A logic suggests itself. Voters dissatisfied with party cues could be reaching for any other cues that are available . . . incumbency is readily at hand" (1974a, 313). The shift from partisanship to incumbency might explain at least part of the high rate of reelection enjoyed by congressional representatives.

This line of reasoning has its limits. First, the theory implies that voters pay virtually no attention to a candidate's qualifications, the issues, the national trends, or a host of other forces that pull them toward a challenger. This perspective demands, as noted by Linda Fowler, "a level of pessimism about democracy that is difficult to accept" (1993, 79). Incumbency theory minimizes the importance of retrospective evaluation and presupposes that weak party identifiers and independents are more inclined to support incumbents than are strong partisans, and this does not appear to be happening (Krehbiel and Wright 1983). An alternative explanation is that voters seek concise messages to explain what the candidate stands for and then relate this information to their own ends. For some voters, party-based appeals might work; for others, incumbency could be the cue; for still others, a host of messages might combine into an effective, multipronged force.

If voters care about factors beyond party and incumbency, campaign themes become critical. It is the easy way for voters to make an informed choice. As Joel Bradshaw notes,

> It is the single, central idea that the campaign communicates to voters to sum up the candidate's connection with the voters and their concerns and the contrast between your candidate and the opponent. It answers the question: Why should your candidate be elected? (1995, 42)

If the candidate is a member of the majority party in a heavily partisan area, party-based appeals might be the key. If the candidate is the incumbent and voters prefer experience, then knowledge of the people and a record of accomplishment could provide the theme. The important point is that voters rarely have time to assess candidate appeals on each and every issue. A well-constructed theme links voter concerns with the candidate's approach.

One of the most effective efforts to drive home a single, well-honed point was the Bush 2004 charge that John Kerry was a "flip-flopper." He votes one way, then other. Almost every day of the campaign, one of Bush's supporters used the words "flip-flop," "flipping and flopping," "flipped and flopped," and so forth. A young man wearing a giant sandal—a giant flip-flop, that is—was seen walking around Boston during the Democratic Convention in Boston. In a post-9/11 world, where Americans wanted resolute leadership, the charge of inconsistency was potent indeed.

While thematic simplicity is important, some candidates fail to see the need for it. They believe voters will make sense of disparate messages. But few voters have the time or energy to do this—and the ones who do tend to confirm a predetermined choice. Campaigns must offer voters a coherent rationale. Indeed, from the perspective of a campaign operation, a central theme guides every message.

Selecting and Implementing a Campaign Theme

There is a certain redundancy to the production of campaign themes. Catherine Shaw, a former Oregon mayor who works as a campaign consultant, has compiled a list of campaign slogans drawn from political brochures: among them, "A strong voice for [Place]," "Taking care of [Place]," and "It's Time for a Change" (2004, 40). The campaign themes seem interchangeable, but Shaw is quick to point out that the choice of an appropriate campaign theme is contingent upon the campaign context. Which is better: "This is about governing . . . and I've done it" or "The Change Will Do Us Good"? (41). The words sound simplistic, but they condense of lot of meaning into a small package. The development of an appropriate theme is an artful combination of what the voters want and what the candidate has to offer, never forgetting what the opponent might say (see Bradshaw 1995, 43).

Finding "what the voters want" is an uncertain proposition. A benchmark poll may indicate a large number of salient issues—perhaps none being mentioned by more than a small number of respondents. When asked to name "the most important problem facing this country today," those who answered a March 2000 Gallup Poll said "education" more often than any other answer. It got a 16 percent score. The AIDS epidemic did not register, getting less than 0.5 percent. Perhaps the numbers would have been higher if the pollsters had prompted the respondents— "Is AIDS an important issue?"—but campaign professionals would then wonder if the poll measured what was really on people's minds.

Although data are always subject to interpretation, theme development must find a message that summarizes voter concerns. Generally speaking, themes are intended to be *inclusive*. They try to encompass a diverse set of issues or a broad range of qualifications. In most instances, it is a mistake to bill a candidate simply as an "environmental leader," even though concerns about pollution might be apparent and the candidate might be well suited to deal with them. Environmentalism might alienate some target voters. Good campaigns find that a more general theme, something like "a candidate concerned about the future," works best for them. A variety of issues can be fitted into this overarching message. Likewise, instead of being the "tough-on-crime candidate," a better tactic might be to say that the candidate favors "a safer community." The fear of crime suggests, at its core, that one is not safe in the community. To make an area secure, many changes could be sought—more cops on the beat and tougher sentences for criminals, surely, but also a better educational system, promotion of family values, more pressure on terrorists, investment in housing and infrastructure, and so on. Broad themes can incorporate several related ideas, thereby appealing to more voters.

Some observers talk about a difference between "positional" issues and "valence" issues (Salmore and Salmore 1989, 112–13). Positional issues are those that have well-defined sides. People have to take a position. Abortion and gun control are divisive issues of this sort. Valence issues, on the other hand, are concerns about which everyone can agree, such as a strong national defense, decreased crime, the elimination of pollution, and the creation of jobs. For the most part, campaign themes center on valence issues. There is an exception, however. A "wedge" strategy—the name comes from a chess tactic whereby an opponent is forced to sacrifice a piece—highlights issues that divide the opposition. A liberal constituency that holds both environmentalists and organized labor gives a Republican the chance to pit a "jobs" message against environmental activists in an effort to bring middle-class workers on board.

The office being sought may also constrain a candidate's choice of theme. Voters may well expect different ideas from candidates for different offices. Candidates for executive posts—governors, county executives, or mayors— might wish to focus on leadership and competence. Rather than merely responding to the needs of particular interests, they are expected to lead. Candidates for legislative posts, on the other hand, might make more hay out of their ability to deliver pork-barrel projects.

The candidate's status—incumbent or challenger—also matters, and incumbents face special restrictions. Judith Trent and Robert Friedenberg suggest that candidate status is a key element in communications strategy (2004, 80–82). An incumbent stressing "change" is asking for his or her own removal. Incumbent campaign themes do better to highlight the need to "stay the course." Unlike challengers, incumbents can use the symbolic trappings of the office—strength, integrity, competence, and legitimacy—but they also have a past from which they cannot hide. Most incumbents try to show a "record of accomplishment."

Challengers enjoy more latitude in their choice of theme—they do not have a record—but the need for a powerful theme is heightened. They must convince voters to change their habits. It is nearly always necessary to attack the incumbent (Trent and Friedenberg 2004, 99–103). As scholars Barbara and Stephen Salmore have noted, "Most challengers must simultaneously erode the favorable reputation of the incumbent and build a positive case for themselves" (1989, 128). Without a cutting edge, voters have little reason to seek change. Thus, in a 1992 U.S. Senate race, Paul Coverdell successfully portrayed himself as an average Georgian, painting his opponent as an extremist. In one powerful television spot, an elderly woman tells voters that Coverdell is "like us," while opponent Wyche Fowler "is just like Ted Kennedy." Georgians are proud of their state; Massachusetts liberalism is not for them.

Whether designed for a challenger or an incumbent, the theme must be readily understood. Once again, voters are more likely to grasp simplicity than complexity. In his successful 1990 bid for the Minnesota U.S. Senate seat, Paul Wellstone developed a straightforward theme, "A man of ordinary means," a not-so-subtle contrast to his opponent, who was ready to spend $6 million on the race. Eight years later, Minnesota voters made former professional wrestler Jesse Ventura their governor, based largely on his defiance of traditional authority. The campaign theme became a no-message message. One political analyst has said, "Unlike the practiced politicians he was up against, he never stayed on message, deflecting the tough questions. That really set him apart." This is not to say, however, that there was no theme: an Independence Day T-shirt screamed, "Retaliate in '98" (Beiler 2000, 128).

CONCLUSION

"Theme is not a word that should have an 's' on the end" (Bradshaw 1995, 42). A theme provides voters with a cognitive shortcut—a simple way to think about the issues—and if there are many paths from which to choose, voters will simply choose none. Ventura's reformist theme gave his campaign a hard cutting edge that fit his strategic goals. If a campaign fails to generate an overall strategy—if it does not think about its strategic position, its target vote, and, perhaps most important, a reason for persuadable voters to cast their ballots, success is unlikely. Then again, it is not enough to know where the votes are and what theme will bring them into the fold; a campaign must undertake a concerted effort to reach its potential supporters. Voter contact is the subject of Part Three of this book.

Part Three

VOTER CONTACT
TECHNIQUES

Chapter Nine

Fund-Raising Strategy and Tactics

Campaigns need money. Volunteers, issues, good looks, and a winning personality can take a candidate only so far. Poorly funded candidates occasionally win, but the shortage of exceptions tends to prove the rule. Campaign expenditures remain a strong predictor of electoral success. This is true of higher-level posts, such as House of Representatives, U.S. Senate, and governor, but it is also true at the municipal level. A long-shot candidate running for a city council seat in Southlake, Texas—population 21,519—won her election by spending more than $18,000 to get her message out (Strachan 2003, 9). That amounts to nearly a dollar per resident, roughly the same ratio as presidential candidates spend. As noted by the former executive director of the Center for Responsive Politics, Leslie Wayne, "Whatever office, whatever level of government, candidates are spending serious money on campaigns" (Strachan 2003, 5).

Money is valuable in part because it allows a campaign to acquire political resources on short notice. Old-style campaigns relied on endorsements and volunteers. But volunteers take time to organize, and they can sometimes be unreliable. The endorsement of a key political figure is helpful on its own—few would deny that the publicity does a campaign some good—but an endorsement carries far more weight if it means a powerful name on a fund-raising letter, access to donor lists, and money calls made on the candidate's behalf. Bankable support has become a necessary precondition of successful electioneering.

Building a campaign war chest is a complex matter. This chapter is designed to acquaint the reader with campaign fund-raising. It provides a brief look at the history of campaign finance, the reasons that people and groups give to campaigns, and some of the strategies and tactics involved in fund-raising operations, including the new frontier of Internet politics and its effect on campaign strategy.

A BRIEF LOOK AT MONEY IN CAMPAIGNS

Campaigns have never been cheap. George Washington's campaign gave away 160 gallons of alcoholic beverage, about a quart and a half per voter, in his first bid for the Virginia House of Burgesses (Dinkin 1989, 3). During most of the nineteenth century, campaigns were conducted in the partisan press and through party organizations. Rallies and events were held, party workers "hit the streets," and handbills were printed and distributed. Party organizations, rather than candidates, raised the necessary funds. In turn, candidates were expected to contribute to the party—frequently, it was a necessary requirement for receiving the party's nomination. When Mark Hanna used millions of dollars, donated in large gifts by wealthy industrialists, to fund the "Front Porch" campaign of William McKinley in 1896, the Republican Party all but purchased the White House. The politics of old were thoroughly scandalous by today's standards.

Although parties would lose ground in the early years of the twentieth century, they continued to play an important role in campaign finance. In most areas, the party leadership still controlled a number of workers, and it was able to manage the nomination process. Parties were still able to amass huge war chests. The money came from a generalized entanglement of cash and clout. To influence government decisions, one would contribute to the party. If money did go directly to the candidate, the candidate was expected to replenish party funds since the candidate was just a creature of the larger party organization. The result was massive party funding by business, labor unions, and wealthy individuals. In 1928, roughly 70 percent of the funds raised by the national parties came from contributions of $1,000 or greater—enough to buy a couple of Model T automobiles (Sorauf 1988, 3).

The political landscape began to shift by the late 1960s. Corruption was still rampant—Vice President Spiro Agnew was forced to resign in 1974 after Justice Department officials happened across kickbacks he was still receiving from his days in Baltimore—but parties were no longer at the center of the election process. The era of candidate-centered campaigns had begun, and money was at the center of this new process. Fund-raising had become serious business by the 1980s, and its burden began to weigh heavy on challengers, open-seat candidates, and incumbents. Many retiring members of Congress suggested that the pressure of raising massive sums for their reelections played a key role in their decisions to leave office. Senator Paul Simon (D-Ill.), who had to raise $8.4 million in his last reelection campaign in 1990, told *60 Minutes,* "When I first came here— man, when there was a Democratic fundraising dinner, I was so eager to go. Now I drag myself. And it's probably a pretty good indication that this is a good time to step aside" (Simon 1995). The price of a Senate seat used to be obeisance to party leaders. In an era of new-style politics, the prize became an endless cycle of campaign fund-raising.

But why are the costs of elections spiraling out of control? There were more people to reach—the baby boomers of the 1940s and 1950s, the Voting Rights Act of 1965, and the Twenty-Sixth Amendment (which gave 18-year-olds the right to vote) expanded the size of the electorate (Adamany and Agree 1975, 21).

The drift from partisan allegiance, a key element of candidate-centered campaigns, has created evermore undecided voters. Put differently, there is a growing number of voters "up for grabs" each election, and in an effort to minimize uncertainty, campaigns avail themselves of new technologies. Sophisticated survey research, direct mail, telemarketing, and computerized targeting, not to mention radio, video, and Web site production, have driven up the cost of getting elected. Campaign consulting has added to the expenses, of course. A top consultant will charge hundreds of dollars per hour, and the introduction of Web-based communications has added a whole new category of campaign consultancy. As noted in Figure 7.1, the cost of winning a seat in the House of Representatives nearly doubled in the past two decades. In the early 1980s, an "expensive" House race might cost of about cross the $1 million. In the 2004, there were 10 races that crossed the $4 million mark.

When Carl Johnson first ran for the state senate of New Hampshire in 1990, he spent $300 on consultant advice. In 2004, this time as an incumbent, Johnson spent more than $10,000 to pay Elevare, a Concord political consulting firm (Milne 2004, 1). "Consultants play a bigger and bigger role," explains Elevare's president. "And it began statewide, races for governor, Senate, House. As we've seen of late, it's gradually working its way down the ballot. Bigger portions of candidates' expenses are being paid to consultants" (Milne 2004, 2).

One might ask whether all this spending is really necessary. Could candidates spend less and still win? Perhaps the cost of campaigning has increased because candidates mistakenly believe that victory requires vast quantities on television, radio, direct mail, and the Internet. While a precise cost per vote might not be calculable, most agree that money *does* make a difference in American political campaigns. For starters, additional money helps candidates reach more voters. Campaigns are won by persuading undecideds and by mobilizing supporters. Money helps on both counts. Second, money helps candidates enlist good help. Campaigns might be run efficiently with volunteers, but money allows candidates to receive professional assistance when needed. Third, a self-fulfilling prophecy is at work: candidates who raise a lot of money are often perceived to be solid, worthy of support. The logic behind this bandwagon effect is that if others are sending in a check, then the candidate must be acceptable. Conversely, candidates without financial resources are often thought to be weak, outside the mainstream, long shots at best. Fourth, hefty war chests can scare off good challengers. Up-and-coming politicians fear losses—and nothing keeps them on the sidelines like an opponent's hefty financial reports. Hiring strong consultants can attract media attention, and of course it takes funds to hire these firms. Finally, and perhaps most important, studies suggest candidates with more resources win most of the time. "[State] legislative candidates who raised the most money for their races won well over 80 percent of all legislative seats in the country in the 2002 election cycle (Institute on Money in State Politics 2005). Campaign riches might not determine victory, but they seem to improve the odds. Few candidates or consultants are ready to gamble on the idea that money is meaningless.

Money and the Incumbency Advantage

Roughly 95 percent of House incumbents were sent back to office in the past decade (Opensecrets.org 2005). Reelection rates at the state legislative level are a bit lower overall, but in most states they are often above 90 percent. So, are campaign finances at the root of high reelection rates? Do incumbents win because it is easier for them to raise money? Or is it the other way around? The answer is difficult to find because the questions are hard to parse. Herrnson's careful study of electoral success shows that challengers are more likely to win when incumbents spend a lot of money on campaign communications (2004, 241). Presumably, a safe incumbent does not need to spend money, whereas an endangered incumbent has to start buying media. One of the first to explore this paradox was Gary Jacobson. When a challenger poses a serious danger, the incumbent can raise the money needed to counter the threat. Jacobson has said, "The electoral value of incumbency lies not only in what it provides to the incumbent but also in how it affects the thinking of potential opponents" (1997, 37). So, is campaign spending a cause or an effect of electoral competition? The record is not entirely clear. Most likely, incumbency and money share a mutually reinforcing relationship.

Herrnson reports that sitting members of the U.S. House raised an average of $369,012 from PAC contributions in 2002, whereas challengers received just $24,635 (2004, 174). Moreover, the Campaign Finance Institute reports that more than 75 percent of PAC money went to incumbents and that in the 2004 election cycle, PAC contributions rose 34 percent over the previous election. Contributions to federal candidates totaled $310.5 million, with incumbents receiving the lion's share (Campaign Finance Institute, 2005). As noted by a former director of the Democratic Senatorial Campaign Committee, "Washington money is, by and large, smart money. Most PACs are not a bit interested in supporting people they don't think will win" (Luntz 1988, 178). Because incumbents usually prevail, they can expect to receive a large share of contributions—and they do.

Other factors may also be in play. Incumbents may have cash left over from their last campaign, making their next effort seem credible from the start, attracting a good deal of "early money" from PACs and individuals. Early money further discourages quality challengers—the ones who can spot the danger signs—from jumping into the race, leaving the field to less qualified contenders (Maisel 1990, 125). Finally, incumbents have fund-raising experience. After all, if they did not know how to raise money, they probably would not have been elected in the first place. Once in office, they maintain a reliable list of contributors, spend time learning from other candidates, and continue to refine their fund-raising operations.

Campaign Finance Law

Federal candidates are subject to strict fund-raising rules. The regulations are extremely detailed, and for this reason wise campaigns keep attorneys and accountants on board to sort through the regulatory maze. That said, the Federal Election Commission (FEC) distributes its rules and regulations in easy-to-digest formats. Virtually all current documents are available on the Web, including a detailed "Campaign Guide for Congressional Candidates and Committees," produced by the FEC. Frequent news releases and various state and local government brochures also provide campaign professionals with up-to-date information on campaign finance and reporting requirements. Campaigns for most offices now file reports online.

Today's disclosure requirements are among numerous reforms designed to reduce corruption in elections. The Federal Elections Campaign Act and a series of amendments in the 1970s, for example, set a $1,000 limit on individual contributions at each stage of the election—primary, runoff (if applicable), and general. PACs could send $5,000, as could the party committees. The parties could also provide assistance through "coordinated expenditures"—usually in the form of voter registration efforts, shared polling, and get-out-the-vote drives. Coordinated expenditures were capped by a formula based on population and inflation. For the 2000 cycle, House candidates in states with more than one congressional district were allowed $33,780 in both state and national coordinated spending. Depending on the size of the state, Senate candidates were allowed up to $1,636,438. Through the years, new financing possibilities were exploited, most notably the use of largely unregulated money intended for "party-building" activities to run political advertisements that were all but indistinguishable from direct campaigning—the "soft-money loophole." By the dawn of the twenty-first century, most had agreed that things had gotten out of control and that new laws were needed.

Reforming the Reforms: BCRA

Leading a bipartisan call for additional reform were Senator John McCain (R-Ariz.) and Russ Feingold (D-Wis.). Both are significant players in national politics, but McCain drew the most attention. He had run for the presidency in 2000, and while he was defeated in the nomination battle by George W. Bush, McCain had become the darling of the media and the growing number of reformers across the nation. As he spoke frequently and passionately about the growing corruption in elections, more Americans were drawn into the controversy. Voters pushed their legislators, and campaign finance became a big issue in the 2000 congressional elections, with most of the successful candidates pledging to do *something*. After much debate and maneuvering by both parties, the Bipartisan Campaign Reform Act (BCRA) was passed by Congress and signed into law by George W. Bush in February 2002.

The new law is sweeping: it outlaws soft-money contributions to the national political organizations and bans group-sponsored advertisements 30 days before primary elections and 60 days before general elections. But the law also raises the contribution limits to $2,000 for individuals and $10,000 for groups and leaves open the ability for wealthy individuals to donate soft money to state and local party organizations. The ban on soft money does not affect PACs, which are still free to raise unlimited amounts.

The law took effect the day after the 2002 midterm election and had a controversial beginning. The very same day that the BCRA was signed into law, Republican Senator Mitch McConnell of Kentucky, a strong opponent of campaign finance restrictions, joined with a host of legislators, interest groups, and minor parties to nullify the measure by filing a federal lawsuit. The core of their argument was that the BCRA represented an assault on free speech. Constitutional arguments in support of the law were that contributions may be regulated without being a burden on the First Amendment because contributions are indirect speech. By the end of 2002, all the complaints had been merged into one case, *McConnell v. Federal Election Commission,* heard in the Supreme Court in the fall of 2003. In a five-to-four decision, the Court upheld the most important elements of the law. It was, according to a *New York Times* account, a "stunning victory for political reform" ("A Campaign Finance Triumph," 2003, 42). The majority reasoned that Congress has a "fully legitimate interest in ... preventing corruption of the federal electoral process through the means it has chosen." Moreover, the majority of the Court suggested that the problem with big, unregulated contributions was preferential access and the influence that comes with it. It was, they noted, not simply an issue of the "appearance of corruption" but volumes of data that strongly suggest real problems.

The exact reach of BCRA is far from settled, however. With the growth of online campaign fund-raising in the 2004 election cycle, many have begun to wonder whether the Internet should be included under BCRA regulation. Presently, the Internet is exempt. Issue advocacy—that is, advertisements that seem, at first glance, to support issues instead of candidates—has come under close examination. Most agree that these ads are designed to support particular candidates, not simply issues. Moreover, numerous reform organizations and even members of Congress have begun to question the propriety of "section 527" money. The reference is to groups organized under section 527 of the Internal Revenue Code, which allowed for unlimited and undisclosed raising of money. As noted by the Center for Responsive Politics, "Most 527s on this list are advocacy groups trying to influence federal elections through voter mobilization efforts and so-called issue ads that tout or criticize a candidate's record" (Opensecrets.org 2005). A great deal of these funds previously went to the parties in the form of soft money.

Two prominent examples of 527s in the 2004 election were MoveOn.org and Swift Boat Veterans for Truth. MoveOn.org was created by a group of activists who were dissatisfied with George W. Bush, and the Swift Boat Veterans for Truth was created with the intention of casting Senator Kerry's past military service in a negative light. As noted by one observer, "Although BCRA cracked down on soft money spending by the political parties, it did nothing to constrain spending by outside groups" (Currinder 2005, 122). Indeed, one estimate is that 527 groups spent (ironically) some $527 million on television ads alone in 2004 (Currinder 2005, 122).

Are 527 organizations just another loophole in campaign finance law? Do the large undisclosed amounts of money flowing in and out of 527s corrupt the democratic process? Or are 527 organizations simply exercising their free speech rights under the U.S. Constitution? The future of 527 organizations remains unclear. The FEC did move forward with rules regulating independent groups, but most agree that there remains enough leeway in the law for these units to operate—and to be key players in the election process—for years to come.

A plethora of rules apply in state and local campaigns, where the growth of special interests roughly parallels the national trend. Insofar as state and local government has become much more involved in regulatory matters, business, labor, and consumer groups have made the decision to get more deeply engaged in the campaign process at this level. According to the Institute on Money in State Politics, parties, PACs, and interest groups in some states provide candidates with the bulk of their war chest (2005). Regulations at the state and local levels vary. Candidates should consult their state's regulatory body for specific information.

REASONS FOR INDIVIDUAL AND GROUP DONATIONS

Whatever one might think of the existing campaign finance system, candidates are forced to live under its rules. They have to raise money if they want to win, and in order to raise money, they must understand why individuals and groups give to campaigns. "The process is bilateral," writes Sorauf; "both contributors and candidates pursue political goals" (1995, 78). In the days when Spiro Agnew charged a percentage on government contracts, campaign donations were easily understood. Campaign finance in the new millennium, however, is more complex. Most constituents would be amazed at the spectacle of a "photo line," in which individuals pay $1,000 or more and wait for a quick "grip-and-grin" snapshot with a Senate candidate. No policy issues are discussed, and those who try to take a moment of the candidate's time for a discussion of a pet project are hurried off by staff. Some aspects of modern campaigning are all but imponderable.

Individual Donors

Of the roughly $661 million raised by all presidential candidates in 2004, some $606 million came from individual donors. Of the $871 million raised by House and Senate candidates in 2004, roughly $553 came from individual contributions (Currinder 2005, 116). Moreover, the FEC reports that in 2004 the national party organizations witnessed a 100 percent increase in individual contributions from 2002. To think that a few "fat-cat" labor unions or corporate sponsors fund campaigns would be wrong. For the most part, campaigns are funded through individual contributions.

But why would anyone give to a campaign? Many people give because they are asked. The act of solicitation greatly increases the chances that an individual donor will produce a check. Without the request, even the most supportive citizen might not offer financial support. It looks like the campaign already has enough money—after all, no one came looking for any. Among those who intend to give, many simply like to hear the request. The solicitation makes donors feel that they are needed and appreciated. Possibly, as Sorauf suggests, "the request for money activates some generalized, even vague, feeling of loyalty or sympathy, whether for the cause or the solicitor" (1988, 49).

Many individuals are interested in government, and by helping a favored candidate win office, they can change the course of political events. Sometimes the contribution is related to a single issue, such as the candidate's stand on the military, abortion, gun control, or economic deregulation. Sometimes the contribution is meant to further a larger set of beliefs, such as a party platform or political ideology. Party activists and those keenly interested in the outcome of government are more likely to give, obviously, but loyalty to nonpolitical organizations may also impel them to send a check. If, for example, a professional association has long opposed an incumbent's political agenda, the association's membership may agree that their best interests lie with donations to the challenger.

Retrospection can be a powerful tool in fund-raising. A candidate who voted for lower property taxes might benefit from contributors who simply want to demonstrate appreciation for these efforts. Retrospective donations can also work in favor of the challenger. One prominent GOP leader has advised GOP fund-raisers, "Ask yourself, who hates the incumbent, who wants to beat him as bad as I do. This starts the donor list process" (Shea and Brooks 1995, 25). Once on the list, some people fall into the habit of giving (Yeutter et al. 1992).

Habit, retrospection, policy preference, and loyalty to the solicitor are powerful forces—but so is celebrity. It is an interesting paradox: as a class, politicians are disdained, while as individuals, many public officials are held in high esteem. Officialdom has its own magnetism. Some people want to be seen at fund-raisers with successful candidates, particularly those who regularly appear on television. Often the contact takes the form of a personal telephone call or an autographed picture. The celebrity factor in politics explains the success of fund-raising events that include popular figures from the worlds of entertainment, sports, and politics. Perhaps for the same reason that some people give to the arts—the chance to participate in the glamour and excitement of a well-known event—many choose to share in the experience of politics by writing a check to a political candidate.

Interest Groups

The incentives for individual campaign contributions apply to interest group contributions as well. The main difference is that groups are more likely to base their donations on policy grounds. Fund-raiser Carl Silverberg lists four reasons that a PAC might give money to a candidate: "The legislator voted with them on their issues. . . . The legislator sits on a committee that has jurisdiction over the majority of the legislation the PAC has set out as its priorities for the year. . . . There is a good following in the district. . . . The corporation represented by the PAC has a good number of employees in the district" (2000, 62). PACs want to elect officials sympathetic to their concerns—to have access to officeholders who handle their issues. This is precisely why incumbents receive the vast majority of group contributions: there is no advantage in funding losers. Hence, it is common to see interest groups giving money to both major political parties to make sure their voices will be heard.

While the donations may be offered out of concern for policy, there is little reason to believe that interest groups are "buying" candidates when they provide funds. Rather, groups contribute heavily out of a desire for access—the hope that they will be allowed to present their position to the elected official. Interest groups seek "a chance to persuade, an opportunity to make a case or argue a point" (Sorauf 1988, 314). Senator Paul Simon put the matter bluntly: "I have never promised anyone a thing for a campaign contribution. But when I was in the Senate and got to my hotel room at midnight, there might be twenty phone calls waiting for me, nineteen from people whose names I did not recognize, the twentieth from someone who gave me a $1,000 contribution or raised money for me. . . . Which [call] do you think I will make?" (1999, 306).

The Decision *Not* to Give

It is important to understand why people and groups might *not* contribute to a given campaign (Yeutter et al. 1992). First, many would-be contributors are not asked. Few people know intuitively that they are supposed to give money to a campaign. Second, sometimes no amount has been specified in the appeal. Without knowing how much is needed, a potential contributor may simply pass up the opportunity. Third, the potential contributor might not have been provided a clear way of giving. A fund-raising letter that does not include a return envelope has wasted a lot of money.

Simple issues can have a profound impact on fund-raising efforts, as can more substantive difficulties. If a candidate uses a racial appeal, many prospective donors may be offended. Sometimes a solicitation leaves the supporter feeling used, belittled, or underappreciated. Along similar lines, the appeal may be unconvincing on its face. Potential contributors need to believe their money will make a difference. If potential donors sense that their money is unneeded or will be wasted—or if they do not trust the solicitor's judgment—they will have no compelling reason to send a check.

FUND-RAISING STRATEGY AND TACTICS

A few years ago, fund-raising expert Mary Sabin was asked to summarize the keys to successful fund-raising: "Work, work, and work. If you are not feeling anxiety and stress, you're not doing your job. . . . This isn't rocket science or brain surgery. [It] is working hard, staying at it, and concentrating on raising the money while feeling completely obsessed about it" (Shea and Brooks 1995, 25). Part of the work is careful attention to planned objectives. Robert Kaplan is adamant on this point: "Once you've bought into the plan, it's your job as a candidate or campaign manager, to work full force to implement it, notwithstanding any midcourse corrections" (2000, 64).

There are four principal elements to a strategic fund-raising plan: quantity, timing, sources, and tactics. Some campaigns mistakenly base their plans on an assessment of the amount of money that can be raised (Himes 1995, 63). The correct approach is to figure out how much money will be needed to implement the overall campaign plan. By setting specific goals, the fund-raising team has clear motivation. Targets and deadlines are strong motivators. If, for example, the campaign strategy calls for a massive television buy in early spring, fund-raising efforts begin well in advance. Traditional sources of money (party funds, local contributors, and the PACs that contributed to other members of the candidate's party) may suffice, but if they do not, the candidate must think about alternatives (regional contributors, PACs that have not contributed to the party, and so forth).

Wealthy candidates have an edge because they can give the money early in the cycle, signaling a concrete commitment. One of the greatest financial obstacles that a campaign faces is "seed money," the funding needed before the campaign can move into full gear, including consultant fees, benchmark poll costs, and money for electoral targeting data. Pro-choice Democratic women often look to EMILY's List. The "EMILY" in EMILY's List stands for "Early Money Is Like Yeast—It makes the dough rise." Without early money, a campaign finds would-be contributors hesitant to give. EMILY's List scouts candidates, trains them, and provides campaign funding, thereby helping selected women get past the first major obstacle to campaigning.

For all candidates, potential sources include family, friends, colleagues, and associates; partisans; PACs; habitual givers; adversaries of the opponent; and political parties at all levels. Many candidates group potential givers, or "prospects," into three general categories: small, medium, and large. Precisely how these categories are defined depends on the specifics of each race. A large contributor in a city council campaign might be considered a small donor in a congressional race. In fact, most candidates prefer that the general public not believe they are relying on "fat-cat" donors. Former Republican senator Rudy Boschwitz, in his 1996 rematch against Paul Wellstone, went out of his way to let Minnesota voters know that he was drawing large portions of his campaign money from "skinny cats" who gave less than $100.

Because fund-raising tactics vary depending on the prospect, broad-based plans work best (Beaudry and Schaeffer 1986, 164). No technique is sure to work in every race, and often the proper mix depends on the candidate and the consultant. Some candidates, for example, are comfortable asking for money, just as some consultants are more skilled in direct mail than in PAC solicitation. Some prospects consider direct mail abhorrent, preferring that someone verbally request the money, while others think that mail is convenient and that phone calls are intrusive. Some will give through online mechanisms, while others worry about security—about giving out their credit card number over the Internet. Not all tactics work equally well for every person or every district. Nevertheless, campaign operatives should be familiar with each of the most commonly used fund-raising techniques.

Personal Solicitation

When GOP representative Rod Chandler of Washington decided to leave Congress in 1992, fellow Republican Jennifer Dunn saw her chance. Having run the

Washington state Republican Party for 11 years, Dunn understood that the best way to raise money is to request it personally. "With help from friends and volunteers, Dunn worked her way through the 5,000 names in her personal files, raising $492,442 from individuals and $168,373 from PACs" (Morris and Gamache 1994, 152). She outraised her opponent by a two-to-one margin the "old-fashioned way"—she asked for it.

"Dialing for dollars" is an unpleasant way to spend an afternoon, but personal solicitation is extremely productive, particularly for up-front money from large donors in a short period of time. In general, a master list of prospects is drawn to include wealthy individuals in tune with candidates' views (Allen 1990b, 49). Personal solicitation can work with small-scale donors, but it takes the same amount of time to ask for $10 as it does for $2,000, with about the same rate of return.

Success often lies in the personal and professional interests of the prospect. Solicitors must be ready to detail precisely where the campaign is going and why the money is needed, offering polling information, campaign brochures, a summary of the candidate's policy stands, and a list of expenses the money would cover. In some instances, it is worthwhile to provide a shortened version of the campaign plan. The goal is to make prospects feel as though they are being asked to join a tightly run, highly organized campaign team.

One of the hardest things that a professional fund-raiser confronts is a candidate reluctant to ask for money. Kaplan calls this phenomenon "fundraising fear" (2000, 64). When making the "ask," Kaplan advises, "choose a number that is 10 to 25 percent in excess of what your research shows contributors should donate" (1991, 54). Some consultants look at the situation from the contributor's point of view: why donate money to the campaign? Consultants often recommend that separate fund-raising accounts be established for each aspect of campaign operations. A donation to underwrite an ad buy shows a specific return for the campaign dollar. A telephone script for a typical request might read, "We're trying to raise $12,000 for some TV spots that have to be bought now for the November election. Would you be willing to make a pledge or send a gift to support our efforts?" (Shaw 2004, 102).

A number of campaigns have profited from the development of "pledge systems," whereby the contributor is asked to donate at periodic intervals. This approach can increase the overall contribution (Beaudry and Schaeffer 1986, 168). The more common technique is contacting those who have given once to give again. Both approaches are risky: it is almost always better to get as much as possible all at once since future donations may taper off. Large-scale fund-raising operations use fund-raising hierarchies. A wealthy donor might promise to sell a table of seats at a high-dollar fund-raising dinner. An individual donor is worth some money; someone who can get others to contribute is worth even more.

PAC and Interest Group Solicitation

To find PAC money, careful strategizing is in order, beginning with a long list of potential donors. At the federal level, PACs are registered with the FEC, and at the state and local levels, most are required to register with the elections commission or the secretary of state. If a candidate is on the wrong side of the policy fence, a donation will probably not be forthcoming. PACs that consistently give to the opponent and the opponent's party are poor prospects as well. Once the list is trimmed, a campaign might look for "hooks"—bits of information that could draw a PAC into the race. An association might count the candidate as a member, an ideological PAC might take note of issues raised in the district, or a business group may be against the opponent's record, as shown in bill sponsorships and floor votes (Yeutter et al. 1992). Developing a PAC list is a time-consuming chore, but the more detailed the database, the better.

From this list, the campaign can develop specific arguments for each PAC, often assembling "PAC kits." A typical kit might place a cover letter on top of biographies, district profiles, prominent consultants, leadership endorsements, and issue papers, along with campaign materials, poll results, and favorable press clippings (see Herrnson 2004, 169; Himes 1995, 66; Yeutter et al. 1992, 24–26). PAC kits are generally mailed, but a follow-up telephone call by either the candidate or a campaign official is made after an appropriate interval (see Silverberg 2000). For "hot prospects," it is often deemed wise to have the candidate hand deliver the packet. In addition, "Nonincumbents who make a PAC's issues among the central elements of their campaign message and communicate this information in their PAC kits enhance their odds of winning a committee's backing" (Herrnson 2004, 177).

Sending or delivering PAC kits is by no means the only way to get special-interest money. Incumbents host periodic receptions on their own behalf, often with the help of colleagues. PAC officials are invited to meet the candidate in a social setting. Receptions in Washington and some state capitals commonly cost $1,000 or $2,000 per person. The more prestigious the incumbent, the higher the price tag.

The process is more difficult for challengers and open-seat candidates than it is for incumbents, but party campaign committees can be tremendously helpful. The campaign committees can provide strategic advice about PACs and the right way to approach them. Most PACs send questionnaires wherein even the slightest mistake can prevent a candidate from receiving funds, so parties tutor candidates on proper completion of these forms. Furthermore, while it is illegal for the parties to "earmark" checks they receive from individuals or PACs for specific candidates, in the past it was common for staffers to highlight candidates on their "targeted race list," thus providing a hit to potential contributors. It was allegations that House Majority Leader Tom DeLay had engaged in a variation on this scheme in violations of Texas law that led to his indictment in 2005. Party organizations also hold "meet-and-greet" receptions, where PAC decision makers and selected candidates are invited to the same gathering, allowing candidates direct access to donors—often a difficult hurdle in the PAC fund-raising process. Like a dating service, the party's goal is to bring the candidate and the PAC together (see Herrnson 2000, 106–7). Party leaders can also prod the news media to see certain races as competitive—leading perhaps to more PAC money. Overall, party committees can be a great help with PAC fund-raising, but to get this assistance, the committee must believe that the candidate stands a good chance of victory.

Direct Mail

Direct-mail solicitation can be a powerful fund-raising tool. The modern approach was developed by Richard Viguerie, who, as an operative in the early 1960s, preferred mailing letters to personal solicitations (Blumenthal 1980, 224). In 1965, "Viguerie hired two employees and the three of them copied [by hand] the names and addresses of the 12,500 major donors to the Goldwater campaign" (Friedenberg 1997, 104). The successful use of direct mail by George McGovern's campaign in 1972 was followed by the rapid growth of Republican National Committee fundraising efforts in the late 1970s. The 1980s and 1990s saw an explosion in the number of mail-service professionals. Dwight Morris and Murielle E. Gamache have reported that in the early 1990s, several dozen direct-mail firms were making huge amounts of money from House campaigns. They note that in 1992, for example, several made more than $400,000 and some more than $1 million (1994, 221). Mail houses flourish because the process of sending direct mail can be complex and confusing, far beyond the familiar task of writing a letter and sending it off. In many ways, direct mail epitomizes new-style campaigning.

Direct mail is a step-by-step process that begins with a "prospect list"—a collection of individuals who have shown "some characteristics or qualities thought likely to make them susceptible to a candidate's appeal for funds" (Sabato 1989b, 88). Often, lists may be available through a government agency (such as the board of elections), the state or local party organization, or prior candidates of the same party (and even for the same office), or they can be pulled together from a variety of nonpolitical lists. List vendors offer the use of magazine subscribers, mail-order purchasers, boat owners, and professional accountants, attorneys, and medical doctors. Everyone is on a list of some sort. Law restricts the use of some lists, so caution is in order.

The trick to profitable direct mail is the acceptance of early losses in expectation of later returns. Assume that the prospecting list contains 40,000 names. Production costs and postage for this large group might run approximately $.70 per letter, for a total of $28,000. The campaign might receive a 2 or 3 percent response rate from a prospecting list, meaning that a great letter will bring about 1,000 respondents. The average contribution from the group as a whole will generally be rather small, maybe $19. The gross income from this mailing would therefore be $19,000, in which case the campaign has incurred a $9,000 loss. Or has it? There is another way to look at the mailing: a list of 1,000 proven donors was purchased for just $1 per name. Once this "house list" has been established, the cost of the next mailing is much smaller (the list is only a fraction of its original size), and the rate of return is much higher. The second appeal will be more refined, with the campaign spending, say, $.85 per letter on production and postage. It is mailed to contributors only, requiring just an $850 outlay. The response rate might be as high as 20 percent, with an average contribution of $18. The $850 investment would therefore gross $3,600—a $2,750 net return. Mailings to the house list can be repeated several times. The rate of return will probably become smaller with each mailing as people grow tired of sending more money, but the contributors will rotate—a different 20 percent or so each time—and check boxes on the donor card set the lowest suggested amount at the donor's highest previous contribution, perhaps pressing a steady donation increase.

Fund-raising consultant Neesa Hart has suggested that a campaign can send the house list a new mailing every week (1992). A direct-mail consultant who worked with Congressman Mark Neumann has noted that his 1998 Senate campaign "grossed over $1.1 million in the mail, and grew challenger Neumann's housefile from 7,000 names in June 1997 to over 36,000 names . . . in-state!" (Thibodeaux 1999, 61, ellipses in original). To increase the campaign's fortunes, "We mailed 28 different prospecting packages, to 756,948 names and grossed over $510,000. And an amazing 70 percent of the prospecting packages netted money!" (61).

One way to enhance a direct-mail program for lower-level races is to begin with a "suspect list" rather than a prospect list. Instead of sending letters to a large group, the campaign looks for specific individuals who are likely to give. For example, it may use a list of habitual party donors or the candidate's business contacts. A candidate for county commissioner may draw up a list of her personal friends. A statewide Democratic candidate might solicit all the Democrats in his hometown. The idea behind the suspect list is to improve the rate of return—to perhaps 15 or 20 percent. Hart suggests a number of other refinements (e.g., weeding out unlikely donors and combining households into one mailing) to improve efficiency (1992). Small lists can be created, personalized, and mailed in-house, perhaps saving production costs.

Increasingly, high-end statistical techniques are being used to improve prospect lists (Johnson 2001, 154). One approach, developed by direct-mail consultant Hal Malchow, is called CHAID (Chi-Square Automatic Interaction Detection; see Malchow 2003). The process begins with a large survey (often upward of 5,000 respondents). Responses are merged with census information based on the respondent's address. The survey reveals the types of voters most likely to give, and the census information suggests where similar prospects can be found. For instance, if young professional women are found to be twice as likely to give to your campaign than other groups of voters, demographic information can be sorted to find the areas where these residents are common. The campaign then mails fund-raising letters into this area.

Whether the campaign proceeds from a big or a small list, several elements of a direct-mail appeal must be kept in mind. The letter must convey an urgent message to the reader. "Dull is dull," writes Ron Kanfer, so "the most successful direct-mail programs are built around [a] compelling story" (1991, 22). Appeals must be personal, or they have to discuss a hot issue. "Addresses are even generated by laser printers," suggests scholar and consultant Dennis Johnson, "to look as though they were addressed by hand, complete with smudged letters" (2001, 156). Readers are given the impression that the campaign is behind in the polls but within striking distance. (Nothing kills a small-donor program faster than the perception that the race is in the bag.) A successful letter will provide a response card and a self-addressed envelope. Often the letter will ask the prospect to purchase something quite specific, such as one television ad or a billboard for one week. Donors like knowing how their money will be spent.

Some have suggested that using a celebrity's name can pay off. The Natural Resources Defense Council mailed a large plain envelope with "Robert Redford" where the return address is normally found, with much success (Johnson 2001, 155). Letting prospects believe they have a "special status" or "insider knowledge" can help, as can inviting prospects to "special" events—that is, in exchange for their financial support. Finally, flattery can also be effective. A recent GOP request suggested it was "up to smart, dedicated, concerned Americans such as yourself to make sure our nation chooses the right course" (cited in Johnson 2001, 158).

As to style, many argue that longer letters, with handwritten notes in the margin, work better than short notes. It seems that, in order to get people to send their hard-earned money, the case must be laid out in detail—even if most do not read beyond the first page. Large donations are often followed up with a personal thank-you note from the candidate—partly out of gratitude but also because the heart of direct mail is the notion that people will give more than once, and one never knows when the candidate will seek higher office. Details matter.

Direct-mail programs are complex and risky. Many candidates and consultants outsource the task to mail houses. These firms are often one-stop units that provide copy, layout, printing, list rental, and postage know-how. Billing is generally handled in two ways: a retainer or a fee per piece mailed (Kanfer 1991). But any investment can go bad. A mailing that costs more than it returns produces out-of-pocket expenses that some campaigns cannot absorb. Good targeting and production are critical. In the late 1980s, Larry Sabato wrote, "Many direct mailers foresee a time when they will commission extensive psychological testing of word patterns, colors, and approaches, and use focus groups and much more sophisticated list selection techniques" (1989b, 99). In the new millennium, variations on these functions are becoming routine.

Events: Big and Small

When the president, the vice president, governors, and members of the congressional leadership travel around the United States, they often stop in at candidate fund-raising events. So do Hollywood stars. At these affairs, the honored guest shakes hands with high-dollar donors, perhaps having a picture taken with the celebrity and the candidate, and then everyone joins the low-dollar crowd for dinner and a few words about the future. Fund-raising events can be large-scale affairs, such as dinners, cocktail parties, concerts, or boat tours, or they can be small events, such as coffees, ice-cream socials, and chicken barbecues. In 2004, "coffees" and intimate cocktail parties proved effective not only for down-ballot races but also for the presidential candidates (especially in the primaries). Done well, these activities can produce large sums of money, demonstrate to the media and the general public that the campaign has momentum, reward past donors, and build a list of contributors (Yeutter et al. 1992). They can also serve an important social function. Many voters and contributors are drawn to candidates for the excitement. Campaigns must know how to build a good event.

Like direct mail, large-scale fund-raisers are a gamble and should be undertaken only after much deliberation. The logistics of an event, particularly a large one, can be overwhelming and can tie up the campaign team for weeks. Ticket sales may falter, and uncontrollable circumstances may threaten success. An event that flops causes financial problems and, more important, suggests to the media, voters, and potential contributors that the campaign is struggling.

Small-scale events do not court disaster in the same way that large-scale events might, but they do risk tedium. Small-group chitchat can be painfully dull. A smart campaign uses some imagination, perhaps holding auctions, wine and cheese receptions, folk dances, and so on. Location is important. Successful event planners go out of their way to find interesting locations, but whether the event is on the waterfront or in a neighbor's backyard, most consultants insist that the setting should have an air of success. Campaigns are cautioned, "Perception is reality—especially in the event business. If you're having a small reception with 20 people, don't book a room that can hold 100" (Meredith 2000, 62). In fact, a good event staff ensures that a room can be "cut" with draperies, movable walls, or greenery, just in case the expected number of tickets is not sold.

Telemarketing

Working in conjunction with direct mail, telemarketing operations can reactivate donors who have not contributed in some time, prompting lost contributors to give again (Himes 1995, 76). Two or three days after the prospect receives a fundraising letter, a campaign telemarketer calls "just to make sure the note from the candidate arrived." Response rates for direct mail can rise significantly, possibly because telephone solicitation gives form letters a more personal appeal.

A critically important element of any telemarketing program is to make the call as personable, as authentic, as possible. The callers must sound like volunteers—preferably a neighbor from the next block over. Americans have grown weary of telemarketers, as the popularity of laws limiting this practice will attest. (Political campaigns are largely except from these laws.) But Americans are not naturally angry, hostile, or anxious to hang up on callers. If the campaign worker sounds authentic, honest programs of this sort can be effective. If they sound as if they are selling credit cards, the exchange will be brief.

Online Fund-Raising

The use of Internet fund-raising in political campaigns has reached new levels. Through mass e-mails and Web sites, candidates can raise a great deal of money at a relatively moderate cost (Katz 2004). In 2000, it was apparent that George W. Bush was the front-runner for the Republican Party presidential nomination. Yet after the New Hampshire primary, another Republican, John McCain, captured the media's attention. Not only did McCain win the New Hampshire primary, but he also raised $1 million during the following week though his Web site.

Although McCain did not win his party's bid, his campaign savvy bolstered the credibility of Internet fund-raising.

When Howard Dean, former governor of Vermont came into 2003 lacking adequate presidential campaign funds, few people took his candidacy seriously. To the surprise of many, Dean broke a Democratic record by raising $14.8 million in a mere three months, much of it on the Internet. In addition, by the end of 2003, Dean had raised more than any other Democratic candidate, including John Kerry and John Edwards (Nammour 2005). According to one account, "Dean [rewrote] the playbook on how to organize, finance and mold a presidential campaign" (Drinkard and Lawrence 2004). After Dean's success with Internet fund-raising, both John Kerry and George W. Bush followed suit—each subsequently raising tens of millions of dollars online.

As Benjamin A. Katz and Cheryl Brummer point out, "While presidential campaigns are often using some of the most exciting technology, these discussions miss the vast majority of online campaigns–those on a congressional, state, and local levels" (2004). In 2004, New York City Council speaker Gifford Miller, for instance, raised more than half a million dollars online for his campaign (McIntire 2005). According to a poll from the Pew Internet and American Life Project, "88 percent of locally elected officials are online" (Larsen 2003, 1). In another instance, when West Virginia Democratic senator Robert Byrd was in need of campaign funds, with the combined help of Senator Barack Obama and MoveOn.org, Byrd received an astonishing $800,000 in online donations in less than 48 hours (Nyden, 2005). It seems clear that as the Internet becomes even more accessible, state and local politicians will come to rely on online fund-raising as a major source of funds.

There is growing speculation about the financial potency of the web blogs. In the November 2005 issue of *Campaigns & Elections,* an article titled "Blogging Down the Money Trail" suggested how campaigns might tap into "netroots"—that is blogs, message boards, and me-zines. Simply put, candidates can post information about themselves, their race, and their opponent on certain blogs. They can keep other bloggers posted about the progress of the race and, when situations arise, post urgent calls for money. The article tells how an Ohio Democratic congressional candidate posted pleas in early August for $30,000 in order to fund his GOTV efforts. He raised $50,000. "Whichever party's candidates manage to get the biggest benefit from blogs," it seems, "the one certainty is that they will be there to be used. Political activists are not going off line" (Weigel 2005, 23).

Because Internet fund-raising is relatively new, many candidates lack the tools to build and maintain a successful online campaign. As one would expect, consulting firms have popped up to help. In the fall of 2005, some 31 Web site consulting firms were listed on the *Campaigns and Elections* yellow pages. Experts have suggested a few basic steps to maximize online fund-raising, which are summarized here in 10 key elements (see Brack 2005; Reich 2005; Straumanis 2004):

1. Create a Web site using the latest technology.
2. Provide a broad range of information about the candidate. Contributors want to know a lot about who they are giving to and why.

3. Promote your Web site persistently, until its URL (Web address) becomes common knowledge. Sometimes direct mail can be used to promote the URL.

4. Make your site user friendly. The home page should be easy to navigate, with a link to the contribution page.

5. Make sure the site is always up to date.

6. Publicize offline campaigning efforts online. Remember, the Internet is not going to be effective unless utilized with other campaigning techniques.

7. Provide a feedback mechanism for any online contributions.

8. Encourage online contributors to prod friends, colleagues, and family to contribute.

9. Post the results of opposition research.

10. Provide useful links.

Understanding how to maximize this new mode of communication, especially when it comes to raising funds, will be critical for new-style campaign practitioners for years to come.

Other Recent Innovations

Some campaigns bridge the gap between personal contact and blind prospecting with a paid canvass. Workers are assigned to potentially productive districts and asked to walk door-to-door in search of funds. As compensation for their efforts, the canvassers receive a percentage of the collection. This process has been used by environmental organizations and Public Interest Research Groups across the nation. It can serve several goals simultaneously: raising money, building a house list, and distributing campaign literature. A drawback to the paid canvass is that many workers are motivated by money, not by the campaign or the candidate. Managers might sometimes wonder if the message is getting out as well as if the money is coming in. Moreover, this technique might signal desperation. The thought of mercenaries scouring the district in search of funds may be too much for some candidates to bear.

CONCLUSION

The precise manner in which campaigns should go about raising money is a topic of much speculation—perhaps more than any other area of new-style campaigning. There is, however, agreement on a few fundamentals. As Kaplan puts it, fund-raising "is about asking—and knowing that one dollar early is better than one hundred dollars late" (2000, 64). Still, while consultants are paid well to give new and improved advice, each has a slightly different spin. One of the most successful conservative fund-raisers, Bradley S. O'Leary, made his name with large events, including a million-dollar affair in an airline hangar. O'Leary says, "For a big fund-raiser, I want the biggest place I can find" (Hallow 1997, 22). At the same time, another consultant confides, "I know a campaign is in trouble when they tell me they are large event driven" (McDevitt 1996, 50). What is the right mix? Few can say for sure. The winning combination can be determined only in light of the campaign's specific time, place, and strategic context.

Chapter Ten

Strategic Communications

Dwight D. Eisenhower aired the first television commercial used in a presidential election, but Richard Nixon was the first master of the medium. While he did not pay close attention to television in 1960—John F. Kennedy's win is often attributed to his performance in the televised debates—the 1968 Nixon team made the first comprehensive use of television marketing professionals. The defining presidency, however, was Ronald Reagan's. One of Reagan's advisers, Michael Deaver, figured out that the medium truly does define the message—and, even more important, that "the message" is conveyed by "the picture." Deaver implemented a communications strategy that made imagery the primary focus of event planning. Deaver understood that "unless you can find a visual that explains your message you can't make it stick" (1987, 141). Because Reagan "knew exactly what he was and where he was going," Deaver has said, the image maker's task was merely to "draw the image around that, so that the public could see it clearly" (Hines 1992).

The idea goes to the heart of campaign communications. While scholars may disparage George Bush Sr.'s decision to hold a campaign event at a New Jersey flag factory, thinking the message shallow, the event was reported faithfully by the news media. It was a powerful image: the vice president draped in patriotic symbolism. Furthermore, the imagery was not necessarily misleading. By appearing at a flag factory, Bush aligned himself with traditional patriotism while setting himself apart from the civil libertarian views of his opponent, Governor Michael Dukakis of Massachusetts. The imagery even had power in the policy arena. When the Supreme Court handed down a decision allowing protesters to burn the American flag, President Bush had no wiggle room. Having used the flag so prominently in his campaign, he could not have backed away from its protection even if he had wanted to. The dangers of such symbolism, however, can be seen in Bush's appearance at Boston Harbor, a polluted body of water that mocked Dukakis's environmental record. The assault on Dukakis was helpful in 1988—Bush became "the Environmental Candidate"—but four years later, with a meager record on environmental issues, the message came back to haunt the president. In 1992, the only people who called Bush "the Environmental President" were derisive Democrats.

Political communication is a complex endeavor. Armchair analysts sometimes think that it is all about money and message—and it *is* about these things, but it is about much else. Communications directors must know the fine points of television (broadcast and cable), radio, print, and new media. They need to appreciate the tactical differences between paid media (advertising) and earned media (news coverage)—how to buy one and how to attract the other. They must also be able to orchestrate all these media into a coherent, strategic unit. This chapter discusses some of the general strategies that campaigns use to maximize the power of their message, the fundamentals of media strategy, the differences among the various types of paid media, and the resources that campaigns use to find the media appropriate to their constituencies. News coverage, which often runs counter to a campaign's strategy, is examined more fully in Chapter Eleven.

MEDIA STRATEGY

Renowned scholar Marshall McLuhan popularized the idea that "the medium is the message" (1964). McLuhan intended his maxim as a critique of a culture that venerates televisions and computers. The written word and its culture would soon give way to more compressed informational structures, and these structures were creating a new culture. Whether the shift is good or bad, it is deeply felt. Print journalists say that television offers less information, while television reporters note that a picture is worth a thousand words. At any rate, research shows that people are more likely to believe what they see on television than what they read in the papers—and in a surprising twist, they are even more likely to believe a news outlet's Web site than the broadcast version of the same information (Pew Research Center 2000). If the medium in any way circumscribes the message that it will convey, then political professionals working in an intensely competitive environment must pay heed to nuance. Professionals must, in short, know how each medium works and how these media can be made to work together.

Coordination is crucial. The overall image of the candidate is created largely by the general strategy of campaign media. If the media do not mesh, then voters will not know where the candidate stands. Will the electorate see this as a reflection on its own inability to understand public affairs? More likely, the conclusion will be that the candidate does not really stand for anything. To build a coherent image, a campaign must commit itself to consistency, efficiency, proper timing, effective packaging, and a well-played expectations game.

Consistency. Media consultants seek "message discipline"—trying to stay "on message" and never getting "off message." During the 2000 campaign, George W. Bush kept the focus on "leadership." Whether the specific issue was foreign policy, the domestic economy, or the need to change the education system, leadership always held center stage. Likewise, Bush's main rival in the primaries,

Senator John McCain, also projected a singular theme. For him, it was good government. All the failings of the political system—high taxes, irrational policy, and so forth—could be tied back to special interests that had an undue influence over American elections. Proof of McCain's determination could be found in his dogged fight on behalf of the McCain–Feingold campaign finance reform bill. While pundits often criticized Bush for his relative lack of leadership experience and McCain for accepting funds that would not be allowed under his legislation, both campaigns hammered home the central message of their respective campaigns over and over again.

Consistency is demanding. A campaign's theme must be communicated up and down the chain of command. Typically, only designated staffers speak for the campaign—the candidate, the campaign manager, and the press secretary or communications director. Consultants are generally expected to stay out of sight. The campaign theme must also be consistent with the candidate's past record. One function of opposition research is to locate discrepancies between a candidate's words and actions. A candidate who says one thing and does another courts misfortune—even if the statement fits the campaign theme. Finally, the theme must be reasonably consistent with the views and actions of a candidate's supporters. Staffers and contributors who may once have worked against the candidate's current policy proposals can become an unwanted part of a news story. Ironically, however, if the staff and contributors are *too* consistent with the candidate's beliefs—if, for example, the candidate's platform is friendly to major donors—then conflicts of interest may be charged. Once again, politics is not an easy game.

Simple consistency is not sufficient. Two of the most unswerving presidential candidates in recent years have suffered the consequences of unshakable regularity—Senator Tom Harkin of Iowa and publishing magnate Steve Forbes, son of the founder of *Forbes* magazine. Forbes made his name in politics by pushing for a flat tax in 1996 and 2000, making the case time and again that his proposal would be equitable for the taxpayers and profitable to the economy. The problem was that Forbes could not talk about much else, and using the same phrases over and over, he was criticized as a "one-note-Johnny" (Tuttle 1996, 3). Much the same problem bedeviled Tom Harkin in 1992. Harkin conveyed a progressive message aimed at unions and other traditional Democratic base groups. He received strong support from these sectors but could not make his case elsewhere. When, in the face of pending defeat, he stuck to his original campaign themes, one political reporter said that Harkin's "solution to the problem [was] to turn up the volume rather than change the tape" (David Yepsen, cited in Kurtz 1992).

Efficiency. Despite complaints that consultants drive up the cost of campaigns, new-style political operatives are known for their efficient use of resources in difficult media environments. They want to eliminate "waste." Consider the problem of a congressional candidate running in Chicago. Credibility demands that the candidate use television advertising—for some people, a campaign is not real until they see it on television—but Chicago stations reach a dozen or more congressional districts, some of them in Indiana and Wisconsin. The viewers who cannot vote in the candidate's congressional district represent wasted media. The job of the campaign professional is to maximize the number of times that persuadable voters can be reached with a campaign pitch, either through paid advertising or through news coverage.

For electronic media, communications specialists think in terms of "reach" and "frequency." Reach is the portion of the viewership that actually receives a given message. The concept is typically bounded by some time frame. For example, a campaign might reach 30 percent of the market in a given week. Frequency, on the other hand, is the number of times that a person is reached. The principal measurement, however, is neither reach nor frequency but a combination of the two, expressed as "gross rating points" (GRPs). GRP is nothing more than reach times frequency. A message that plays three times on a show having an 11.2 percent reach adds up to 33.6 GRPs. These notions offer communications personnel a powerful means of analyzing media efficiency.

Demographics matter. ESPN may offer a large viewership, but would it be the right show for a campaign that wants to reach upscale women? The Food Network might be a better buy—a much smaller audience but a tighter demographic (see Mentzer 2000b). However, the demographic of the Food Network tends to represent good consumers, and a campaign would have to compete with commercial marketers who want to reach the same audience. For the same reason, some programs with a small audience can be worth the money. MTV's audience is not large, but it is valuable to some advertisers because it skews toward a narrow, youth-based demographic. If people of all ages watched MTV, its audience would be less valuable—even if it attracted more people—because fewer advertisers would be interested in a scattershot viewership.

As a rule of thumb, a political campaign thinks not in terms of simple GRPs but in terms of the "cost per point" of persuadable voters. Everything outside the district is waste. Everything outside the targeted demographic is inefficiency. The more precisely a campaign can aim its message at targeted voters and the more options that it has for reaching them cost effectively, the more efficiently the campaign can spend its money.

These principles are relevant for news coverage as well as paid advertising, for print as well as electronic media. Ads consume campaign cash, whereas news coverage consumes the precious time of the candidate, staff, and consultants. A congressional candidate in Chicago has to work hard to win a profile piece in the *Chicago Tribune,* and if this widely circulated paper eventually decides to run the story, many of the candidate's new admirers will be in northern Indiana. Additionally, the *Tribune*'s demographics may be all wrong. For some campaigns, an interview with a reporter from *Crain's Chicago Business* would be a far more efficient use of a candidate's time. More likely, however, the best investment would be a neighborhood weekly, which might reach targeted voters more efficiently.

Dealing with the press is a profession of its own. Likewise, purchasing of media time and space is so complicated that most midlevel and some lower-level campaigns delegate media strategy to outside consultants. Where advertising is concerned, many of these consultants subcontract the purchasing of ads to professional ad buyers who take a commission on every dollar spent. The cost of expertise is presumably recouped in the efficiency gains of carefully targeted ad purchases.

Timing. Part of the efficiency equation is the timing of the message. A standard sequence for a challenger's campaign might be to introduce the candidate to the public with a series of press interviews combined with "establishment" ads—those designed to let viewers know who the candidate is in the broadest terms. Once a positive impression of the candidate is created, the campaign might build credibility with a series of "issue" ads, laying out the high points of a candidate's agenda. If the incumbent starts to respond, the challenger might return fire with "attack" ads. At the end of the campaign, it is the responsibility of the strategists to decide whether the challenger should go negative, go positive, or stay the course. Incumbents might follow roughly the same pattern, but they generally start off with better name identification, so they may not have to get into the business of establishment ads. Incumbents must, however, decide whether they want to strike back at a challenger who attacks their record.

Timing is important to message development for another reason. Ad buys and news coverage require advance planning. Reporters do not sit down with a candidate at a moment's notice; relationships take time to build. Moreover, an opponent who enjoys a long-standing association with a reporter might have been subtly dropping insinuations about the candidate since the beginning of the campaign year. If the challenger waits too long, there may be no way to erase the bad impression that has been built over time. With paid electronic media, the problem is far more acute. Buying ad space in a newspaper is a simple matter of phoning the advertising department and requesting display space. Electronic media, on the other hand, represent a limited resource. Only a fixed number of radio and television spots are available during the course of a race. Timing becomes critical. A campaign must make early determinations about how much money it will be able to raise and when it will be able to get the cash in hand. A campaign's income and outflow must match an odd quirk in the tactics of ad buying: the last days have to be purchased first. Because every campaign wants to grab the last few days before the election, a campaign that waits until a month before Election Day to buy the final slots will likely walk away empty handed—another reason for raising early money.

Packaging and Effectiveness. A voter who always votes Republican need only be informed that the candidate is a member of the GOP. Signs, radio ads, endorsements, and television spots might make the candidate's party affiliation explicit: "Jones: Republican for U.S. Senate." Sometimes, however, the cues must be more subtle, and metaphors can help make the case.

In the 1980s, there were few issues in national politics more difficult than the nuclear standoff between the United States and the Soviet Union. Between Democrats and Republicans, the question was whether the appropriate strategy was a buildup, a freeze, or a drawdown. President Reagan stood firmly with those who sought to increase U.S. nuclear superiority. The 1984 Reagan team needed a way to make its case in simple terms. The campaign used a well-constructed metaphor. A Native American faced a "bear in the woods." Noting that there was disagreement as to whether the bear is dangerous, the well-armed hunter forced the bear to literally back away. The message was clear: "the best way to avoid a military confrontation with the Soviets was for America to be stronger than [its] Cold War rival" (Weaver 1996, 204).

Campaign ads fall into three general categories: positive, comparative, and negative. Advertising designed to establish a candidate's credentials and to lay out a policy agenda are usually positive. The Reagan ad is a good example, but there are others. In a 1998 Georgia race, Republican Dylan Glenn was trying to become the first black Republican congressman from the South since Reconstruction. To introduce himself, he ran a biographical sketch—"From Georgia; for Georgia." Comparative ads lay out differences between the candidates. In the 1998 Ohio race between Congressman Ted Strickland and Lieutenant Governor Nancy Hollister, one 30-second ad was literally split in half. It began with a harsh attack on Hollister's record ("41% Income Tax Increase"), complete with black-and-white imagery and a discordant musical score; then, in midcommercial, the music lifted, the colors flowed, and the ad turned decidedly positive ("Ted Strickland is working to cut taxes"). Across the Ohio River in Kentucky, the 1998 Senate campaign of Republican Congressman Jim Bunning included a fiercely negative ad against his opponent, Scotty Baesler. Baesler was shown shouting into the microphone at a campaign rally, to which was added Richard Wagner's "The Ride of the Valkyries," a score often associated with Nazism. According to scholars who followed the election, this ad helped make the race "one of the nastiest in the nation" (Gross and Miller 2000, 190).

From this same part of the country emerged one of the most contentious campaigns of the 2004 cycle. In southeastern Ohio, former Beirut hostage Terry Anderson challenged incumbent Joy Padgett for a seat in the state senate. Padgett attacked Anderson with a piece of direct mail that featured a picture of her opponent next to an actual terrorist. The photograph was real, but the implication was misleading: "Missing from Padgett's advertisement was any mention that the terrorist pictured with Anderson was the secretary general of Hezbollah, the group that abducted him in 1985. Anderson [had] confronted and interviewed the terrorist leader for a television documentary years after he was freed" (Simonich 2004, A1).

Skeptics would be forgiven for believing that the increasing use of media in American campaigns stems, in part, from the fact that ad buyers and consultants receive a percentage of the ad buys. George Stephanopoulos, discussing the huge sums that Dick Morris made from the 1995–1996 campaign cycle, said, "It's inarguable that there's a conflict of interest. . . . That doesn't mean it was bad advice, but it certainly wasn't disinterested advice" (Harris 1998). Some consultants advise that campaign polling be kept institutionally separate from the purchasing of campaign ads. At least one pollster believes that those in his profession can serve as "independent auditors," making sure that the candidate knows how well the media efforts are working (Friedenberg 1997, 56).

Expectations. An important element of communications strategy is something that political professionals call the "expectations game." "News" is that which is new, and if a front-running candidate wins, then there is not much new news. If, however, a dark-horse candidate finishes the race a close second, then there *is* real news—though not the type that the actual victor desired.

George W. Bush suffered from inflated expectations early in the 2000 campaign. Through most of 1999, Bush was the presumptive winner of the next year's primaries. He had nowhere to go but down. When Steve Forbes ran just 11 points behind Bush in Iowa and John McCain won New Hampshire by 19 percent, virtually all attention shifted to Forbes and McCain. The question was whether the front-runner had hit a roadblock. More realistic observers saw that neither Forbes nor McCain had sufficient money and organization to win. Forbes had no genuine organization outside of Iowa. McCain had some people beyond New Hampshire but nothing to rival Bush's national web of established Republicans and financial donors. Yet operatives for Bush's nationwide campaign—ahead in virtually all the post–New Hampshire states—were forced to call supporters with reassurances that Bush still had good prospects.

The expectations game demonstrates the relative nature of news. The question is not, Did Bush win Iowa? but, rather, Did Bush win Iowa by the number of votes anticipated? Critics say that the outcome is all that counts, but sometimes the failure to meet expectations signifies an underlying problem. Even though Forbes had little hope of eventual victory, his strength in Iowa exposed weakness in the Bush camp. His advocacy of the flat tax forced Bush to respond with his own tax cut plan. Forbes' effort *was* news. But the deeper meaning of the story is that political campaigns must work in an environment where perception tends to become reality. Campaigns must therefore do their best to control expectations.

There is a routine cycle to the effort. At the beginning of a campaign, a challenger wants to give the impression that victory is possible, hoping to get at least minimal coverage. An incumbent, on the other hand, seeks to show that victory is inevitable, hoping to scare off challengers. Once a competitive election begins, both sides claim that the race is close. To make sure that voters go out to the polls, front-running candidates highlight the possibility of a loss so that their supporters do not just sit out the election. Even an incumbent with a commanding lead tells supporters on Election Eve that the race is not yet won, that there is still plenty of work to do. It is a message that wise campaigns will press through both news coverage and paid campaign advertising.

PAID MEDIA

Paid media give campaigns the ability to control their message. Unlike news coverage, which puts a reporter between the campaign and the public, paid media allow campaign operatives to script the message, target the audience, and, for the most part, select the timing that best suits the needs of the campaign. The downside is that paid media cost money (by definition). Television ads can run tens of thousands of dollars. Even a small display ad in a college newspaper can cost hundreds. According to congressional scholar Paul Herrnson, "Hopeful challengers committed an average of $660,000 to campaign communications" (2004, 244).

Campaigns must be efficient in their targeting, and they must choose the right medium for their message.

Communications consultant Craig Shirley says, "When I first began doing public relations in Washington back in the '70s, media options were the large city daily newspapers, the secondary city newspapers, the wires, the three networks, some radio . . . and the local affiliates" (1997, 22). Campaigns in the new millennium have a wider variety of options, from new broadcast channels to cable systems to Internet media. Each has its own advantages. Cable allows for narrow targeting. Broadcast television and radio have wide reach and are required to sell ad time to candidates at bargain prices. Newspapers are doing their best to remain competitive by offering deep discounts. Campaign Web sites, unknown before 1996, are becoming a critical means of voter outreach.

Television

Television is a powerful medium. Combining audio with visual imagery, it absorbs its viewers in ways that radio and print cannot. Joe McGinniss wrote more than three decades ago that television was "something new, murky, undefined," that "the mystique which should fade grows stronger. We make celebrities not only of the men who cause events but of the men who read reports of them out loud" (1969, 28). Why? Because television makes its images more "real" than do any of its competitors. Thus, "the medium is the massage and the masseur gets the votes" (29). Most political consultants would agree.

Production costs are high, to be sure. Assembling a television spot requires the assistance of a producer, photographer, assorted gaffers, and a postproduction house to edit the raw footage. An independent filmmaker warns campaign consultants, "In the quick turnaround, high-pressure world of media production, there are few situations where margins of error are smaller, time crunches more acute and smooth sailing more essential than in the production of political ads" (Arnold 1999, 62). The process is complicated, taking time that campaigns can barely spare. The competitive nature of politics puts a premium on speed, and television is the slowest and most expensive of the media to produce. It is cumbersome and resistant to real-time changes, but no campaign turns down the opportunity to use television ads if it has the money to do so.

Communications scholar Robert Friedenberg has noted that consultants see 300 to 500 GRPs as the minimum threshold for going on television (1997, 174). Because each GRP represents a percentage of potential audience tuned in at any given time, 300 GRPs means that, theoretically, everyone saw the campaign ad three times. With GRPs priced into the thousands of dollars, the costs add up quickly, and consultants are upping the ante. After the 1996 elections, a campaign that crowded the political marketplace with political ads, recommendations started to exceed the 1,000-point boundary (1997, 175). One consultant whom Friedenberg interviewed said that "he would like to see every voter exposed to his ads 10–14 times or more, to help account for the problems inherent in the new media environment of the 1990s" (175). Of course, this kind of advice may well have the self-fulfilling effect of causing upward-spiraling campaign costs.

In the race to reach the right viewers, political campaigns enjoy advantages not shared by commercial advertisers. Federal candidates have a legal right to buy ad time at discount rates in the days immediately before to the election. Prior to 1992, there was some question as to whether nonfederal candidates were entitled to the low rate; the Federal Communications Commission determined that they were not. Even for federal candidates, there is a catch. Low-cost purchases provide no guarantee of placement. If a candidate buys a spot at a certain time using anything less than the higher "nonpreemptable rate," another of the broadcaster's clients can pay top dollar to bump the candidate's ad from its time slot. To use low rates well, ad buyers must pay attention to day-to-day fluctuations in the broadcast marketplace.

Close monitoring is possible because candidate ad-buy records are public by law. Everyone has a right to view up-to-the-minute reports and to make copies for a reasonable fee. Researchers who look at the files can find everything from purchase orders and canceled checks to scribbled notes of phone conversations. If a campaign is making a heavy ad buy on daytime soaps early in the electoral cycle, all the paperwork related to the acquisition, right down to the specific time slot request, is supposed to show up in the file. What the researcher might not find, however, is documentation as to whether the buy went through. Was the requested spot actually run at the date and time ordered? Or was it bumped by a higher-paying customer? The answer might be inferred by totaling up invoices, but inferential measurements in lieu of after-the-fact affidavits are mere approximations. In addition, the station rep and the ad buyer might rearrange time slots over the phone, leaving no paper trail. Furthermore, not all stations fully understand or comply with the rules. It is not uncommon to find that a media outlet has failed to keep its records current. The researcher may end up waiting at the reception desk while the designated file keeper assembles the relevant documents on immediate notice.

In the digital age, some campaigns might wish to avoid manual records searches. Fee-based ad detection systems claim to track television spots by their audio signature, but even if the system works well, its use is expensive and alerts the campaign only after the opposition's ads were run. It is important to trace the station's sales ahead of time. Despite the incompleteness of public records, frequent trips to broadcast stations can serve as a distant early warning system. A campaign that buys early has tipped its hand. Its strategy is out in the open. An additional reason to watch the opposition's ad buys in advance is to monitor broadcasters' compliance with the "Equal Time Rule" (technically, the "Equal Opportunities Rule"). Generally speaking, if a broadcaster sells time to one candidate, it must offer time to any other candidate in the race. Keeping a close eye on public records can let a campaign know when it should jump into the market.

Broadcast Television. The most familiar means of receiving television is via broadcast. In the mid-1970s, it was practically the only way to see a television program, but with the rise of cable in the 1980s and 1990s, broadcast lost a significant share of the video audience. Videocassette recorders, digital video recorders, and video games reduced the broadcast television audience further still. With more and more viewers recording their favorite shows for later viewing, there is a greater likelihood that the commercials, including political spots, will be "zapped."

Nonetheless, broadcast television continues to be a mainstay of larger, new-style campaigns. The reason is reach. A campaign can send a powerful message to wide swaths of the electorate with a single ad buy. Many homes are still not wired for cable. This fact causes a problem for consultants who think about skipping broadcast television. As noted by one media specialist, "To be successful, we must obtain a market share of 50 percent plus one of the potential pool of political customers. This fact requires us to be mass marketers. We want market share, not unit sales" (Hutchens 1996, 42). Especially for candidates who must reach lower-income voters, broadcast remains a powerful medium.

Cable Television. Broadcast television reaches the widest audience, while cable television targets the most specific selection of voters. At the turn of the twenty-first century, just under 70 percent of homes in the United States were wired for cable, providing ad buyers with a whole new category of paid media. On the one hand, there is no difference between broadcast and cable advertising. Viewers watching a major-network television show transmitted via cable might be unable to distinguish between ads run by the network and those inserted by the local cable company. On the other hand, the ability to run ads in a single cable market fundamentally changes the tactics of video ad placement. Cable offers narrowly defined markets. Local cable companies have fixed borders—towns, cities, counties, and other municipal entities—and these boundaries are contiguous with many electoral districts. Waste is minimized. Moreover, because cable offers dozens, even hundreds, of channels, each one is forced to "narrowcast" their programming. The History Channel, A&E, BET, and MTV each seeks a thin slice of the pie. Many candidates take advantage of Spanish-language networks. As if to emphasize the tremendous ability of cable to segment a political marketplace, some campaign organizations have even chosen to run different ads in different locales within a single electoral district. The 2004 Bush campaign even used closed-circuit feeds into health clubs.

The benefits of cable are not without cost. First, the cable audience tends to be highly desirable to product marketers. Cable is a fee-based system, so the demographics of the cable viewership skew up the economic scale. While it has been reported that cable customers vote more regularly than broadcast viewers (Friedenberg 1997, 184–85), campaigns that wish to target these voters are competing with powerful economic interests. Second, the cable marketplace is decentralized. Because there are many cable companies across the country, buying cable ads can be a tough job. Media buyers often feel compelled to use the services of "spot reps" to facilitate the acquisition of ad time in more than one market. Finally, as noted earlier, there is some question as to whether an all-cable strategy is politically wise. Cable penetration is deep but not total, and many people are opting for satellite dishes instead of traditional cable hookups. Says Hutchens, "Excluding any significant-sized audience from receiving your communications only invites peril" (1996, 42).

The distinctive value of cable, however, is revealed by Hutchens's own experience. In 1992, Hutchens was working for Democratic Congressman Jim Bacchus, whose redrawn district made for a precarious reelection cycle. To lift its prospects, Bacchus's people targeted a small area of his Florida district, Indian River County, that had not been with the congressman in the past but that seemed to offer a fair amount of opportunity. Writes Hutchens, "In addition to direct mail, we bought heavily on Indian River cable (25 spots per day on all available networks) and supplemented our reach with local, non-metro radio" (1996, 43). On Election Day, "the additional vote out of Indian River County made the difference in what turned out to be a very close race" (1996, 43).

Changes in the cable industry are helping to make it more competitive with broadcast. Cable availability has continued to increase, while network market share has decreased. As local cable companies are absorbed into larger systems, billing and invoicing are centralized. The advantage to a campaign is paperwork efficiency: a single phone call can request ad time on several cable systems, and at the end of the process, the campaign receives just one bill. For a political campaign, which must operate on speed, any decrease in complexity is appreciated.

Radio

Radio obviously lacks the visual element of television, but in some ways it offers the best of broadcast combined with the best of cable. Like broadcast, it has a powerful reach, and it follows the same discount rules as broadcast television. Like cable, it can be used for precision targeting and constant repetition. For example, talk radio attracts a decidedly more conservative audience than pop stations. A radio-based strategy is therefore low cost, allowing a campaign to buy a great deal of time. Moreover, fast production means that radio is suitable for rapid response. Campaigns can react to events in a matter of hours. Moreover, a radio-based strategy helps a campaign "fly under the radar," escaping the sorts of "ad watch" scrutiny that sometimes makes negative advertising difficult. As Friedenberg points out, "Generally, radio ads are not taped, nor are the transcripts of them closely analyzed by the press" (1997, 143).

Radio has intimacy: "the images it conveys exist in the listener's minds" (Sweitzer and Heller 1996, 40). Radio imagery can be seen in a pair of ads that the Senate campaign of John Warner produced for the 1996 elections. The *Washington Post* described Warner's predicament in the GOP primary: "He must drive up turnout dramatically. He hopes to do that with an aggressive media blitz aimed at mobilizing women, moderates, and especially Northern Virginians, while giving reason to doubt his rival's credentials as a true believer" (Baker 1996). Evidently in an effort to tweak the demographics, "Warner aired a radio commercial featuring a male voice assailing his Republican primary opponent for masquerading as a conservative. It ran just once before being taken off the air. A few days later, it resurfaced—but this time with a woman's voice" (1996). The Warner campaign, it seems, wanted to paint a more feminine picture in the mind of the radio audience.

Newspapers

Once the primary means for propagating partisan ideas, newspapers have lost a great deal of market share. Fewer people are reading newspapers, and less money is spent advertising in them. There are, however, a few reasons that newspaper ads remain part of new-style campaigns. First, ad space is always available. Whereas television and radio are scarce commodities, newspapers can always find space for display ads—even if they have to add a few pages to accommodate an end-of-the-campaign advertising blitz. Second, newspapers are responding to market pressures by segmenting their markets. High-tech printing operations allow for geographic variations in advertising content whereby each suburb in a metropolitan area might receive its own set of display ads. Finally, there is a fear factor at play. Many political operatives believe that failure to buy newspaper ad space can lose a campaign its rightful endorsement and might even affect decisions about news reporting. This economic pressure is presumed to work both ways. One former elected official recommends the following to candidates in local races: if a paper never runs with a campaign's news release, "threaten to cancel [campaign] ads and ask for your money back. . . . The editors will hate me for telling you this, but for a small paper on a tight budget, this is an effective technique for your campaign" (Grey 1999, 182).

New Media

Newspapers are old media; campaign Web sites are new media. In the 1980s, such resources did not exist, but now a presence on the World Wide Web is considered essential to campaigns at almost all levels. A candidate without a Web site appears to lack seriousness. A candidate with a disheveled site gives the impression of having a disorganized campaign. A visually attractive, user-friendly Web site that offers an abundance of informational content—one early study showed that visitors spend the most time with "issue sections, candidate biographies and comparative sections" (Hockaday and Edlund 1999, 14)—can help deepen voters' impression of the candidate. During the 2000 campaign, it became common for campaign Web sites to post news releases, calendars of upcoming events, and even streaming video and audio, showcasing the ads being run through more traditional media.

During the 1996 cycle, the reason to have a campaign Web site might have been to avoid newspaper stories about the lack of a Web presence. In the new millennium, when far more people have access to the Internet and when campaign Web sites offer a wealth of information about candidates, the new wisdom is that the Web can offer a strong foundation for campaign communications. The campaign Web site became feature rich, filled with policy papers, pictures, and streaming video.

The difficulty with campaign Web sites is that people must make a conscious effort to travel to the site. Radio and television reach all the listeners and viewers who do not zap the ad. They are "opt-out" media. The Web, however, is an "opt-in" medium, meaning that some sort of off-site marketing is necessary to bring a substantial surfer base to a Web site. Media consultant Mike Connell points out that the Web can serve as an extension to broadcast media. Campaigns try to purchase "30-second spots in which the candidate must explain to all the electorate who they are, what they have done, their vision for the future and why they are the best candidate. But put the campaign's Web site address on the advertisement and suddenly you've given the electorate access to complete, in-depth information on the candidate" (Connell 2000, 58). Donald Dunn, running for Congress in 2000, "ran a list of [Utah residents] who are owed money from their 1998 tax returns on his Web site." It proved to be a smart strategy: "The Dunn campaign then held a press conference announcing that they would be posting the names, after which the Web site had nearly 20,000 hits" (Jalonick 2000, 62).

FINDING THE MEDIA

Finding media outlets requires careful research. Take, for example, the search for print media. While just about everyone knows the major papers in a big city, a number of smaller publications might go unnoticed. With geographically large districts, such as rural congressional districts, just getting a handle on the television stations that serve the electorate can become a chore. Media advisers must inventory the outlets that serve a district—not just those that are published in the district but all those that reach the district's voters. The principal resources are Editor and Publisher's *International Year Book, The Gale Directory of Publications and Broadcast Media, SRDS TV & Cable Source, Broadcasting & Cable Yearbook,* and *SRDS Radio Advertising Source.*

The *International Year Book* lists publications from major daily papers down to shopping guides. A researcher studying the Miami Beach market will find a handful of major newspapers serving the metropolitan area, including the *Miami Herald* (in the "Dailies" volume) and the Spanish-language *el Nuevo Herald* (listed in the "Hispanic Newspapers" section). For each paper, the *Year Book* lists circulation, advertising rates, special editions, special weekly sections, and the newspaper's magazine. In addition, technical specifications—ranging from the width of a paper's columns to the types of software and printers in use—help a media consultant plan the details of an ad buy. To find smaller papers, the researcher looks to the "U.S. Shoppers" section of the *Year Book* or to the *Gale Directory.* There one finds that Miami Beach has the *SunPost,* affiliated with the Post Newspaper Group. Contacts and ad rates are supplied. Even with all these resources, a prudent operative will actually travel the district to see what publications are sold at the newsstands and offered at the local libraries. Perusing news boxes on the sidewalks makes clear that the *Miami New Times,* which focuses heavily on Miami's young, urban scene, is widely read in the South Beach area.

Radio stations can be found in the *Gale Directory, Broadcasting & Cable Yearbook,* or the *SRDS Radio Advertising Source. SRDS* divides the state of Florida into markets. Miami Beach lies in the "Miami–Fort Lauderdale–Hollywood" market. In the section devoted to this region, the researcher learns about a variety of radio stations, including WLYF, a 100,000-watt "adult contemporary" station licensed out of Miami. It has women aged 35 to 44 years as its primary audience and men and women aged 25 to 54 as its secondary audience. Television resource information is structured in much the same way. *SRDS TV & Cable Source* shows that the Miami–Fort Lauderdale market is served by a number of broadcast stations, including WFOR, a CBS affiliate out of Miami. All contact information necessary to set up a rotation of campaign ads can be found in the directory. With a little investigation, the astute researcher can map out a rigorous media strategy.

CONCLUSION

The point of media research is purely strategic. Media buying has as its primary goal the purchasing of spots and ad space that will most likely move the candidate closer to electoral victory. The business of paid advertising—the most controllable form of voter contact—becomes unpredictable as soon as the opposition candidate enters the fray. Charges are followed by countercharges as each campaign seeks to push the other side off message. To reinforce its own themes, a campaign must use all available means of reaching the voters, including news coverage, in the quest for an integrated campaign message.

Chapter Eleven

News Coverage

A sizable war chest, a strong message, and a smart strategy each help a campaign present its candidate in a positive light. Paid media offer control over timing, audience, and message, but few campaigns have unlimited funds, and while news coverage is not truly free and while it carries inherent risks, it has the benefit of credibility (Herrnson 2004; Salmore and Salmore 1989). The message is coming from a seemingly neutral observer. It also comes within a context—on the television news, in the newspaper, or during a radio news segment—where people are thinking about politics. In other words, the news media reach people when they are in the market for political information. Getting into the news is a wise use of campaign time. Indeed, a campaign that fails to court reporters may leave the impression that it has something to hide.

Political consultants talk about "earned media." The term refers to coverage on television, on radio, and in the newspapers. Consultants call it "earned media" rather than "free media" in order to emphasize the hard work that goes into the quest for coverage. Perhaps the only office for which candidates are guaranteed regular news coverage is the presidency—and even then, front-running candidates complain that they are not getting enough attention or that the coverage they are getting is not entirely fair. For years, reporters have objected that politicians try to "manage" the news, even as candidates feel put upon by an unwieldy press. Moreover, while pundits grumble that candidates offer nothing more than "sound bites," the news media continue to run snappy political phrasing as real news.

Positive coverage is never assured. When Democrat Bob Graham of Florida decided to run for the U.S. Senate, he planned a large press event to kick off the race—a multicity, satellite-driven extravaganza that unfortunately coincided with the explosion of the *Challenger* space shuttle. During the 2000 campaign, George W. Bush was taken aback when an on-air radio personality asked him to name the leaders of various foreign nations, and the candidate's inability to do so raised questions about his knowledge of international affairs. Whether the line of questioning was fair or not, the damage was done. As noted by one observer, "If you are brilliant, the media will make you appear even better. If you are foolish, incompetent, indecisive, or wimpy, the media can cripple you" (Phillips 1984, 77).

To understand how campaigns operate, it is important to know how candidates, consultants, and campaign staff view the media. The press is a blessing and a curse, an opportunity and a danger—a necessary part of the campaign process but one that always looms as a threat. Among political operatives, there is little confidence that the press is "objective" in the sense that it merely reports the facts. Rather, a campaign understands that the news media are forced to pick and choose which facts are going to be reported. To say that a paper contains "All the News That's Fit to Print" merely begs the question, What counts as "news"? Likewise, it is too easy to assert that reporters are generally liberal while editors and publishers are conservative, that news organizations are just profit-seeking enterprises, or that reporters always base their stories on personal opinion. Political reporting is complicated. This chapter tries to comprehend news-based campaign strategies by discussing the history of news reporting, with an eye to "newsworthyness," and the tactics that campaigns bring into play.

A SHORT HISTORY OF NEWS REPORTING

A *Gazette* or *Intelligencer* of early America looked nothing like today's *New York Times*. Without a drive for objective, dispassionate reporting, the "news" was unabashedly partisan (Dinkin 1989, 7–9). Newspapers, such as they were, aligned themselves with one side of a debate or the other, and they did so according to the whims of the parties that funded them. In the first half of the 1800s, however, publishers began to understand that people who wanted to read the news might be willing to pay for it. The "penny press" was born. For one cent, readers could get the news of the day along with feature stories to keep things interesting. More readers meant more profit, so there was little reason to restrict a paper's viewpoint to that of one particular party. Thereafter, publishers came to understand that even more money could be made if space was sold for advertising. With the rise of profit-driven "yellow journalism" in the late 1800s—which gave front-page coverage to crime, scandal, and tragedy—newspapers became big business.

The profit motive was not the only force in journalism. In much the same way that broader sales freed newspapers from their partisan roots, the Associated Press (AP), a national wire service, started to release the press from its local, parochial points of view. The AP was formed in the late 1840s and the early 1850s as a cooperative that pooled the resources of New York newspapers. Instead of having dozens of reporters on a single site, the publishing community could save money by recycling the story of a single, local journalist. As the AP co-op spread across the United States, reporting on the Civil War and other domestic news, the regional interests of AP reporters gave way to a more national perspective. At the end of the nineteenth century, a backlash against yellow journalism reinforced the idea that "objectivity" should be the guiding principle of journalism. Progressives in the early 1900s hailed the arrival of "muckraking" journalism, which sought to expose corruption in government and greed in the private sector. Advocating a form of reporting that focused on journalistic responsibility, the muckrakers paved the way for the new professional standards—a form of journalism that distinguished "facts" from "analysis" and "editorializing"—a form that would later be taught in schools of journalism around the country. A strong ethical framework that would have seemed foreign to the early partisan press had taken hold in American journalism.

The difficulty with the concept of journalistic objectivity is that the meaning of reportable news has fluctuated considerably in the past 100 years. In the first part of the twentieth century, politicians were often treated with kid gloves. Many journalists accepted what they were told and rarely scrutinized the private lives of candidates. Larry Sabato aptly labels this a time of "lapdog" journalism (Sabato 1991, 25). During the 1960s and 1970s, the news industry entered a period of "investigative journalism." Shocked by revelations of government misinformation, reporters who covered the Vietnam War and the Nixon administration no longer took for granted the sincerity of politicians. They scrutinized the words and behavior of candidates. Reporters dug to find the dirt, leading some to call this period one of "watchdog journalism" or even "attack-dog" journalism. For campaigns, there was a growing interest in the horse race—who is ahead and who is behind—and even the internal workings of campaign operations. In a sense, "the mechanics of campaigning have become a better story than the campaign itself" (Luntz 1988, 33).

Most criticism of the media is reserved for television news. In the early 1900s, radio started broadcasting news events, but unlike print outlets, which cover news in depth, radio reporting was exceedingly condensed and required all the day's news to be delivered in a few moments. Radio was criticized for its superficiality. Nevertheless, the medium was given credibility by serious journalists like Edward R. Murrow, whose voice gave urgent, passionate reports from Europe at the onset of World War II. After the war, a number of radio reporters, including Murrow, moved to television news, which suffered the same time constraints as radio. Indeed, the cost of television production and transmission meant that viewers had limited options: three broadcast networks decided what constituted "the news." Lacking depth, the medium was open to attack by the likes of Marshall McLuhan, Joe McGinniss, and, before them, Daniel Boorstin. Boorstin wrote, "Our national politics has become a competition for images or between images, rather than between ideals. The domination of campaigning simply dramatizes this fact" (1964, 249). The news media, Boorstin thought, were full participants in the problem, having allowed themselves to become mesmerized by "pseudo-events".

Boorstin's critique can be directed at all news media. Journalists chafe at the idea that their profession is anything less than objective, but objectivity is an elusive ideal. The fact remains: media outlets that go out of business are not able to inform the public, so news content must be able to hold consumer interest. Some stories are more interesting in one medium than another. When Republican candidates in 1994 walked in front of the U.S. Capitol to sign the GOP Contract with America, almost every detail was staged for the television cameras (Tron 1996).

Although the story was fed to other media, the event was designed for video. At the same time, complicated stories that involve detailed information work better in print. In the middle of the 2000 campaign, the *New York Times* ran an extensive biographical profile on U.S. Senate candidate Rick Lazio, analyzing the congressman's policies, his personality, and his approach to politics. It is difficult to imagine that a drawn-out life history of any nonpresidential candidate could have attracted a sufficient television audience to warrant a producer's approval.

Even if publishers did not have to worry about the bottom line, the problem of journalistic preconceptions would linger. Reporters cannot help but bring their outlook on the world to bear on their coverage of the news. Reporters work hard to separate political partisanship from news coverage, and they are perhaps more aware of the distinctions between facts and analysis than most. Still, they are forced to make decisions on the credibility of sources and the importance of events. Are politicians, as a class, believable sources of policy information? In the early 1960s, the answer was yes, but no longer. Does money corrupt politics? Perhaps. Furthermore, the history of the profession requires journalists to write stories that are both fair and newsworthy. But what happens when fairness is not newsworthy? Some would argue that, when the news media reported Dan Quayle's mistaken spelling of "potato," they should have made clear that the vice president had been reading from a cue card given to him by a schoolteacher. The event was newsworthy, but was the reporting fair? To the vice president's office, the episode reconfirmed its fear of the "liberal" press. But more likely, the news media thought that the vice president's mistake was indicative of larger questions about the vice president's intelligence.

An additional problem facing contemporary campaigns is the blogosphere. Campaign-generated blogs, which hew the official line, tend toward tedium. Most devotees of political blogs prefer the independent variety—and here a campaign must ready itself to contend with helpful (and not-so-helpful) allies and the serious possibility of an Internet smear campaign. Sometimes the smears are intentional, and sometimes they are simply the product of overzealous partisans. The best a campaign operative can do is present the facts quickly and back them up with firm documentation.

COMMUNICATIONS TACTICS

The history of earned media bears directly on communications tactics. For a campaign to attract media attention, it must understand the needs of the press. Stories must be newsworthy. A campaign-related item must be fresh, and it must usually relate to public affairs in a way that is likely to affect the lives of readers, but two caveats are in order. The first is strictly economic. The media marketplace is highly competitive, with an array of vehicles ranging from newspapers to cable opinion shows to Web sites offering up-to-the-minute news reporting. Without good stories, readers and viewers will not consume the information, and advertising dollars will dwindle. Dull pieces are a hard sell to reporters, producers, and editors. Similarly, because every news organization operates on a budget, stories that are expensive to cover will not get much play. A story that would require a television crew to lug its equipment over a mountain pass is far less likely to get covered than one conveniently situated near the television station. The second caveat goes to journalism as a profession. Reporters are trained to uphold standards acquired over a century and a half of professional development, complete with heroes like Bob Woodward and Carl Bernstein, who literally changed history with their reporting of the Watergate break-in and the subsequent cover-up. Indeed, journalists view themselves as professionals, and they share similar views of newsworthiness, appropriate press scrutiny, and the relative importance of stories. Campaigns that fail to recognize the tenets of journalistic writing and the economic demands of the news industry are unlikely to gain the attention of reporters.

The News Release

A good new-style campaign knows how to market stories to the news media. The campaign operation puts its best foot forward, even if it can never really manage the news. The most important tool for selling a candidate is the news release. Releases are used to issue statements, announce upcoming events, spin breaking news, highlight endorsements, respond to attacks, and provide background facts that help reporters make sense of the race. This form of communication, inexpensive in both production and distribution, plays a central role in any campaign's earned media strategy.

The difficulty is that media outlets receive countless news releases from businesses, organizations, and individuals, not to mention other campaigns. A major paper might receive hundreds of news releases daily. Some are selected, but the vast majority are not. The cardinal rule in release writing is that one should make the text newsworthy to the editor and informative to the reporter. Few editors wish to have boring, unimportant articles in their papers or on their radio or television news broadcast. Still, puffery is the single most common flaw in news releases (Randolph 1989). Facts are best. To make life easy for reporters, campaigns provide everything needed to write a positive story. Many find that the best approach is to write the release exactly the way the campaign would wish the news to appear in the paper. Press secretaries are advised to employ the same notation that reporters use, adding, for example, a "###" or a "-30-" to indicate the end of the release (Hewitt 1999, 57).

The reason campaigns imitate journalistic style is twofold: (1) it helps fit the story into the mind-set of a reporter, editor, or broadcast producer, and (2) some smaller newspapers will run the story word for word. Thinking like a reporter, press secretaries will include at least one quote from the candidate or some other pertinent figure (clearly identifying name and title). Usually, the quote will be in the form of a "zinger"—a pithy remark with a powerful message. News releases stand a better chance of unedited publication if they contain a headline, a strong lead sentence, and relevant photographs, particularly when they are written in the journalist's inverted-pyramid format—with the most important information at the top and the less important information farther down. Many consultants suggest brevity. The shorter the release, the more likely it will be run. Of course, it is also possible that long news releases are more helpful to reporters.

In format, campaign news releases follow a distinct style. They are written in the third person, using action verbs as much as possible, relying on facts instead of opinionated generalities. To the greatest extent possible, they are written in simple language. The style of good releases tends to match that of the targeted outlets. Radio, newspaper editorial pages, and Sunday morning magazines each have their own manner of speaking. Furthermore, candidates must establish credibility with the media so that reporters feel comfortable using their releases. If a campaign maintains accuracy, it will not lose the trust of news organizations. In addition, the name and telephone number of a campaign "contact person" are usually noted at the top of each release as well as the recommended timing of the story. Some stories are "embargoed" for later release. "For immediate release" indicates that the story can be run as soon as the editor sees fit.

As to how many releases should be sent, the profession seems divided. Some believe "the more the better," arguing that the campaign can never tell when an outlet will have a slow news day. Every press secretary can point to favorable news stories that followed releases they never expected to see picked up. Frequent releases also keep the election at the forefront of an editor's mind and let reporters know what is going on in the race. But daily releases can lead to summary dismissal. Reporters and editors who receive bundles of releases from the same campaign quickly tire of them and assume, perhaps rightly, that the releases contain fluff. The most important releases are rejected with the rest. Media consultant Steve Snider recalls a time when an opponent was overzealous with his releases, leading a columnist to write about the waste: the releases were used as a scratch pad for the columnist's three-year-old (Snider 1990).

Actualities and Feeds

While radio and television stations also receive news releases, the odds of the message being run are increased dramatically if the candidate goes directly to the station. Many radio news editors appreciate the fact that a candidate went to them, and as a consequence they sometimes feel obliged to provide some airtime. At the very least, the candidate might be allowed to give a quick statement to be used at the station's convenience.

This type of contact requires a fair amount of time and trouble. There are easier ways—rather than walk into a studio, a campaign can send clips. To get radio air, a campaign distributes news advisories in advance, allowing for any necessary planning and preparation on the station's part. The press secretary then calls and asks if the campaign can send an "actuality." The actuality will be a short recorded statement from the candidate (just a few seconds, definitely not more than 20 or 30). The press secretary also provides the reporter with a written account of the information so that the news director has something from which to write the story. Many radio stations use the process heavily because it gives the listener the impression that reporters went into the field to get the story when in reality the campaign came to them.

There are several ways to provide radio stations with actualities. The simplest is the spoken word. The candidate phones in a quick statement that is recorded on tape at the station. Although effective, this approach generally yields metallic-sounding audio. Worse, calling all the stations ties up the candidate's schedule. To save time, a candidate might tape a statement that the press secretary would then use with each radio station, holding the recorder to the telephone so that the station can capture it. But this approach merely worsens the quality of the transmission. In the 1990s, candidates would overcome problems of sound quality through "electronic couplers" and actuality machines. The candidate's statement was recorded on tape, and the statement was transmitted over telephone lines wired directly to a playback unit. Today, campaigns will make sound bites available digitally by posting sound files on the Internet.

For television, the process is much the same, but the technicalities are far more complex, and the costs of satellite time are much higher than telephone charges. To do satellite feeds, studio production must be moved to an uplink station—all of which requires professional assistance. For this reason, many campaigns still rely on "sneaker" connections, running a tape to the station and handing it off.

A masterful use of actualities and video feeds was the distribution of the Contract with America signing. According to Barrie Tron, who built the event, "We produced a multicamera live broadcast" that was distributed to news departments around the country (1996, 51). Writes Tron, the "signal was distributed live, via satellite . . . to every television station around the country. The feed was free and produced as if we were feeding our own network" (51). The whole event, from start to finish, was offered to the media because "news directors want the most options—especially in the midst of a campaign" (51). For radio, "an audio bridge fed the audio portion of the program, [accessible] via telephone and made available free of charge to radio stations" (52). As a result, the hard work that went into setting up a massive, tightly choreographed event on the Capitol steps paid off with a day's worth of heavy, nationwide coverage. "Demand was so high" for the audio feed, Tron says, "we even scheduled a highlights replay for additional stations" (52).

Mass distribution feeds have become commonplace, and, as such, news directors are beginning to ignore them. As the Internet opens new channels for the distribution of audio and video—both to stations and to the public at large—campaigns must find new ways to distinguish themselves. One strategy is virtual personalization, by which the candidate goes to each station electronically. "Satellite media tours" allow the candidate to reach a large number of stations in a short period of time with each appearance tailored to the individual station. From a single studio, a candidate can be interviewed by one television reporter after another. A media specialist notes that "in one hour you can talk to ten stations, each getting an exclusive interview," and "radio is done in much the same way, only you can be anywhere there is a phone" (Ouzounian 1997, 51).

News Conferences

If the news release is the earned media workhorse, the news conference is the show horse. News conferences bring reporters into a controlled environment so that the candidate can talk about a significant campaign development. They allow for personal explanations of complex issues or dramatic new developments as well as an opportunity for the press to ask questions about the matter. Although the odds of coverage are poor for run-of-the-mill political items, many candidates use news conferences to announce their candidacies. News conferences are also used to level attacks against the opponent, defend the candidate against charges level at him or her, introduce new rounds of campaign commercials, announce important endorsements, highlight fund-raising activities, introduce celebrities, and so on.

Deciding whether to cover a news conference, assignment editors undertake a cost-benefit calculation. They weigh the merits of getting the story firsthand with the price of sending a reporter into the field. To the campaign press team, this balancing act suggests that the issue must be exceptionally important and that it must be easy for the press to cover. When these two conditions are met, most candidates for lower-level offices still have a hard time getting coverage. If reporters choose to cover a candidate's news conference, chances are better than not that they will run a story—though not always the message that a campaign has in mind.

A waste-of-time news conference is scorned by the media and will, in all probability, be the last one that reporters cover. Campaigns are warned, "If you call a press conference and it ain't news, they might not cover you again" (Shirley 1997, 23). The campaign may even be written off or, worse yet, ridiculed. After all, the campaign wasted precious time; someone has to pay. Before a conference is called, the campaign communications team must be certain that the topic will be found newsworthy. If so, and it chooses to proceed, a notice is sent to each outlet, outlining the importance of the issue, where and when the conference will be held, and the name and telephone number of the contact person. Campaigns follow up with a telephone call or even a visit to the assignment editor or reporter. Occasionally, this sort of prodding tips the scales in a campaign's favor. Pushing too hard, however, can have the opposite effect.

The days of the informally prepared news conference are long gone. In new-style campaigns, close attention is paid to the backdrop behind the candidate. Good visuals are a boon to both the candidate and the media—a powerful shot helps convey the right message while giving an incentive for the media to run the story. Well-prepared campaigns help the shoot go as smoothly as possible. A "mult box" is provided so that several television and radio stations can plug directly into the candidate's microphone. Good angles are established in consultation with camera operators, and the distance between the press stand and satellite trucks will be paced off beforehand so that there are no surprises. A wise press secretary keeps an eye on deadlines. If, for instance, the campaign wishes to make the local 6:00 P.M. news, the event might be held before 3:00 P.M., giving the stations plenty of time for editing. The same logic applies to newspaper deadlines.

It is a matter of convenience. Asking reporters to drive an hour out of town is a sure way to minimize press participation. Finally, coverage is sometimes affected by limited parking and inadequate electrical power, insufficient seating, and the failure to provide room for tape recorders, lights, and cameras, even the lack of a proper lunch.

Media Events

The struggle for media attention has led candidates to walk across states, work blue-collar jobs, sleep among the homeless, serve food at soup kitchens, clean up neighborhoods, visit toxic waste sites, meet with senior citizens, greet workers at factory gates, and climb into hot-air balloons. Creativity is vital. One candidate who was attacked for putting campaign posters on public utility poles called on the local Boy Scouts and Girl Scouts to help him take them down, offering a dollar for each poster. Nearly all the district's media outlets covered the cleanup day. There was little doubt that the few hundred dollars paid to the Scouts was well worth the coverage. Not all press events go as planned. During his 1994 gubernatorial race, George W. Bush participated in an annual ritual, the opening day of dove-hunting season. He invited the press along to take a few pictures. One of the birds he felled, however, was not a dove but a protected songbird. Bush paid a $130 fine.

What distinguishes a media event from a simple news conference is that the focus of the news conference is the spoken word, whereas the focus of the media event is the action and context. The signing ceremony for the Contract with America was among the best media events of the 1990s. In the 1980s, the best events were scripted by White House aide Michael Deaver, who defines the essence of a quality event by example:

> We were searching for any development that we could showcase to reflect a good trend. A staffer walked into my office one day and said housing starts were up for the first time in five years and we ought to get the president down to the press room to make an announcement.
>
> At such moments, you go with your instinct. This was mine: "No, find me a city with the most dramatic increase in housing starts in America. And get it back to me fast."
>
> The city turned out to be Fort Worth, Texas. I had the president fly to Fort Worth, and he made the announcement at a housing development there, surrounded by a bunch of construction workers in hard hats. (1987, 140–41)

Deaver adds, "My standing joke with Bill Hinkle, the head of the advance team, was: If you can't give me a good visual, give me a big sign" (141).

There is an art to the construction of media events. All the rules for advancing news conferences apply—there must be enough chairs to seat the attendees but not so many that the event looks poorly attended, and the lighting must be sufficient to allow for video but not so bright that the candidate starts to sweat. But, unlike a standard news conference, the idea behind a news event is that the action itself is the message. If things go right—as when, during the 2000 campaign, George W. Bush went to the nation's most prosperous border town, San Diego, to say that he would reduce immigration waiting times—the result is positive press. When things go wrong, the message can be disastrous. During the 1996 presidential campaign, Bob Dole, leaning forward to shake hands, pressed against a railing that gave way, and Senator Dole fell into the crowd. The accident was portrayed as a metaphor: Dole's campaign had lost its balance. Good advance staffers check every detail of event staging. It is not beneath them to jump up and down on a riser to check for squeaky joints or weak spots.

As Michael Deaver's work taught, the image must convey the message before a single word is spoken. "I am sure the purists, who want their news unfiltered and their heroes unrehearsed, gag on the word *visuals*," he wrote, "but in the Television Age, [an event] hasn't happened, or at least it hasn't registered, if people can't see what you see" (1987, 141). Matthew Bennett, former trip director for Al Gore, says the reason that visuals are so important is that "we can't control the decisions made by the writer or editor about what will be covered" (Bennett 2000). But, he adds, if the media wanted to run a "horse race story" and Al Gore wanted to talk about policy, the advance team can at least convey the intended message visually.

Debates

For many local candidates, debates are the only opportunity to get free press. Reporters cover most of these events, perhaps from a desire to "inform voters," and they might feel obliged to print a few lines about each candidate. Coverage is generally balanced, meaning that each candidate gets about the same amount of ink. Unlike higher-profile presidential or gubernatorial debates, there are few "winners" or "losers" at the local level. Not enough people see them to make a difference. If, however, the coverage complements themes articulated in paid media, the one-two punch can prove effective. Debates can help poorly funded candidates get their names out—precisely why candidates ahead in the polls are often reluctant to debate. Why give the challenger this kind of exposure?

Candidates who want to maximize press coverage gear most of their remarks to the press, not the audience at home. A vast majority of those who attend debates personally or watch them on public television have already made up their minds and merely wish to see their candidate fight the good fight. Very few uncommitted voters watch debates, but reporters and editorial boards pay close attention. Candidates strive to make clear, brief, novel, and sometimes confrontational statements. It is important to reinforce the campaign theme, but simple repetition can be interpreted as "old news" (Hershey 1984, 23). New wrinkles and off-the-cuff deviations can draw media attention. Reporters realize that nothing is more boring than a photo of two candidates standing stiffly on stage, so anything out of the ordinary catches their eye. A candidate who knows this tactic might hold up a piece of the opponent's campaign literature to highlight a contradiction—but if a candidate uses this tactic too aggressively, as when Rick Lazio walked a petition right up to Hillary Rodham Clinton's lectern, media backlash can be the result.

Candidates generally want to be well prepared for debates because the media will seize on gaffes. Candidates who deviate from prepared material place themselves at risk. When Ronald Reagan suggested in a debate that trees were the major cause of air pollution, the press pounced. George W. Bush's seeming lack of preparedness for the first 2004 debate was deemed utterly disastrous. There are few things in politics more fearsome than a media attack on live television. It has become commonplace for campaigns to prepare briefing books on the issues and to work with the candidate on sharp replies, cutting attacks, and strong defensive maneuvers.

Interviews, the Editorial Page, and Nonattributed Information

News conferences and media events are open invitations for candidate interviews. Other earned media possibilities include radio and television talk shows and community service programs. When Democratic senator Dianne Feinstein of California struggled to hold her U.S. Senate seat in 1994, she faced an increasingly conservative electorate and a multimillionaire opponent. When her lead began to slip, the Feinstein team went on the offensive. Feinstein's opponent, Michael Huffington, had endorsed Proposition 187, which was designed to limit the flood of illegal immigrants into the state. It was discovered, however, that he had employed for some time an illegal immigrant as a houseworker. The hypocrisy was sure to drain support from Huffington, but getting out the word quickly and inexpensively was problematic. Feinstein decided to lead the attack on CNN's *Larry King Live,* and the charge was then picked up by California news media. Huffington's negatives skyrocketed; Feinstein was returned to the Senate.

Candidates for local office are rarely invited to appear on national television talk shows, but there are opportunities on local radio and television programs, and there is always space on the editorial page. The prevailing wisdom is that "placing an op-ed is one of the most difficult things to do in public relations. Especially if your client or candidate is not a well-known figure" (Shirley 1997, 23). But the reason that editorial pages are so difficult to break into is that they are so influential: everyone wants to get his or her opinion in the paper, so editors have a large number of op-eds from which to choose. An alternative route is a letter to the editor. Campaigns routinely coordinate letters to all the newspapers in the district. In addition to being a means of easy access, letters to the editor are one of the most heavily read parts of the newspaper (Beaudry and Schaeffer 1986, 138).

A campaign that does not have to fight for coverage can get its message out with nonattributable backgrounders. The messages might be called "leaks," except that the term sounds devious and underhanded—perhaps even unauthorized. The fact of the matter is that a large portion of news presented to the public as independent research is actually given to reporters by authorized parties who strike a deal to remain anonymous. Campaigns that have gained the trust of a reporter can disseminate their ideas "on background."

While the boundaries are hazy, there are four general levels of reporter–source communication. First, "on-the-record" conversations can be printed with direct attribution to the source. All conversations with a reporter are assumed to be on the record unless another agreement has been made ahead of time. Second, "background" conversations are those that can be attributed to a nonspecific source. The campaign staffer might, for example, negotiate for references to "a campaign official." Third, "deep background" exchanges cannot be attributed at all, but they can be used to guide a reporter's research. The most famous example is "Deep Throat," the hidden voice behind the *Washington Post*'s coverage of Watergate (who turned out to be an FBI official). Finally, "off-the-record" conversations cannot be used in any way. For the most part, the only remarks that are kept off the record are discussions about family and other personal matters—friendships between reporters and political professionals are included here—and in any case, conversations off the record often turn up in the paper.

Nonattributed conversations—talking to reporters "on background"—can be used to help reporters write their stories. One consultant says, "On background is useful to outline a complex plan yet to be announced or to explain something not generally understood by the media in which the speaker is not the primary source" (Scudder 1997, 25). Research on nonattributed sourcing will always be sketchy, but the anatomy of "backgrounders" can be seen in the Clinton White House's handling of the fund-raising controversies that followed the 1996 elections. White House special counsel Lanny Davis was in charge of handling press inquiries. His job was not to deflect reporters' questions but rather to answer them as fully as possible. The idea was to establish a "baseline": "Help the reporter write the first story, make sure it's complete, with everything in it," Davis says, and "from that point on, other reporters will find it when they search the LEXIS-NEXIS database of published newspaper stories, and so it will become the starting point for all future reporting" (1999, 43). Many of the campaign finance stories that appeared to have been leaked by Republican investigators actually got their start at the White House.

As Election Day nears, most daily and weekly newspapers declare their preferred candidates in editorial endorsements. New-style consultants are mindful of the fact that reporters play only a supporting role in the endorsement process. Although the exact steps involved in the endorsement decision vary from paper to paper, most often the decisions are made by the editors and, occasionally, by the publishers. Reporters are sometimes asked for their opinions, but the final determination is not theirs to make. Special efforts are made to win the favor of decision makers. Periodic visits help, as do personal notes from the candidate thanking the editor for a "fair and accurate" story, and certainly the candidate will attend any meeting requested by the editorial board. Campaigns that get the nod will reprint the endorsement for last-minute literature drops. Democratic state senate candidate Gordon MacInnes was given an immense boost when the leading paper in the district called his opponent, among other things, "a walking argument for term limits." The piece was reprinted and dropped to swing areas throughout the district (Beiler 1994). Of course, there is always a possibility that an editorial decision will go the wrong way. In this case, media consultant Robert Shrum once recommended the value of a paid media counteroffensive, saying, "500 gross rating points of media can answer largely unread editorials" (1997, 24).

CONCLUSION

James Carville has called news media "the Beast"—if the campaign does not feed it, it feeds on the campaign. Whether or not this assessment is accurate, the media play a critically important role in new-style campaigns. As 24-hour news has erased the old deadlines, with regional and statewide news networks doing the same transformation to statewide and congressional races and with bloggers creating and rehashing news in real time, the political world is truly changing.

Chapter Twelve

Returning to the Grassroots

New-style electioneering is expensive. Whereas in the past candidates might expect legions of party activists to help carry the banner, today money and professional campaign services are funneled in from Washington and the state capital. Local party volunteers are not the force they once were.

Yet grassroots campaigning is far from obsolete, and it has seen a resurgence in recent years. The 2004 election witnessed one of the most successfully orchestrated get-out-the-vote grassroots campaigns in recent history. Both Democrats and Republicans worked hard to mobilize voters, both sides could claim success, but it was the Republicans who dug their heels in deepest. Not only did they conduct a successful grassroots campaign at the state and county levels, but they penetrated individual voting precincts—an aspect of electioneering usually managed with greater dexterity by the Democrats. Journalist James G. Lakely of the *Washington Times* said, "More than 13,000 volunteers [were] at work in Oregon, the highest number of Republicans ever in that normally Democratic-leaning state" (Lakely 2004, 1). Even more impressive were the efforts of more than 85,000 volunteers in Ohio, a key battleground state (Farhi and Grimaldi 2004). According to one account, "Bush's Ohio campaign used targeted mailings, phone calls and doorstep visits to talk about values" (Farhi and Grimaldi 2004, A01). Some have speculated that 2 million telephone calls were made in support of the president, 349,000 doors were knocked on, and 3,254 parties were thrown. Some boasted that Bush volunteers in Ohio made more than 2 million contacts (Blogs for Bush 2004, 1).

As suggested by Ken Mehlman, the Bush/Cheney campaign manager, "One of the advantages we had is that the president had millions of supporters all around the country. The most effective endorsement you can get is not someone talking on TV, but by a neighbor walking up to you and saying 'Here's why I support George W. Bush'" (Lakely 2004, 2). Mehlman criticized the Kerry campaign for failing to gather enough activists and for relying too heavily on 527s and labor

unions for support. Nothing can replace the hard work of a solid grassroots organization, suggests Mehlman, and in 2004 the Republicans drove that point home.

Barack Obama's successful U.S. Senate bid in 2004 offers another example.
Among other things, Obama's multicultural heritage helped his campaign forge
an effective grassroots network. With a mother of Cherokee Indian descent and
a father who is Kenyan, it is little wonder that an eclectic group of voters flocked
to his campaign. Numerous groups were organized, and waves of volunteers were
sent into targeted areas. Yet Obama's grassroots activities were not limited interpersonal communications. He took full advantage of the Internet. With a personalized campaign Web site and various supporter-sponsored Web logs, Obama was
able to reach targeted voters with sophisticated messages. He also used the Internet to organize "Obama Communities" in specific areas and neighborhood needs.
In numerous counties and cities across Illinois, groups such as "Asian Americans
for Obama" or "Educators for Obama" took on voter registration, fund-raising,
canvassing projects, and much else (Obama for Illinois, Inc. 2004). Generating
a massive grassroots following, spanning political parties and even state lines,
Obama successfully used volunteer-based tactics to win a seat in the Senate.

Every election season produces new examples of grassroots campaigns that
prevail on Election Day. Personal contact remains the single best means to win
votes, and grassroots efforts are important in any new-style campaign. A team
of dedicated volunteers can help compensate for weak finances and, at times,
help push a well-financed race over the top. This does not mean that grassroots
campaigning is simple and unsophisticated. To the contrary, in order to optimize
the help of volunteers, careful attention must be paid to planning, targeting, and
resource allocation. All the basic principles of new-style campaigning apply to the
grassroots operation. Because the "soldiers" in the grassroots effort are generally
untrained, they often need supervision.

This chapter discusses reasons why direct voter contact works, describes various types of grassroots activities, and outlines some ways to optimize the aid of
volunteers and other direct-contact activities, often termed "fieldwork." Volunteers who rely on sheer grit and determination can help their candidates. Still,
poorly planned grassroots efforts can prove disappointing. The old-fashioned way
of getting votes remains one of the best but only if it is combined with new-style
strategies.

THE POWER OF DIRECT VOTER CONTACT

Direct voter contact works for a number of reasons. First, it brings the voter to
a different cognitive level than that of other campaign communications. There is
a qualitative difference between a volunteer talking with the voter on the front
porch and a piece of campaign literature in a mailbox. The voter becomes more
engaged and is more attentive for a longer period of time. Second, direct contact
allows two-way communication. Voters are given a chance to share their own
views. When voters have the opportunity to meet the candidate, they become
more invested in the campaign (Trent and Friedenberg 2004, 318–19). Additional

benefits of direct contact are physical cues not otherwise afforded by indirect means. For example, a voter may be persuaded by the physical appearance or body language of the candidate or volunteer. Facial expressions, hand movements, and voice inflections can mean a great deal in interpersonal communication.

Grassroots campaigning also humanizes the candidate. Campaigns conducted over the airwaves can seem distant and impersonal. When a candidate or volunteer makes direct contact with the voter, a better connection is made. In the new millennium, voters need to be reminded that candidates are people, not products. Along similar lines, fieldwork can give the impression that there is a groundswell of support for the candidate. Voters like being on the winning side. An enthusiastic volunteer effort leads them to believe that others in the community are supporting the candidate. This, in turn, can bring in still more volunteers as well as support on Election Day. There are few better ways of getting the bandwagon rolling than with a visible outpouring of help by members of the community.

Fieldwork costs money, but the wise use of volunteers can keep expenses low. If the campaign is out of funds and receives a last-minute endorsement, for instance, a massive volunteer literature operation can spread the message quickly. Grassroots campaigning offers one of the most narrowly targeted voter contact activities available. With careful planning, it can bring the right message to the right voters without the waste that normally accompanies broadcast media.

Finally, fieldwork can lead to greater enthusiasm in the race, bringing increased media attention and easier fund-raising. Campaigns engulfed by hordes of volunteers are conspicuous—they stand out and send a positive message. Potential contributors take notice, as do editors and reporters. An air of grassroots popularity can be a self-fulfilling prophecy.

The advantages of direct voter contact are numerous. But is grassroots organizing easier said than done? How does a campaign recruit the number of volunteers necessary for a strong campaign? The first place to start is always the candidate. It is difficult to ask others to lend a hand if the candidate is unwilling to do so. Again, the most persuasive message is the one delivered by the candidate, and the candidate's family and network of friends are the next logical resource. Often this effort takes some prodding—those close to the candidate presume that their efforts should be geared only to "strategy" as opposed to implementation. Successful campaigns revise this notion early in the race.

Some local parties are as robust as they have been at any time in the past 30 or 40 years. Local party operations can offer a deep reservoir of potential volunteers. Many party workers have campaign experience. Grassroots campaigning is not difficult, but there are some "tricks of the trade." Local organizations and interest groups can provide volunteers as well. Many Democrats are assisted by labor unions, and many Republicans get a boost from business organizations and church groups. If the candidate is a member of such a group, certainly fellow members can be approached. Yet another source is the pool of student organizations at the local college or university, and at the other end of the age spectrum are senior citizen groups. Older Americans are a rapidly growing demographic group, are politically active, and often have a good deal of spare time.

TYPES OF GRASSROOTS ACTIVITIES

Contemporary fieldwork is systematically targeted. While direct voter contact is often the best means to win votes, it is also the slowest—and time is a precious campaign resource. In addition to standard measures of persuadability, grassroots organizers look to reachability. For example, geography is an important factor in door-to-door campaigning. Suburban areas are more amenable to a precinct walk than rural areas, where the number of households approached might be only four or five an hour. The benefit of a well-targeted grassroots effort is that it can be aimed very narrowly.

A media-based campaign that relies on radio might reach listeners across an entire county, including many of the opposition's base voters. A carefully planned door-to-door effort might have the candidate walking right past the homes of opposition loyalists.

The Candidate Walk Plan

In congressional campaigns and races further down the ballot, candidates themselves often canvass the prime target areas—the most electorally significant neighborhoods in the district. This effort entails more than just sending the candidate out to meet voters with a handful of literature. It is meticulously planned, down to the finest detail. A good candidate walk plan consists of several elements.

Walk Sheets. The first step is to acquire walk sheets. These lists contain the names (and in some states the party affiliations and limited biographical data, such as date of birth and occupation) of voters at each house on each street in the area. They exclude those not registered and list the households along each side of the street rather than in numeric order. For example:

1. Alma Jones (R), Morris Jones (R); 1 Maple Street
2. Bert Smith (D), Carol Smith (R), April Smith (D); 3 Maple Street
3. Andrew Johnson (I); 7 Maple Street
4. Betty Hill (D), Stephen Fisher (D); 9 Maple Street

This format allows the candidate to skip households without registered voters and to work one side of the street at a time. Voters enrolled with the opposing party are also skipped. Walk sheets can usually be purchased from the board of elections, the office of the secretary of state, or a commercial list vendor.

A Local Volunteer. The candidate rarely goes into the field unaccompanied. A volunteer, preferably one from the area where the candidate is assigned to walk, can serve many roles. Volunteers can introduce the candidate to the resident, provide some background information on each voter ("Mrs. Smith is a retired teacher who loves to bird-watch"), or give a quick rundown of the neighborhood ("We used to have a toy factory here"). The volunteer can carry the walk sheet, allowing the candidate to shake hands with the voters. He or she can keep the candidate on task, provide directions, and, most important, serve as the "bad cop" if needed. If the voter is eager to have the candidate in for coffee, the candidate might appear accommodating, but the volunteer will suggest that they need to be moving along. In all likelihood, the voter will blame staff for the misfortune.

Prewalk Cards. Approximately two weeks prior to the candidate's walk in an area, prewalk cards are mailed to each household (or, if the campaign is short on funds, the materials are hand delivered). These cards might contain a picture of the candidate and a small note, something like the following:

> I'll be stopping by in the next few days to visit. I hope we get a chance to chat about your concerns and what I might do in the state legislature to help.

These cards serve several purposes. They get the candidate's name and message out, prime the voter for the visit, and maybe provide a picture of the candidate so the voter knows who is at the door. Even if the voter will not be home on the day of the visit, the cards suggest that the candidate is willing to "listen to average folks." Once the cards are sent, the candidate is obligated to walk in the area. Accordingly, the prewalk can also serve as a strong motivator for the candidate.

The Drop-Off Pamphlet. After shaking hands at the door, the candidate often provides an informational pamphlet in the hope that after the candidate has departed, the voter will return to the couch and read the material. This one-two punch of meeting the candidate at the door and then scanning the pamphlet generates powerful repetition, the heart of voter contact.

Careful Notes. Immediately after the candidate departs from each voter's doorstep, the volunteer takes notes about the conversation: the name of the person contacted, the voter's concerns, the voter's comments about the candidate, and so forth.

The Follow-Up Card. If the voter is not at home, the candidate leaves a *handwritten* note on the back of the literature:

> Sorry I missed you. I stopped by to say hello and chat about your concerns, but you were out. Perhaps we can get a chance to talk another time. Please feel free to call.

The cards are written in advance so that the candidate and the volunteer can move along on the night of the canvass. To those voters who were home, a follow-up mailing is sent about a week after the visit. It thanks the voter for his or her time and highlights the candidate's commitment to voter input. If, for instance, the voter was concerned about environmental issues, the follow-up might outline the candidate's environmental priorities.

Additional Follow-Ups. As a final step, any requested information or material is mailed, delivered, or telephoned to the voter immediately. This chore can be done by a volunteer.

A multistep program of this sort is time and resource intensive. But if it is done in the prime target areas of the district, the costs are justified. Repetition and careful attention to message distinguish this type of walk plan from traditional canvasses, in which the candidate simply knocks on doors.

The Canvass

In many ways, the canvass mirrors the candidate walk plan. Here, however, other members of the campaign team walk door-to-door. Instead of mailing a candidate prewalk card, a note is sent indicating that "a volunteer will be stopping by soon." Door-to-door workers usually have a clean-cut appearance and are familiar with the themes of the campaign. Training sessions and scripts are an excellent idea. The importance of careful records as to who was home and the interests of the contacted voters is stressed. A follow-up note might say, "Thanks for chatting with one of my volunteers." At crunch time, this sort of canvass can serve as a "rapid-response" operation, a so-called door-to-door blitz. If the opponent levels a powerful charge during the final days of the race, a canvass blitz might help limit its impact.

Voter Registration Drives

Volunteers are frequently used to find and register new voters. While the number varies greatly from one district to another, often only 50 percent of the voting-age residents are registered to vote. According to U.S. Census data, citizens age 65 and older have the highest registration rate—roughly 75 percent—while those age 18 to 24 had the lowest—about 40 percent (U.S. Census 2005) A voter registration process is a relatively uncomplicated affair. On a walk sheet, nonregistered voters will be in houses not listed. A campaign volunteer might visit these homes and try to persuade the resident to fill out a voter registration card. The volunteer brings the completed cards back to campaign headquarters, where they are compiled into a list and then delivered to the local board of elections. (Campaigns must check state laws carefully.)

Registration does not necessarily imply a vote on Election Day. Nevertheless, previously unregistered voters tend to be less partisan and, as such, less committed to opposing candidates. Moreover, because these are new voters, it is possible that they will not be listed on opposition lists. If so, the only campaign material that they receive during most of the race may come from the candidate's headquarters. Voter registration drives are time consuming and somewhat unpredictable, but they are a good way of keeping volunteers busy, and they can be a big help if the campaign faces an uphill battle. In districts with a large, mobile college student population, registration drives can make or break candidates.

Absentee Ballots and Mail-In Voting

As technology continues to advance, new voting options have emerged. The use of absentee-style voting has skyrocketed. Because of the relative ease of mail-in ballots, many opt to vote this way. Early voting at defined locations has also become quite popular. A "no excuses voting" plan, for example, gives voters three weeks prior to the election to vote at satellite voting stations. In some states, residents can now cast their ballot week ahead of the election. As of 2004, some

19 states allowed in-person early voting. Advocates say that increased ease of voting is a boon for the democratic process and that absentee-style processes are quick, convenient, and less costly than traditional go-to-the-polls-on-Election-Day voting. Moreover, the public seems willing to move in this direction.

Changes of this sort mean a great deal to campaign operatives. One possibility is that a distinct set of voters will cast votes early—a group defined by the campaign. Mail-in ballots can be used to encourage participation among low-frequency voters—those who are registered but either have skipped a few elections or vote only in presidential contests. Senior citizens often fall into this category. They should be mailed a packet containing an absentee application and, if allowed by law, information on the candidate. This can lead to added votes, but one should bear in mind that the other side will likely understand the potency of mail-in ballots. Any time a new pool of voters is added to the electorate, uncertainty is created. Will electoral targeting prove accurate? Will uncertainty drive up campaign costs? Will new voters break for candidates of one party more so than the other? New-style campaign operatives loathe uncertainty, but no-excuse absentee and early voting options will likely increase the vagaries of electoral strategy in the coming years.

Early voting procedures also shift strategic timing. Campaign workers must note the deadline for the submission of absentee and early voting ballots, making sure that every would-be voter has this information as well. Next, in jurisdictions that provide such information, absentee lists can be secured from the board of elections or the secretary of state's office. Volunteers carefully review these registries and mail literature to absentees throughout the race. For those not then residing in the district, it may be the only concrete information they receive. Campaigns that engage in this kind of activity might find that "Election Day" is elongated to three or four weeks. Instead of building up to a single moment in time, a campaign must spread its most intense efforts—media buys, news events, and campaign mailings—over a monthlong period, with particular attention paid to the first few days after the voting window opens.

Ballots are sent to electors usually up to the week before an election is held and are typically counted on Election Day, but the rules vary from state to state. Problems with absentee ballots can easily arise, mainly in two different forms: vote suppression and vote reduction. Vote suppression occurs when outgoing ballots to voters in key precincts are lost, forcing a replacement ballot to be sent. Vote reduction occurs when incoming ballots are lost or need to be replaced for voters in key precincts. According to political writer and analyst Mary Mostert, some ballots never reach their intended destination, and in other cases, ballots are infiltrated in the mail and filled out by others and subsequently submitted illicitly. Mostert explains that "I have had reports from various areas about absentee voter fraud in the last election. One of the charges has been the absentee ballots simply not getting to voters—especially voters in the military. In my own household, a young woman from Florida who stayed with me while in school was unable to vote because, although requested, her absentee ballot never arrived. In a couple of cases, absentee ballots have been stolen from the mail, filled out and sent in" (Mostert 2000, 1).

Literature Drops

Literature drops are also targeted to swing areas. Unlike the canvass, drops entail not meeting the voter but simply placing a piece of campaign literature on the porch or in the doorjamb. It can be done by anyone, including volunteers unfamiliar with the candidate—even kids. The idea is to cover an area quickly and provide material somewhere other than the mailbox (which is illegal). Drops are much less expensive than mailings (no postage is needed), but their overall effectiveness is debatable. They are perhaps most helpful in improving early name recognition or during a last-minute push.

Telephone Banks

Telephone banks are an excellent way to reach a large number of voters in a short period of time. They keep volunteers busy, particularly those not able to walk door-to-door, and they are relatively cheap. There is new empirical evidence suggesting that telephone contacts made by local volunteers may well be the most cost-efficient means of turning out voters (Green and Gerber 2004).

There are three functions in a full-service telephone operation: persuasion, identification, and activation. A persuasion pitch simply targets voters with a brief message. A script is devised, and a volunteer conveys this information. Similar to an indirect voter contact activity, such as a television ad, the voter is not called on to respond. The goal is to provide the voters with information. In a voter identification process, a pitch is provided, followed by a few short questions regarding the voters' preferences in the coming election—who they will be voting for, what their primary concerns are, and so on. This information is carefully recorded, and the voters are marked "for," "against," or "undecided." Sometimes a numbering scheme is devised along the same lines. Voters labeled "against" are removed from the phone list, and if they demonstrate a serious dislike for the candidate, they may be removed from the mailing lists. Let sleeping dogs lie. "Undecideds" are given another call, mailed information on the candidate, and perhaps even visited by a volunteer. This group is cultivated extensively throughout the race. Activation calls are placed in order to urge persuaded voters to go to the polls on Election Day. At a minimum, this list is made up of those noted as "favorable" during the identification phase, but it can include others deemed likely to support the candidate. This can be done a few days early or on Election Day itself.

Telephone banks allow for tight control. Callers are given a list of voters and a carefully honed message. The number of contacts projected during a given time period can be predicted with a good deal of accuracy. This is done by multiplying the number of volunteers and the number of hours each volunteer will spend on the phone and dividing the product by the number of calls a volunteer can make in an hour. Some nights will have more volunteers than others, and some nights will see fewer hours in service, but in general terms, a campaign can calculate about how long it will take to make a series of telephone contacts in a given period—helpful information when the campaign maps out its overall strategy and the timing of campaign activities.

There is an advantage to hiring a telemarketing firm to carry out this operation, mainly, speed. At the end of the race, it may be necessary to complete 5,000 contacts over one weekend. This task would be difficult for most volunteer teams, but it could be accomplished easily by a large telemarketing firm. Such firms generally charge a fixed rate for each completed call, perhaps $.50 or $.75, depending on the length of the script.

There are a number of benefits to keeping the operation local—and volunteer based. It is much easier to monitor the callers, perhaps leading to better quality control. Often a local law firm, real estate office, or labor union donates the use of its phones during the evening. This approach offers greater security and more flexibility as to when calls are made (Yeutter et al. 1992). Most important, voters often snub professional telemarketing pitches. If the call is coming from a volunteer, perhaps even a neighbor, the voter is more likely to listen. In a way, it bridges the gap between efficiency and effectiveness. It is quick, somewhat personal, and relatively inexpensive.

Direct Mail, E-Mail, and Blogs

"Persuasion direct mail" can be a powerful weapon in new-style campaigning because of its precision and because it takes place below the radar. GOP consultant Richard Vigurie believed that "direct mail is like a water moccasin—silent but deadly" (Meredith 2004, 37).

The strengths of persuasion direct mail are numerous. First, it can be targeted to a very narrow range of voters. If the campaign finds that Jewish women under 40 represent a pool of undecided voters and if a list containing these voters can be assembled or purchased from a list vendor, then the campaign can send several messages to this narrow group. The number of list vendors and the breadth of variables they use to create precise groups has mushroomed in recent years. New-style electioneering is about sending the right message to the right group of voters, and direct mail makes this possible.

Second, direct mail allows the campaign to create a running narrative where each letter builds on the prior mailing. Through the course of the campaign, a detailed story can be told—that is, a tale can be constructed about your candidate or the opponent. Direct mail can also complement other outreach activities, such as radio and television advertisements. Voters hear the message on the way home from work and then read the same cue as they open their mail in the evening. It also allows for the use of creative pictures, graphics, charts, and nuanced messages. For instance, a piece of direct mail might reproduce a newspaper editorial or an endorsement. It might offer a picture of the candidate or the opponent, or it might present a telling graphic. Television can also do these sorts of things but often to a less targeted audience and at a higher expense. Direct mail is not cheap, but it is less expensive than many other outreach techniques.

Direct mail can also be a wonderful volunteer project. An increasing number of campaigns hire direct-mail services to produce, label, and mail literature, but some still call on volunteers to do some of this work—especially labeling. Large tables can be set up in one location, and a team of helpers can eat pizza, drink soda, and affix labels. Many actually enjoy the camaraderie. If a campaign is fortunate enough to have a legion of volunteers, it might consider hand addressing particular mailings. While most people discard mass-produced mailings quickly, everyone opens hand-addressed letters. In fact, hand-addressed letters may represent the single best way to communicate a specific message to a targeted group of voters. It works, but it is very labor intensive for even small target lists. Careful attention should be paid to regulations regarding return-address information and bulk-rate fees.

There are downsides to persuasion direct mail, however. Repetition is important for all forms of campaign communications, but it is especially necessary for direct mail. A campaign should never assume that a single mailing (or even a handful of mailings) will make hay with voters. Less sophisticated candidates and operatives will often want to do one or two mailings "just to introduce a topic." This is a mistake, a waste of resources. A small direct-mail program is almost an oxymoron. Likewise, voters often pitch campaign literature in the trash rather quickly—along with the pile of credit card offers and fast-food coupons they receive each day. Direct mail can work—but only slowly and through innovative, creative ways of drawing the voter's attention. Finally, direct mail is generally not considered a rapid-response technique. It often takes several days to produce, label, and mail a piece of literature. Radio and television spots, on the other hand, can be produced and aired in the same day.

Persuasive e-mail has been used with some effect in recent elections—especially the 2004 races. The advantages over snail mail are time and cost. Bulk messages can be sent in a matter of minutes at no cost. The use of attachments and links has opened up a range of possibilities as well. For instance, a campaign might ask an e-mail recipient to follow a link to new polling, a particular news story, or another group's Web page, or it might attach a short video.

The real downside to e-mail is reaction of the recipients. Many open their accounts each morning, only to delete a large percentage of the messages. Unlike junk snail mail, trashed e-mails are not even viewed for a few seconds. Perhaps the best use of e-mail is to excite and mobilize supporters and to organize events. MeetUp.Com took the political establishment by storm in 2004 not because it turned voters to progressive candidates and causes but rather because it brought already progressive voters out of their living rooms to rallies and campaign headquarters. E-mail can organize and motivate the faithful and thus has become a key piece of grassroots campaigning.

Coffees and Handshakes

Opportunities for direct voter contact activities are vast. A growing number of candidates are using coffees or cocktail parties. These events are popular with state and local candidates and with higher-level campaigns. In 2004, the Bush and Kerry teams orchestrated thousands of small gatherings. A supporter invites his or her neighbors to his or her home, and the candidate drops by for a visit. Hosting several get-togethers on the same evening allows the candidate to touch base with a large number of voters. This can be a rather pleasurable form of campaigning. Knowing when a factory shift changes can mean a lot of voter contact over a short period—several hundred workers might pass by 15 minutes. Factory gate and commuter station activities can be especially effective if the candidate hands out coffee and donuts, for example, as well as a small piece of literature. Moreover, shift and commuter changes usually occur at times when little else is going on in the campaign, perhaps as early as 7:00 A.M. Giving voters an opportunity to chat on a train platform helps candidates build strong connections.

It is possible to go overboard with handshakes, however. Some consultants deal with candidates who believe that the best way to meet voters is to visit the local mall or fair or to stand on the street corner. "Thousands of folks go to the fair," the candidate exclaims, but this type of shotgun approach is antithetical to new-style campaigning. The candidate has no sense of people's residency, partisan predisposition, or even registration status. Untargeted activities are an inefficient use of precious time. Productive campaigning is not about meeting as many people as possible but rather about meeting the right folks and providing the right message.

GET-OUT-THE-VOTE DRIVES

Efficiency is critical because time is the enemy. An excellent illustration of the importance of last-minute campaigning is the Oneonta, New York, school board election of Rosemary Shea, the late mother of *Campaign Craft*'s coauthor Dan Shea. With one hour to go before the polls closed, the campaign team had exhausted its list of favorable voters. In fact, two or three calls had been made to each. Determined to work until the last minute, the candidate scoured the list of those who had not voted. With 15 minutes to go, she drove across town to visit a household of three would-be Democratic voters. She convinced them to get into her car and be driven to the polls so that they could fulfill their "civic duty." With seconds to go, all three cast their votes. Out of the thousands of votes cast, Shea won that election by the same number: three votes.

Get-out-the-vote (GOTV) efforts can be the most important activity undertaken during a campaign. The history of campaigns is filled with elections won and lost by a handful of voters. In every election, scores of congressional, state legislative, and even senatorial and gubernatorial races are decided by less than 1 percent of the votes cast. Carefully orchestrated, last-minute pushes can mean the difference between success and failure.

While democracy calls on everyone to vote on Election Day, the goal of a GOTV drive is to concentrate on those most likely to vote for the candidate. There are a number of ways to determine this, including voter ID calls, demographic and survey research, and electoral history. Party enrollment is often used. All things being equal, a person's party enrollment is the best single predictor of his or her vote choice. Conceivably, the canvass records will produce a list of favorable voters. A good rule of thumb is to target roughly 10 percent of the votes needed for victory: "If you are running a state legislative race and need 15,000 votes to win, you must have at least 1,500 identified supporters whom you will push to the polls" (Allen 1990a, 38). Whatever criteria are used, it is important to remember that last-minute pushes are designed to get the candidate's voters to the polls, not simply to kick up turnout.

Effective GOTV Techniques

In 2004, Yale University scholars Donald Green and Alan Gerber's book *Get Out the Vote* presented evidence based on scores of studies showing what works and what does not work when trying to get voters to the polls. Perhaps more important, the book carefully charts the cost-effectiveness of different techniques. Are automated "robo calls" worth the time and money? Likely not. Does it help to have a celebrity make the voice recording? No. Are in-person visits effective? Yes. But are they more cost effective than telephone-based programs? Sometimes. There are limitations to the book—many of their experiments rely on a random selection of voters, whereas real-world campaigns rarely use random selection procedures. Still, Green and Gerber have added empirical sophistication to the folklore about GOTV. In the field, techniques that rely on volunteers have proven to be quite effective, particularly when the efforts are organized methodically, step-by-step.

Early Planning. The team might begin planning the GOTV about 30 days before Election Day. This means establishing a written plan of action and assigning a coordinator. The plan lays out specific tasks, deadlines for accomplishing these jobs, and the people responsible for completing them. Moreover, it lists the resources needed for implementation.

GOTV Mailer. Three to five days before the election, a mailer is sent to voters in swing and favorable election precincts throughout the district. If the swing group is not needed, it may be dropped. This mailing stresses the importance of the election and the difference that every vote can make. It is a good idea to include an anecdote of an election won by just a few votes. If the campaign is strapped for cash, a pamphlet can be dropped in target areas during the weekend prior to the election.

Telephoning. On the eve of the election, the telephone operation shifts into full gear. The target group for this phase is more refined than the mailer group. If at all possible, the entire 10 percent GOTV group is contacted. The message on the phone is similar to the message in the mailer.

Poll Watching and Pickup. Many jurisdictions allow for "poll watching." On the morning of the election, volunteers go to each polling place, find a comfortable place to sit, and then record the names of each person who votes. The resulting lists are picked up throughout the day, perhaps at about two-hour intervals, and then brought to headquarters. The names of those who have voted are scratched off a master list. This process indicates which registered voters have gone to the polls, letting the campaign know who should get reminder calls.

Reminders and Assistance. Most people vote early in the morning or just after work. By about 4:00 P.M., a smart campaign puts a telephone operation into action, focusing on those in the target group who have not yet voted. Very often people need assistance to get to the polls: child care and rides to the polls are commonly offered. This process continues throughout the evening, relying on updated lists from the poll watchers in order to scratch off recent voters. Prospective supporters are called until the polls close.

Other GOTV Aids

The mailer/poll-watching/telephoning/assistance operation forms the core of a GOTV drive, but several other activities might help. A rally might be held in a targeted area the weekend prior to the election. Massive literature drops can work, as can yard sign blitzes. Unless the candidate is down in the polls and a large turnout is deemed the only chance, the campaign steers clear of untargeted activities, such as waving signs at intersections, handing out leaflets at shopping malls, and blanket canvassing.

As for the candidate, this can be a difficult time. Months if not years of work are coming to an end. It is a good idea for consultants to give the candidate a specific task, perhaps calling his or her best supporters and thanking them for their work. An alternative is to have the candidate walk door-to-door in the highest swing neighborhood in the district. More than anything else, he or she needs to be kept busy—for everyone's sake.

Some Thoughts on Recount Procedures

The gravity of recount procedures held the public's attention during the six weeks following the 2000 presidential contest. Many were surprised with the complexity of recounts and the fragility of election results. Every time the ballots were counted, the vote totals changed. In 2002, the Help America Vote Act was passed to standardize voting procedures and to correct many of the problems encountered in 2000. Most agree, however, that while the act moves the election process in the right direction, the system remains flawed in many respects. The potential for irregularities and miscounts abound.

In a well-prepared campaign, laws structuring the applicable recount procedures should be compiled ahead of time. An attorney with a working knowledge of state election law should be brought on board. Legal questions should be clarified well before Election Day—in terms of both initiating a recount (if the campaign loses) and opposing a recount (if the campaign wins). Among those who would sit on a recount team, both legal and political, responsibilities should be clear, contact information shared, and all the necessary addresses and telephone numbers of election offices, election commissioners, and appropriate judicial authorities readied.

The reason: recounts are generally initiated in rapid order, usually on Election Night or the following morning. (Some jurisdictions have automatic recounts for close elections.)

Often, the first step is to secure the ballots and voting machines. In New York State, for example, a court order from a county justice is necessary to impound all voting machines in a given county. This step is critical, especially if the campaign suspects fraud. From this point, the work of the lawyers begins. A recount process is time consuming and labor intensive; attention must be paid to the details. The focus is often on mistakes in voter tabulation. In 2000, the problem in Florida was a combination of poor ballot design, voter error, faulty voting procedures, and improper instructions. There were even allegations of voter intimidation. Less frequent is outright election fraud (Sabato and Simpson 1996). In any event, attention must be paid to both the legal implications of the recount and the attendant communications issues, for the court of public opinion is no less important than the court in which the lawyer's arguments will be heard.

Operatives on all sides should understand that election results are very hard to overturn even when the evidence seems clear. One attorney relates the story of a election that his client lost by 30 votes. A precinct that went 55 votes to 125 for the opposition showed clear indications of machine malfunction, even if the exact problem could not be located in the device itself. With a seeming undervote of 100 votes,

> we canvassed the precinct and got about 150 affidavits from people who said they had voted for the Democrat. I checked them against the precinct sign-in list and every one of them had been there. At the hearing, I proffered the affidavits to show that my client had been the victim of a machine malfunction. The judge said he trusted the machine. My client decided not to take an appeal. (Still 2000)

Indeed, at times, candidates believe it is more dignified to simply bow out gracefully than to fight to the end, as it seems John Kerry did in 2004, even after questions were raised about the ballot process in Ohio.

GRASSROOTS IN CYBERSPACE

One of the most promising new aspects of grassroots electioneering is what now can be accomplished over the Internet. No one knows this better than the chair of the Democratic National Committee, Howard Dean. In his bid for the Democratic presidential nomination, Dean undertook one of the best run online grassroots campaigns in history—and in doing so changed the nature of electioneering. His campaign manager, Joe Trippi, believes the 2004 election "was the opening salvo in a revolution, the sound of hundreds of thousands of Americans turning off their televisions and embracing the only form of technology that has allowed them to be involved again, to gain control of a process that alienated them decades ago" (2005, xviii–xix). Although the Internet had been used as a political tool prior to 2004, it did not become such a powerful grassroots mechanism until Dean. Today, the use of the Internet to generate volunteer support is no longer considered exceptional. Nearly every serious statewide or congressional campaign develops a sophisticated Web site boasting the candidate's biography and policy positions, a schedule of events, how to give donations, chat room opportunities, and concrete ways that volunteers can join the fight. Often, professionals construct these Web sites, but sometimes volunteers rise to the challenge. After the sites are established, volunteers input data, upload and download material, and answer and send e-mails. Grassroots has moved into cyberspace.

As noted by one observer, "The Internet's impact is most likely to be felt in those races where a lot of information is not available to the public, specifically, for local and state races. . . . The Net can be used not only to bring information to voters, it can be used to foster interaction between candidates and voters online and offline" (Anderson 2002). Web logs present a medium for the exchange of ideas and information 24 hours a day. The Internet is clearly not an end-all, a substitute for more effective, proven campaign efforts. Joe Trippi might be animated by the power of online campaigning, but his candidate lost. Candidates who see the Internet as a magic potion and neglect tried-and-true tactics will be bitterly disappointed on Election Day. Online campaigning will *not* revolutionize the electoral process, but it will reshape some of its elements—including the scope and nature of grassroots activism.

CONCLUSION

As with all other facets of electioneering, political judgment in grassroots campaigning is vital. In some places, it is common to find door-to-door volunteers on Sunday; in others, this is taboo. On any day, campaigns should be wary of calling before 9:00 A.M. or after 8:30 P.M. Yard signs are acceptable in some places but considered in bad taste elsewhere. Professionals must understand the social, religious, and political norms of any area in which they campaign.

Political wisdom is usually learned on the job—often through mistakes. Take, for example, the crisp Saturday morning in October when a zealous campaign operative rounded up a team of volunteers to walk door-to-door. Their race was located in the Long Beach area of New York's Nassau County. After two hours of work, the group became increasingly discouraged. Although cars were in the driveways, no one appeared to be home. Those who did answer the door refused to open it more than a few inches. The canvass was soon canceled. Later investigation found that the area contained a large number of Orthodox Jews. Saturday was their Sabbath, and they were insulted by insensitive campaign workers. Repairing the damage took considerable effort.

Campaigns must channel volunteer enthusiasm properly. A strong volunteer workforce is a rare commodity in politics. Smart campaigns bring the candidate to many of the volunteer functions in order to express gratitude and maintain interest. Pizza, bagels, soda, and coffee are served, and on Election Night there will be an extravagant blowout.

Smart electioneering uses this model throughout the campaign operation. To win an election, the race must be fun. Sour looks and hot tempers corrode the relationships necessary for a smooth campaign. Even as targeting and media politics have overtaken many traditional campaign activities, politics remains a very human endeavor. As such, campaigning can be one of the most rewarding missions that anyone can undertake. The rush on Election Night is unmatched. Candidates, consultants, and campaign staff always want to win, but professionals never forget that it is only an election. Win or lose, life will go on.

Chapter Thirteen

Conclusion: The Future of Political Campaign Organization

Political strategists speak in terms of military planning because "politics and war follow the same principles: armies face off in battle, each with different plans, different strengths and weaknesses, limited resources, generals with different styles, and all sharing the same goal of crushing the enemy" (Sweitzer 1996, 46). For a political strategist, campaigns are civilized warfare. For a political tactician, however—the one who must implement wide-ranging battle plans—a different conceptual model is required. Tactical operations take the form of commercial marketing (see Newman 1999). The language of voter contact speaks of "gross rating points," "spot production," "list management," and "demographic research." Each electoral cycle brings new marketing tools—novel methods of segmenting the electorate and selling the candidate. As the new millennium began, consultants were talking about the marketing power of the Internet and how it might help campaigns target voters in ways never imagined in the 1950s. Adlai Stevenson, who railed against those who "merchandise candidates for high office like breakfast cereal," would be astonished at the present state of affairs.

For the past half century, political campaigns have absorbed innovative technologies with amazing speed. Databases, video editing, digital phones, and laptop computers have become standard equipment. Advanced technologies, such as Geographic Information Systems (GIS), are used widely in high-profile campaigns and some down-ballot races. As with all other areas of life, the tools that an organization uses tend to transform the organization itself. To see the future of American political campaigns, one need only look at the leading edge of the technological revolution. This chapter provides a conceptual framework for the microeconomics of consultant-centered campaigns, highlights some of the technologies that reinforce new-style electioneering, and discusses the implications of these forces on the relationship between candidates and the electorate.

PROFESSIONALISM AND MASS CUSTOMIZATION

As party identification became a less important determinant of voting behavior, individual politicians had to build identities of their own. Television was the preferred means of promotion. The congressional class of 1974 had a whole new look—young, energetic political outsiders with blow-dried hair. Tammany-style politics were gone. To win, candidates had to go on television, a costly medium requiring specialized expertise. Few pols knew how to backlight a candidate without creating a "halo effect." The language of ad production—with its "Nagras," "Chroma Keys," and "crystal syncs"—was foreign to old-style campaign managers. Furthermore, the moving arts require forms of creativity not found in other visual media. Television demands professionals. Political campaigns were forced to outsource the production of campaign ads to those who already knew the business.

The microeconomics of the situation enabled consultants to penetrate the campaign market. Direct mail illustrates the point: learning postal regulations for a mass mailing requires scarce time; turning to a professional can significantly shorten the production schedule. But figuring out how to size, sort, and seal a mailing is only the beginning. Direct mail depends on clean data, efficient stuffing machines, and expertise in building productive lists that yield high-dollar contributions. Database professionals must know how to "merge and purge," "de-dupe," and practice "good data hygiene." Once a campaign operative has mastered the legal, technical, creative, and organizational demands of the mail business, there is no point in restricting the expertise to a single candidate. Working on a number of campaigns at once helps distribute the costs among a larger group of clients, thereby reducing per-unit overhead and increasing profits. The organizational structure of campaigns is thus forced to change.

In the 1970s, a competitive U.S. Senate campaign wishing to send out a mass mailing would rely on a volunteer coordinator who would assemble a team of supporters and spend an evening folding letters and stuffing envelopes. In the new millennium, the job is outsourced to a professional mail house. Consulting firms like the Strategy Group in Chicago can manage the entire process. Professionals target the recipients, develop the artwork, write the copy, arrange for printing, and then ship the mailing. Not only does professional administration reduce the number of volunteer hours needed by the campaign, but mail houses quite possibly save raw dollars and cents. A direct-mail consultant counsels, "A lettershop is cheaper than pizza and beer for your volunteers" (Malchow 1990). The new economics of electioneering devalues the role of the volunteer coordinator—a position once filled by itinerant college students and battle-hardened party members—while it increases the need for independent fund-raisers. (The money to hire professionals is itself raised by professionals.) While a pool of talented volunteers might be persuaded to go without pizza during the final hours of a campaign, a direct-marketing firm will not forgo its consultancy fees.

In the golden age of parties, campaigns were constituent parts of a centralized chain of command. In the early days of new-style campaigns, the breakdown of party structure meant a trend toward multiple hierarchies, with each candidate running his or her own operation. As this transformation toward candidate-centered campaigns was taking place, the candidates came to rely on dispersed outside consultancies. Even the resurgence of the national parties reflects this trend. The parties are no longer just a pecking order of elected officials and staff. They are clearinghouses for money, expertise, information, and political intelligence. The result is a party structure in which campaigns are far more adaptable to changes in the political environment.

One way to reconceptualize new-style operations is to look at a recent development in the private sector: mass customization. This seeming oxymoron was popularized by B. Joseph Pine II, who advocated a convergence of mass-production efficiency with the individualized attention of hand-tailored craftwork. "Through the application of technology and new management methods," Pine wrote, manufacturers are "creating variety and customization through flexibility and quick responsiveness" (1993, 44; emphasis omitted). The rise of mass customization has distinct parallels with the rise of new-style campaign techniques, and in many ways the future of political campaigns can be divined from the history of industrial manufacturing.

American industrialism arose from a major transformation in economic organization—a movement from the craft of individual artisans to the repetition of mass production. "Economies of scale" could reduce a product's cost per unit by increasing a factory's quantity of output. In this way, development costs were distributed among a large number of identically produced items. The downside of mass production was its lack of flexibility. Focusing on a single product hobbled a firm's ability to generate "economies of scope"—its capacity to enter new product lines. Furthermore, to maintain market share, large manufacturers *dictated* consumer demand rather than *responded* to it. But as consumers began to insist on a wider variety of goods, the old "stability and control" model began to fall away as the new marketplace demanded a "better understanding of customer requirements" (Pine 1993, 44).

Manufacturers reacted by "developing, producing, marketing, and delivering affordable goods and services with enough variety and customization that nearly everyone finds exactly what they want" (Pine 1993, 47). The retail computer industry has been completely reconfigured by mass customization. In 1964, the only mass-market computer was the IBM System/360 (36). In the new millennium, customers design their own systems online. Shoppers looking to buy a Dell or a Gateway machine go to a Web site, choose a computer that meets their needs, and then configure the system according to their personal requirements. Network devices, hard drives, external storage, and screen sizes are selected one at a time—all according to the customer's personal specifications. Thousands of combinations are possible.

The parallel with politics is clear. Political consultants routinely mix and match preexisting campaign slogans, color schemes, policy stands, and media strategies to suit a range of clients. Campaigns are neither handcrafted nor mass-produced. Most are created by adapting pretested components to the needs of new localities, candidacies, and constituencies.

"Modularity" is the key. New-style industries use parts that are interchangeable not just within a product line but across product lines as well. Standardized components are fitted to a variety of manufactured goods, meaning that costs can be contained by producing a multiplicity of modules that are combined into a wide-ranging diversity of items for consumption. Writes Pine, "Economies of scale are gained through components rather than the products; economies of scope are gained by using the modular components over and over in different products; and customization is gained by the myriad of products that can be configured" (1993, 196). In the political world, CNN creates short news segments that can be played on any of its many outlets, including Headline News, CNN International, CNNMoney, CNN Airport Network, CNN en Español, CNN Radio, CNN en Español Radio, and affiliated Web sites. The modular construction of video news reporting has increased the scope and flexibility of the journalistic environment.

Campaign scholars Judith Trent and Robert Friedenberg write that "candidates adapt" to varied political audiences with "speech modules" (2004, 182). Each module is "a single unit of speech," they write, and "typically, candidates will have a speech unit, or module, on each of the ten to twenty issues on which they most frequently speak" (192). These "talking points," as they are called in the industry, are recycled from one event to the next, with only small variations in phrasing. They can be used in letters, brochures, op-eds, debates, or any other textual form of communication.

But speech modules are only the beginning. Modularization can be seen throughout the campaign process. Campaign data come in standardized formats, and campaign commercials have a consistent regularity. A presidential advance staff can quickly assemble an immense campaign rally—with satellite trucks, lights, and a handsome backdrop—because each piece of the puzzle has been used several times previously. When a campaign staffer learns how to coordinate sound and video at small events, this expertise can soon be fitted to larger and larger settings. A smart advance person figures out which pieces of the technology—electronic equipment, wiring, and so forth—are unique to local vendors and which are standard nationwide. Once the transferable elements of sound and video production are understood, the technique has been, in effect, modularized, and the swift production of large events becomes possible.

Modularization requires political wisdom. A mass-production approach would demand only that the procedures that created a successful campaign event be repeated step-by-step for each venue. An artisan's approach would tailor each campaign event to the specific needs of every campaign stop. A mass-customization approach, however, merges the efficiency of repetition with the power of individualization. Political professionals must distinguish the elements of a successful event that could work only in a particular time and place from those that can be transferred to other contexts. This task demands a broad knowledge of campaigns or, at the very least, close attention to industry trends. Communications consultants can learn how to build a Web site from hard experience, but the smart professional looks to the modularized advice collected from the experience of others: "Tell voters what others are saying about you," "Translate into Spanish," "Make the site personal, but relevant," "Use entertaining features to get people's attention," and so on (Jalonick 2000, 56, 58). Over time, campaign professionals learn what works and what does not—and, more important, what can be reused time and again.

The professionalization of political campaigns stems partly from the efficiency of well-executed modularization. A whole industry of consultants has arisen—an industry that profits most when it recycles techniques from one campaign to the next. Political professionals develop "formulas" to guide electoral targeting and get-out-the-vote operations. They specialize in particular types of campaign messages or field tactics. One consultant who has written "around 150 speeches" notes that he "regard[s] all of those speeches as variations on one single speech": "[Each speech had] six parts. Four parts were set in advance, and the remaining two were prepared especially for each event." Hence, in the introduction, "the candidate would . . . recall the crowd's nostalgia and say something like, 'I remember how once upon on a time the situation was such and such. . . . (filler N. 2)'" (Maor 2001, 35; ellipses in the original).

As James Carville has said, "In campaign politics an idea is like a fruitcake at Christmas—there's not but one, and everybody keeps passing it around" (Matalin and Carville 1995, 35). There is a danger to being overly predictable—the general who fights the next war like the last risks defeat—but if the modularized components of campaign management are continually remixed and rematched, with new techniques replacing those that have become outmoded, a consultant's general methods of operation can remain strategically viable. To win—and profitability is maximized by repeated victory—campaign operatives must keep their techniques current. They must continually broaden their knowledge by working on a variety of campaigns, meeting with other consultants, and keeping up with the most recent changes in their chosen field. In other words, consultants must become "professionals" in the sense that their careers revolve not around individual candidates or the nuances of democratic governance but around campaigns and elections per se.

Indeed, political consultancy has evolved into a mature profession. It has a professional organization, standards of conduct, an industry magazine, and a collection of norms and practices that set consultants apart from the old party bosses and even their own candidates. Professional consultants seem to have more in common with their colleagues on the other side of the partisan aisle than with outspoken ideologues within their own party. But most important, the profession has been locked in place by the increasing complexity of new-style campaigns. This was true as far back as 1980, when Sidney Blumenthal wrote, "The arrival of new techniques based on computers—direct mail, voter identification methods, sophisticated polling—reinforces the role of consultants" (1980, 3). The reason, according to Blumenthal, was simple: "In order to have access to the new technology, a candidate needs a consultant. He can't run a viable, much less a respectable, campaign without one" (3).

CUTTING-EDGE TECHNOLOGY

Mass customization of political campaigns depends on the increasing power of database management and the astounding proliferation of communications technologies. These two developments go hand in hand. Database management produces lists of voters, and these voters can be targeted by new modes of communication and made available to campaign operatives online. At the beginning of the new millennium, advisers to down-ballot races still understand that managers need to rely on hard-copy records: "If you are using index cards, place all information for each volunteer on a single card" and do the same for all campaign contacts (Shaw 2004, 55). These sorts of tactics make sense for small races insofar as the start-up costs for computer databasing remain fairly high. As the costs of data management decline, however, even down-ballot campaigns will enter the digital age.

Database Management

The 1996 presidential primary effort of political commentator Pat Buchanan was, in many ways, an early version of a new-millennium campaign. At its heart was a technological advance the campaign called "Electronic Field Operations." The idea was to integrate data from a wide variety of sources—donors, 1-800-GO-PAT-GO callers, and phone bank operations—and then use the database as the foundation of all voter contact, updating it in real time as the race moved forward. The campaign set up a military-style "Tactical Operations Center," which "contain[ed] representatives of all the major staff sections to ensure that all parts of the force [were] supporting and communicating with one another" (Hathaway 1996, 43). The database team was able to monitor all campaign plans, intervene when necessary, and quickly retrieve data. As a result, the Buchanan campaign was able to react to late-breaking events as they occurred. In Alaska, for example, partway into caucus voting, it was learned that the Wasslia polling site would be open later than expected, so the database "was queried for all the eligible voters in the district and within 10 minutes the in-house phone bank had a list of over 1,500 voters which they called in the final 90 minutes of the election." The result: "Wasslia reported a 2:1 Buchanan win, a vote margin that accounted for almost half of his statewide margin of victory" (43).

The key to information management is data integrity. Each data record must correspond to a prospective voter, and all the data appended to the voter's record must (1) be accurate and (2) be in a form that corresponds to all the other records in the database. In Buchanan's campaign, for example, all the imported data had to fit into a standardized file structure and then be deduplicated "by building a match-code based on zip code, name, gender, and [commercially obtained] addressing information" (Hathaway 1996, 43). The process becomes more complicated with the addition of each new record. The first record in a database has no match, obviously, but the second will be matched against the first, the third against the first and second, and so on. The cost of data integrity increases incrementally. By the time a database has reached 100,000 or so voters, deduplication can become a troublesome and time-consuming job.

The high capital costs of databasing are eventually recouped by the benefits of reduced operating expenses and increased reaction speed. With individualized records, campaigns can combine polling, voter identification calls, electoral targeting, and voter contact results into a unified operation. And demographic clustering is becoming more and more precise. Consultants are now using the highly refined data and statistical approaches developed for commercial marketing. High-end pollsters can boast of careful segmentation of dozens of "lifestyle clusters" derived from "millions of pieces of data" that include "grocery purchases, automobile preferences, magazine subscriptions, charitable donations, and many others" (Usher and Mellman 2004, 36). Once the target groups are identified, the campaign can use traditional voter contact techniques to persuade and motivate the voters.

While some may look forward to the use of increasingly sophisticated statistical technologies—neural net pattern recognition and genetic algorithms that model the evolution of "selection formulae" through "thousands of 'generations'" (Malchow 1997, 39)—new-style campaigns are already putting data to good use in the form of innovative list management. A database marketing consultant says, "Political fundraising can learn a great deal from commercial database marketing where analysis and overlaid information provide insight that would be literally impossible without the process" (Halatyn 1998, 48). New donors can be identified by looking at the statistical characteristics of existing donors, just as persuadable voters can be identified by looking at persuaded voters. In a North Carolina Senate campaign, one candidate "utilized database overlays" in an effort to locate "soccer moms": "Public voting records, U.S. Postal Service sequencing lists and local directory information provided a target list of more than 10,000 priority voting targets," and an "intensive mail and phone campaign" was combined with voter ID calls to "find likely supporters and undecided voters to continue last-minute mail communications" and even a traditional door-to-door canvass operation (Crone 1998, 51).

Data overlays form the basis of "tactical cartography." One of the reasons that Geographic Information Systems (GIS) are becoming an important part of campaign operations is their ability to represent numerical data in a comprehensible format. For example, "by overlapping the boundaries of TV coverage with the location of a targeted voter group, campaigns can better understand the need to reach segmented audiences" (Lindauer 1999, 49). Data overlays can give a political operative a statistical listing of targeted precincts, relating the numbers to demographic characteristics and past campaign operations. Numerical readouts, however, are sometimes difficult to understand at first glance. But when strategists can see clusters of support, opposition, and uncommitted voters waiting to be persuaded, the full force of database technology comes into view.

In the recent past, the use of GIS was constrained by lofty hardware requirements, but in the twenty-first century, desktop computers can easily handle most off-the-shelf GIS software. As such, the visual display of campaign data began trickling down to lower-level campaigns and elections.

While GIS provides long-term efficiency benefits, the capital costs of building an integrated political GIS database remain high. Traditional campaign structures cannot be expected to develop the necessary technological resources over the course of a single election cycle. As a result, campaigns become increasingly dependent on outside consultants and vendors. The contemporary political marketplace offers clean voter lists, demographics, electoral histories, and consumer data, along with the data management tools that can help build donor, supporter, and voter contact files. As the cost of technology declines and as more campaigns take advantage of digital campaign management, the days of the three-by-five file card are giving way to outsourced data management.

Campaign Communication

With powerful database management tools, the nature of traditional voter contact changes dramatically. No longer are voters targeted just by ward or precinct. They can be targeted individually, according to their own particular voting and demographic patterns. Mailings can be tailored with an eye to market segmentation, and telephone campaigns can be personalized to individual voters. "Call center" technology moves beyond the phone bank, tracking consumer data and configuring appropriate messages for each contact they make. Predictive dialers get the target voter on the line before transferring the call to a call center agent.

New-style campaigns depend on sophisticated Web sites. The 2000 campaign demonstrated a quantum leap in Web site design. One of the most sophisticated sites in 1996 was that of the Clinton–Gore campaign, which, in addition to informational material, also gave visitors the chance to map their own Electoral College victory. Four years later, the Clinton–Gore site seemed positively archaic. Web sites for both Al Gore and George W. Bush offered policy information on virtually all subject areas, used streaming audio and video so that visitors could watch new ad campaigns, and sought contributions via secure Web transaction systems. So confident was the Gore campaign of the Web site's completeness that its chairman could tell a conference call of top advisers that all necessary talking points could be found on www.algore2000.com. In 2004, all the major candidates assembled cutting-edge Web sites. Not only did they offer text, audio, and video, but they started to become part of the organizational structure of the campaigns, helping volunteers stay coordinated and stay on message. For the Howard Dean campaign, the very idea of the Internet received iconic status. Dean volunteers saw themselves as part of a technological revolution that was changing the way American campaigns were run.

Capital Costs

Mergers of communications and technology require substantial funding. Telemarketing seats cost money, and sophisticated Web design costs money. Voting lists cost money. New-style campaigns cost a lot of money because they rely on specialized expertise. A consultant's article in *Campaigns and Elections* titled "Can Political Candidates Afford to Allow Their Data to Be Managed by Anyone but a Professional?" suggests that professionals "can take the burden of mission critical database management and related targeted communications off of the plate of the campaign manager" (Grefe 1998, 18). Consultants have a vested interest in outsourcing, but the logic is nonetheless compelling. Competition necessitates technical competence; technical competence is capital–intensive; and because campaign operations cannot afford to absorb the start-up costs, competitive campaigns must rely on outside consultants.

Consider Web site design. User-friendly software can help almost any techno-savvy supporter build a candidate's Web site. The difficulty is that Web sites built by amateurs end up looking amateurish. Web surfers are accustomed to visually attractive sites that never crash. They will inevitably be disappointed with a poorly designed site. Even worse, unless the designer is thoroughly familiar with a variety of server platforms and the fine distinctions among Web browsers and versions, the candidate's Web site may crash a user's computer—quite possibly losing a vote in the process. Top-notch sites require first-rate talent if for no other reason than that Internet security is a growing necessity. To be hacker-proof—a particular concern for political sites, which are prime targets for mischief—the designer must know more about server technology than do nearly all other Internet users. When the campaign starts to deploy e-commerce applications to collect campaign contributions, the need for paid professionals becomes even greater. The campaign can hire an outside consultant, or it can contract with an existing e-commerce firm that has experience in political contributions. The relative value of volunteer Web designers is diminished, and it is becoming more and more doubtful that an in-house campaign staffer will be capable of designing a stable, secure, and up-to-date campaign Web site.

The capital costs of research, development, and experience cannot be shouldered by any single candidate operation. A candidate's loyalists might not be able to build professional Web sites, manage complex databases, layer demographic and electoral variables on GIS, and develop an integrated television, radio, Internet, call center, and mail outreach program. Polling and electoral targeting are becoming more sophisticated. The abundance of information available at the turn of the twenty-first century made opposition research an advanced skill. The new resources do not make campaigning much easier. Rather, campaigning becomes more complicated. The competitive nature of electoral politics ensures that each new technology escalates the need for campaigns to be faster, stronger, and more capable of doing battle with other techno-savvy campaign operations. In the new millennium, only the uninformed would try to run a major campaign without drawing on experienced consultants using.

Knowledge comes at a price. In the late 1800s, the capital costs of campaign management were borne by the major parties, as knowledge was stored in Tammany-style organizations. If, in the new millennium, traditional parties were still intact, there might be no need for the consultant industry. But in the 1960s and 1970s, with the rise of individualized campaign operations, party structures loosened, and consultants picked up the slack. Consultants, for their part, are loyal to party organizations insofar as they represent certain political ideals and a ready stock of clients. They have little interest in joining party hierarchies, and they treat their selection of candidates as a business decision. James Carville's minimalist criteria are representative: "I will work for a Democrat who I can get along with who is neither a bigot nor a crook" (Matalin and Carville 1995, 55).

The decline of parties led to a fragmented marketplace and the rise of independent consultancies; the resurgence of political parties can be attributed partly to the parties' recognition that they can serve as consultancy brokers, harnessing the power of professional expertise by distributing money and referrals to candidates in targeted races. But even as parties respond to the new environment, the fact that they are using, not remaking, consultant-based campaign techniques demonstrates a concession to the new reality: independent campaign operatives have taken over the management of American political campaigns.

The value that campaign consultants provide is specialized expertise. Imported from the private sector, television advertising and research-driven market segmentation were used heavily in the 1952 Eisenhower campaign, which used the services of television advertising pioneer Rosser Reeves, whose best-known slogan was "M&M's—Melts in your mouth, not in your hands." In 1968, Richard Nixon relied on a handpicked media team, including Roger Ailes, executive producer of the popular *Mike Douglas Show.* In 1996, Bill Clinton used Bob Squier of Squier Knapp Ochs, a Washington-based media firm that handled a wide variety of clients. As if to demonstrate that the component parts of media consultancy truly are interchangeable, Ailes, who also worked for Ronald Reagan and George Bush, would later return to television as president of Fox News Channel, and Bob Squier, whose knowledge of damage control was virtually unrivaled, helped America Online respond to bad publicity when customers complained about busy signals interrupting their online service. Political professionalism, borne of private-sector marketing, had returned to its point of origin, carrying new tools useful in the business world.

George Stephanopoulos, when he first met James Carville, reflected on the changes that had taken place since Kennedy's time:

> Theodore H. White's *The Making of the President, 1960* described the major political advisors of the day as a few dozen Washington lawyers, "who in their dark-paneled chambers nurse an amateur's love for politics and dabble in it whenever their practice permits." By 1991, that description had the dated feel of a sepia-toned photograph, harking back to an era when political consultants, like tennis players in long pants, were not paid for their work. There were still amateurs who loved the game in 1991, but campaigns were now run by professionals. (1999, 45)

From 1991 to the turn of the twenty-first century, the campaign marketplace began to require increasing specialization.

According to one observer, general consultants like James Carville, who supervised a political campaign from top to bottom, "are dinosaurs of the consulting world" (Glasser 2000a). The tremendous profits that can be made by skillful entrepreneurs and the increasing complexity of political campaigns make for a campaign context in which specialization is sometimes prized over broad-spectrum talent. A large campaign might find itself hiring a strategist who bills by the hour, a pollster who charges a flat fee per survey, an opposition researcher who runs up billable hours, a media consultant who bases costs on a mix of production fees and commissions, an ad placement consultant who takes an additional cut of all media buys, a telemarketer who will invoice the campaign for a retainer plus a cost per call, and a direct-mail consultant whose fees will vary according to the type of mail requested, the lists used, and the size of the mailing sent. The strategist, in turn, might purchase demographic data from an outside contractor and voter lists from yet another, and the media consultant might work with a Webmaster who subcontracts visual production, site hosting, and e-commerce services to yet another set of professionals. Campaign management becomes the business of integrating subcontracted professional services.

Americans have been campaigning so long and so well that overseas consumers are taking notice. Elections in Europe and the emerging democracies of the former Soviet bloc are assisted in large part by Americans. They bring the technology of new-style campaigns with them, along with a strong understanding of strategy. While Americans must work hard to learn the culture in which they are working—"The American approach with hard-hitting contrast ads may prove counterproductive in cultures that prefer to avoid confrontation" (Panagopulos and Dayanand 2005, 45)—the idea that voters must be segmented and prioritized has global appeal. Indeed, "Latin America, with its culture of *presidentialismo,* is one of the hottest markets for U.S. consultants" (45). So powerful has been the American professional move into to foreign markets that political consulting has been drawn into debates over the politics of economic and cultural globalization (Sussman 2005).

Mitigating Forces

Despite the powerful centrifugal forces that break up campaigns and distribute their parts to a wide range of outside contractors, campaign decentralization is limited by a variety of constraints inherent in political operations. In most small, municipal-level campaigns, the economic benefits of consultancy are not realized. Examples of consultant-free campaigns abound. Councilman Ed Baum, a Republican in a small Ohio city, gained his seat with a self-run campaign that cost only a few thousand dollars. Baum's team was made up of friends and acquaintances, and his strategy was developed by reading a few good books. He built name recognition with yard signs and ran ads in the local paper. After his victory, Baum sat down and figured out what went right and what did not so that he could do even better next time. The need for a political consultant in this sort of race seems remote. Little if any efficiency would be gained by turning to a professional. But aside from pure economic calculations, a number of other factors mitigate against the power of consultants in campaigns and elections.

First, the public is not infinitely malleable—some candidates just do not persuade voters. In media-driven California, both Michael Huffington's losing 1994 campaign for Senate and Al Checchi's disastrous bid for the gubernatorial nomination in 1998 suffered from backlash against candidates who seemed to be buying the election through paid media. Huffington was seen as an "empty suit" whose $30 million campaign was orchestrated by his then-wife, Arianna. Checchi's advertisements and campaign materials, coordinated by top consultants Mark Penn and Bob Shrum, reflected the sort of corporate professionalism that one might expect from a $40 million campaign run by an airline executive, but they were never able to connect the candidate with the voters. Said media consultant Alex Castellanos, "You know, sometimes the problem is not the label on the can, it's the dog food. And sometimes there's just dog food dogs don't like" (1998). In campaign politics, media makes a difference, but rarely can it make *all* the difference.

Second, loyalty counts. Even as candidates look to outside consultants, they continue to rely on inside advisers. Wise candidates form kitchen cabinets of trusted friends and colleagues. During the electoral season, the group might become a formal campaign committee. In office, a few of these loyalists might go on the official payroll. Even in the off-season, public officials depend on the counsel of their close advisers. Both major party presidential candidates in 2000 commanded this sort of loyalty. Al Gore had long depended on his former chiefs of staff—Peter Knight, Roy Neel, Jack Quinn, and Ron Klain—all of whom worked high up in the vice president's campaign. George W. Bush's inner campaign circle was filled with staffers who had demonstrated their loyalty for years in the governor's office. Candidates turn to intimates for confidential advice, alternative interpretations of a consultant's polling data, and a listening ear to hear the musings and frustrations of candidates in the middle of a tough campaign. Consultants, who must treat politics as a business, who may be employed by a party committee, who are probably working for several clients at once, and who may well fade from view days after the election, are not always privy to the internal decision-making processes of candidates.

Third, the same technological forces that complicate campaigns can also simplify, to a degree, the campaign process. This is achieved by the production of off-the-shelf solutions to standard campaign problems. With more than 500,000 electoral offices in the United States, there is a rich market for campaign advice and technology. Again, no one size fits all, but the similarities that allow professional consultants to modularize components of their campaigns also create a mass market for the tools of the trade. Campaign books provide generalized advice. The cable industry reminds professionals that it can simplify ad placement. With respect to campaign data, a new-style candidate at ease with computer technology can, over the course of a long weekend, download a county's demographics, retrieve voter lists, layer this information on top of prior electoral data, and then display the results on a computer-generated map. In this way, candidates and their loyalists have the ability to maintain campaign operations close to the vest as they contain the costs of electioneering.

Fourth, good management demands that the number of consultants be limited. As more consultants get involved in a campaign, management issues come to the fore. With each layer of consultants comes a new possibility of media leaks, cost-control problems, and an overall inability to manage a large and growing operation. With respect to out-of-state consultants, campaigns are well advised to weigh the benefits of "a broad, national perspective" against the reality that "overextended national consultants delegate important work to second and third tier assistants" (Faucheux 1996, 56). Simple communication can become problematic. Even if the consultants are drawn from within the state, the task of bringing a large number of profit-driven consultants to work together can sometimes overwhelm even the ablest of political candidates. That was one of the problems on the Checchi campaign, it seems, where battles reportedly broke out among consultants who became overly aggressive in seeking fees (Glasser 2000b).

For an electorate that demands authenticity in its candidates, there will always be something untoward in the hiring of people whom James A. Thurber and Candice J. Nelson call "campaign warriors" (2000). Mercenaries are little more respected in politics than in battle, and the very fact that a campaign has hired a high-priced, out-of-state consultant can be used against the candidate. Is it a sign of desperation? Does it mean that the candidate is trying to buy the election? And there are larger issues. If consultants use the same tricks of the trade over and over again, will American politics become homogenized at the expense of originality? Given the propensity of the electorate to seek out authentic candidates—Arnold Schwarzenegger's recall campaign against Gray Davis succeeded partly because the Terminator so often departed from the routine campaign messages. Any hint that a campaign is mass-customized tends to chip away at a candidate's image. For many, the rise of political consultants signifies a move away from the politics of personal connection and toward an era of hypermediated political connections.

POLITICAL CONNECTIONS

Did the people of earlier times have a closer connection to power than those of the new millennium? In some ways, they did; in other ways, they did not. At no time did a golden age of politics truly exist. Never did money fail to provide some degree of access, nor was there a moment when campaigns did not attempt to change the public mind for purely political reasons. The Civil War was a violent extension of partisan and sectional politics. Later, Mark Hanna, William McKinley's strategist, took in $250,000 from John D. Rockefeller's Standard Oil, the fortunes of which were endangered by William Jennings Bryan. What passes for mean-spirited politics at the beginning of the new millennium pales in comparison to the partisan witch hunts of Joseph McCarthy. But there is a sense in which all these comparisons are quite irrelevant. First, each tends toward the extreme. The Civil War, Rockefeller, and McCarthy are outliers in the American experience. Second, the forms of voter contact provided by campaign organizations have changed so radically that any comparison of old- and new-style campaigns is problematic.

One of the most common bases of comparison is the infamous political operation of George Washington Plunkitt. Plunkitt boasted personal knowledge of everyone whom he represented. While there may be self-aggrandizement in his claim, certainly the urban political machines, which merged social and political affairs, fostered a more personalized connection between voters and elected officials. The old party hierarchies had a one-to-one connection with many of their members. But a close read of *Plunkitt of Tammany Hall* (Riordon 1995) shows a far more attenuated relationship between candidates and constituents.

Plunkitt got his start when he built a political following of voters who would cast their ballots the way he wanted. The voters in his base of support became Plunkitt's "marketable goods" (Riordon 1995, 8). Plunkitt used his newfound assets to link up with party leaders at district headquarters, which, in turn, was beholden to the city and state organizations, respectively, on up to the national party level. In the world of the old party machines, hierarchies of power were stratified through multilayered echelons. The idea that one of Plunkitt's loyal supporters might speak with a Democratic governor or president is all but unthinkable. On the one hand, the old party structure was highly personalized. Plunkitt had an immediate relationship with his initial supporters, as indeed his first loyalists were a cousin and his friends. On the other hand, there was virtually no contact between low-level supporters and leaders up the chain of command. Party hierarchies mediated relationships between leaders and voters by inserting many layers between them.

New-style campaigns have fundamentally changed the old-style party relationships, bringing novel forms of voter alienation. As campaign scholar Christopher Arterton has noted,

> Modern politics have eviscerated [the old party] networks, replacing them with polling and mass communications. In the process, the individual voter has become a cipher, a statistical construct rather than a living, breathing person. Targeting involves creating an electoral majority by sending out messages to voters on the basis of the probability of support, depending on certain demographic characteristics or known "facts" about the individuals in a given group. Given the large number of citizens involved, campaigners cannot treat (or even conceptualize) these voters as individuals. In fact, to some degree, the individuals themselves are unimportant. As long as the total number of supporters can be pushed over the 50 percent mark, one voter is more or less substitutable by another. (2000, 22)

Depersonalization was a hallmark of American politics in the period that followed the decline of traditional parties.

In some ways, however, the fall of old party hierarchies resulted from the forging of new relationships between voters and candidates. When Ronald Reagan campaigned in the 1980 primaries, he "went over the heads" of the party leadership by speaking directly to Republican voters. The appeal was made on the airwaves—it was in no sense a personal, one-to-one relationship—but Reagan's politics were a great deal more personalized than the "smoke-filled rooms" of Plunkitt's day. Nixon could run apart from the Republican establishment because television allowed him to bypass the party leadership. George McGovern received the Democratic nomination in 1972 in large part because he had mastered the art of direct mail. Jimmy Carter made effective use of television to present himself as an outsider at precisely the moment when the political marketplace demanded such a president. In 1992, Bill Clinton used the "town hall" format to great effect, dispensing with the probing questions of skeptical reporters. In 2000 and 2004, Bush "connected" with the voters far better than did his adversaries.

The handpicked audiences of George W. Bush's campaign events in 2004 are instructive. The real audience was the television viewership—in this sense, it was a mediated event. And yet, the questions were posed to candidates by supporters who came to the event outside the usual channels of party politics. They were not party officials, just good upstanding campaign workers. Does this make politics more or less distant? In a curious way, the randomly selected recipients of a survey call or the carefully chosen subjects of a mall intercept have become powerful new voices in the electoral process. The nature of democratic representation has truly changed.

Blumenthal noted that "consultants . . . embody many of the virtues espoused by the turn-of-the-century Progressives. They are usually dispassionate critics of politics, wary of control by party bosses" (1980, 7). The corrosive power of new technologies in the hands of independent consultants has, for better or worse, sealed the fate of traditional party hierarchies. Precision targeting and sophisticated marketing techniques hold out one-to-one customer relationships as their main goal. New-style campaigns do not foster the warm relationships that one finds in sentimental depictions of American politics in which public officials know each voter personally, but neither do they promote the remote interactions of mass-media advertising. Arterton sees a possibility, at least, that Internet technology may help "establish a new, more personalized connection between candidate and voter," perhaps even helping to "restore some balance and mutual respect to the relationship" (2000, 22).

Of course, it is possible to romanticize new-style politics. Dick Morris, a consultant who turned pundit, sees the Internet as a new "*vox populi* in cyberspace" that will change government by reforming elections and reducing the power of money in campaigns (1999b, 27). A serious review of elections and campaigns, however, suggests that technology has neither brought candidates and voters closer together nor pushed them apart. Rather, the nature of the relationship has been so profoundly altered that comparisons between old- and new-style politics are difficult to render. When a candidate's voter contact strategy targets swing voters, does it make politics more or less personalized? When party leaders enlist independent consultants to win state senate races, have the parties consolidated their power or ceded it to outsiders? The critical transformation that has taken place in American elections has filtered down from presidential campaigns to mayoral races, and as students of politics seek to appreciate changes in American government, they must unravel the nature of new-style electioneering.

Central to the new understanding of political campaigns is the recognition that professional electioneering is a new craft. It is no longer a high art, if it ever was such, in which the intuitive faculties of candidates would impress the electorate with spontaneous oratory and principled debate. Nor is it a science in which the voter is held up for detached observation by pollsters and then manipulated by media consultants. Instead, in the competitive environment created by America's two-party system, campaign operatives must constantly refine their expertise, mixing technology and creativity in the search for electoral success. Consultant-centered campaigns are less beholden to the old party structures than their predecessors were, as candidates have released themselves to set up their own campaign operations and have come to rely on professionals who know the strategies and tactics of campaign management. In this sense, new-style electioneering is both art and science—the product of ingenuity as well as research, experience, and analysis. Consultant-based campaigns are best understood as a new campaign craft.

References

Abramson, Paul R., John H. Aldrich, and David W. Rohde. 1999. *Change and Continuity in the 1996 and 1998 Elections.* Washington, DC: CQ Press.

Adamany, David W., and George E. Agree. 1975. *Political Money: A Strategy for Campaign Financing in America.* Baltimore: The Johns Hopkins University Press.

Agranoff, Robert. 1972. *The New Style in Election Campaigns.* Boston: Holbrook.

Ahuja, Sunil, Staci L. Beavers, Cynthia Berreau, Anthony Dodson, Patrick Hourigan, Steven Showalter, Jeff Walz, and John R. Hibbing. 1993. "Modern Congressional Theory Meets the 1992 House Elections." *Political Research Quarterly* 47: 891–908.

Alford, John, Holly Teeters, Daniel S. Ward, and Rick K. Willson. 1994. "Overdraft: The Political Cost of Congressional Malfeasance." *Journal of Politics* 56: 788–801.

Allen, Cathy. 1990a. "GOTV." *Campaigns and Elections,* October.

———. 1990b. "Peer-Pressure Politics." *Campaigns and Elections,* June.

American Political Science Association. 2005. Symposium on the 2004 Presidential Vote Forecasts. *PS: Political Science and Politics* 38: 23–40.

Anderson, David M. 2002. "Primaries and Local Elections Need the Net." Maryland Internet Politics Week. Available at http://www.mdipw.org/05_10_2002_Gazette.html. Accessed 10 August 2005.

Anderson, Margo J., ed. 2000. *Encyclopedia of the U.S. Census.* Washington, DC: CQ Press.

Ansolabehere, Steven, and Shanto Iyengar. 1995. "Winning through Advertising: It's All in the Context." In *Campaigns and Elections American Style,* ed. James A. Thurber and Candice J. Nelson. Boulder, CO: Westview.

———. 1997. *Going Negative: How Political Advertisements Shrink and Polarize the Electorate.* New York: Free Press.

Arnold, Marguerite. 1999. "TV Spot Production: A Political Campaign Primer." *Campaigns and Elections,* September.

Arterton, Chris. 2000. "New Relationships." *Campaigns and Elections,* April.

Atlas, Mark. 1989. "Gambling with Elections." In *Campaigns and Elections: A Reader in Modern American Politics,* ed. Larry J. Sabato. Glenview, IL: Scott, Foresman.

Backstrom, Charles H., and Gerald Hursh-Cesar. 1981. *Survey Research.* New York: Macmillan.

Baker, Peter. 1996. "Contrasting GOP Strategies Mark Senate Primary in Va." *Washington Post* (26 May).

Bayer, Michael J., and Joseph Rodota. 1989. "Computerized Opposition Research." In *Campaigns and Elections: A Reader in Modern American Politics,* ed. Larry J. Sabato. Boulder, CO: Westview.

Beaudry, Ann, and Bob Schaeffer. 1986. *Winning Local and State Elections.* New York: Free Press.

Beiler, David. 1990. "Precision Politics." *Campaigns and Elections,* February/March.

———. 1994. "The Harder They Fall." *Campaigns and Elections,* May.

———. 2000. "The Body Politic Registers a Protest." In *Campaigns and Elections: Contemporary Case Studies,* ed. Michael A. Bailey, Ronald A. Faucheux, Paul S. Herrnson, and Clyde Wilcox. Washington, DC: CQ Press.

———. 2002. "The Misadventure of Tom Sawyer: How the Free Trade Issue Turned a Presumed Congressional Lifer into a Democratic Primary Loser." *Campaigns and Elections,* September.

Benenson, Bob. 1995. "Jesse Jackson Jr. Wins House Seat." *Congressional Quarterly Weekly Report* 53: 3836.

Bennett, Matthew. 2000. Telephone interview with Michael John Burton, 17 July.

Berelson, Bernard R., Paul F. Lazarsfeld, and William N. McPhee. 1954. *Voting.* Chicago: University of Chicago Press.

Bike, William S. 1998. *Winning Local Elections: A Comprehensive Guide to Electoral Success.* Juneau, AK: Denali.

Blakely, Ed. 2001. "Cable TV: How Good for Campaigns?" *Campaigns and Elections,* December.

Blogs for Bush. 2004. Available at http://www.blogsforbush.com/mt/archives/002715. html. Accessed 10 July 2005.

Blumenthal, Sidney. 1980. *The Permanent Campaign: Inside the World of Elite Political Operatives.* Boston: Beacon Press.

Bogart, Leo. 2000. "Politics, Polls, and Poltergeists: A Critical View of the 1996 Election." In *Election Polls, the News Media, and Democracy,* ed. Paul J. Lavrakas and Michael W. Traugott. Chatham, NJ: Chatham House.

Boorstin, Daniel J. 1964. *The Image: A Guide to Pseudo-Events in America.* New York: Harper and Row.

Bovee, John. 1998. "How to Do Opposition Research on the Internet." *Campaigns and Elections,* September.

Brack, Andrew C. 2005. The Brack Group. Available at http://www.brack.net/tips/ tips_campaign.htm. Accessed 10 July 2005.

Bradshaw, Joel. 1995. "Who Will Vote for You and Why: Designing Strategy and Theme." In *Campaigns and Elections American Style,* ed. James A. Thurber and Candice J. Nelson. Boulder, CO: Westview.

Braun, Gerry. 1999. "Bilbray Catches Heat from Assembly Woman over Trip Down Under." *San Diego Union Tribune* (12 August).

Broder, David S. 1971. *The Party's Over: The Failure of Politics in America.* New York: Harper and Row.

Brown, James, and Philip M. Seib. 1976. *The Art of Politics: Electoral Strategies and Campaign Management.* Port Washington, NY: Alfred.

Brown, Ron, and Nello Giorgetti. 1992. "Downballot Doldrums." *Campaigns and Elections,* June.

Bryan, William Jennings. 1913. *Speeches of William Jennings Bryan.* New York: Funk and Wagnalls.

Bumiller, Elisabeth. 2000. "Giuliani Accuses Mrs. Clinton of Negative Calls, Disguised as Polling." *New York Times* (23 February).

Burton, Michael John, and Daniel M. Shea. 2003. *Campaign Mode: Strategic Vision in Congressional Elections.* Lanham, MD: Rowman & Littlefield.

———. "Campaign Strategy." In *The Electoral Challenge: Theory Meets Practice,* ed. Stephen Craig. Washington, DC: CQ Press. In press.

Campaign Finance Institute. 2005. Available at http://campaignfinanceinstitute.org. Accessed 22 August 2005.

"Campaign Finance Triumph, A." *New York Times,* 11 December 2003, 42.

Campbell, James E. 2000. *The American Campaign: US Presidential Campaigns and the National Vote.* College Station: Texas A&M University Press.

Castellanos, Alex. 1998. Interview, PBS, *The :30 Second Candidate.* Available at http://www.pbs.org/30secondcandidate. Accessed 10 May 2004.

Center for Public Integrity. 2005. Available at http://www.publicintegrity.org/default.aspx. Accessed 13 August 2005.

Center for Responsive Politics. 2005. Available at http://www.opensecrets.org. Accessed 13 August 2005.

Connell, Mike. 2000. "A Guide to Finding a Smart Internet Strategy for 2000." *Campaigns and Elections,* December/January.

Cover, Albert D. 1977. "One Good Term Deserves Another: The Advantage of Incumbency in Congressional Elections." *American Journal of Political Science* 21: 523–41.

Crone, Brad. 1998. "Finding Priority Precincts with Database Overlays." *Campaigns and Elections,* December/January.

Currinder, Marian. 2005. "Campaign Finance: Funding the Presidential and Congressional Campaigns." In *The Elections of 2004,* ed. Michael Nelson. Washington, DC: Congressional Quarterly.

Daves, Robert P. 2000. "Who Will Vote? Ascertaining Likelihood to Vote and Modeling a Probable Electorate in Preelection Polls." In *Election Polls, the News Media, and Democracy,* eds. Paul J. Lavrakas and Michael W. Traugott. Chatham, NJ: Chatham House.

Davis, Lanny J. 1999. *Truth to Tell: Tell It Early, Tell It All, Tell It Yourself.* New York: Simon and Schuster.

Dawidziak, Mike. 1991. "Use Ethnic Targeting to Focus Mailings." *Campaigns and Elections,* November.

Deaver, Michael K., with Mickey Herskowitz. 1987. *Behind the Scenes.* New York: William Morrow.

Diamond, Edwin, and Stephen Bates. 1992. *The Spot: The Rise of Political Advertising on Television.* Cambridge, MA: MIT Press.

Dimock, Michael A., and Gary C. Jacobson. 1995. "Checks and Choices: The House Bank Scandal's Impact on Voters in 1992." *Journal of Politics* 57: 1143–59.

Drinkard, Jim, and Jill Lawrence. 2004. "Online, Off and Running: Web a New Campaign Front." *USA Today.* Available at http://www.usatoday.com/news/politicselections/2003–07–14-online-cover-usat_x.htm. Accessed 2 August 2005.

Dinkin, Robert J. 1989. *Campaigning in America: The History of Election Practices.* New York: Greenwood.

Duggan, Dennis. 2005. "Is Political Suicide a Crime?" *New York Newsday* (4 May): A17.

Dulio, David. 2004. *For Better or Worse?: How Political Consultants Are Changing Elections in the United States.* Albany: State University of New York Press.

Dunn, Anita. 1995. "The Best Campaign Wins: Local Press Coverage of Nonpresidential Races." In *Campaigns and Elections American Style,* ed. James A. Thurber and Candice J. Nelson. Boulder, CO: Westview.

Egan, Timothy. 1996. "Of Marriage, Money and a Lawmaker's Woes." *New York Times* (2 May).

Ehrenhalt, Alan. 1991. *The United States of Ambition.* New York: Random House.

Farhi, Paul, and James V. Grimaldi. 2004. "GOP Won with Accent on Rural and Traditional." *Washington Post.* Available at http://www.washingtonpost.com/ac2/wp-dyn/A23754–2004Nov3?language = printer. Accessed 28 July 2005.

Faucheux, Ron. 1996. "Should You Hire Out-of-State Consultants?" *Campaigns and Elections,* February.

———. 1998. *The Road to Victory, 2000: The Best of the Best from* Campaigns and Elections. 2nd ed. Dubuque, IA: Kendall/Hunt.

———. 2002. "How to Win Modern Elections: New Insights for Today's Candidates." In *Campaign Battle Lines: The Practical Consequences of Crossing the Line between What's Right and What's Not in Political Campaigning,* ed. Ronald A. Faucheux and Paul S. Herrnson. Washington, DC: Campaigns and Elections Publishing.

Faucheux, Ronald A., and Paul S. Herrnson, eds. 2002. Chapter 1/ *Campaign Battle Lines: The Practical Consequences of Crossing the Line between What's Right and What's Not in Political Campaigning.* Washington, DC: Campaigns and Elections Publishing.

Feld, Karl. 2001. "Online Polling and Survey Research." Available at http://web1.infotrac.galegroup.com. Accessed 21 June 2005.

Fenno, Richard F. 1978. *Home Style: House Members in Their Districts.* Boston: Little, Brown.

Ferejohn, John A. 1977. "On the Decline in Competition in Congressional Elections." *American Political Science Review* 71: 166–76.

Ferguson, Andrew. 1996. "Live Free or Cry: The Truth about New Hampshire." *The Weekly Standard,* January, 42–47.

Finkel, Steven. E. 1993. "Reexamining the 'Minimal Effects' Model in Recent Presidential Elections." *Journal of Politics* 55: 1–21.

Fiorina, Morris P. 1981. *Retrospective Voting in American National Elections.* New Haven, CT: Yale University Press.

Fowler, Linda L. 1993. *Candidates, Congress, and the American Democracy.* Ann Arbor: University of Michigan Press.

———. 1995. "Campaign Ethics and Political Trust." In *Campaigns and Elections American Style,* ed. James A. Thurber and Candice J. Nelson. Boulder, CO: Westview.

Fowler, Linda L., and Robert D. McClure. 1989. *Political Ambition: Who Decides to Run for Congress.* New Haven, CT: Yale University Press.

Frantz, Douglas. 1999. "Plenty of Dirty Jobs in Politics and a New Breed of Diggers." *New York Times* (6 July).

Frendries, John, and Alan R. Gitelson. 1999. "Local Parties in the 1990s: Spokes in a Candidate-Centered Wheel." In *The State of the Parties,* ed. John C. Green and Daniel M. Shea. Lanham, MD: Rowman & Littlefield.

Friedenberg, Robert V. 1997. *Communication Consultants in Political Campaigns: Ballot Box Warriors.* Westport, CT: Praeger.

Friedman, Lawrence M. 1993. *Crime and Punishment in American History.* New York: Basic Books.

Gaddie, Ronald Keith. 2004. *Born to Run: Origins of the Political Career.* Lanham, MD: Rowman & Littlefield.

Glad, Paul W. 1964. *McKinley, Bryan, and the People.* Philadelphia: Lippincott.

Glasser, Susan B. 2000a. "Hired Guns Fuel Fundraising Race." *Washington Post* (30 April).

———. 2000b. "Winning a Stake in a Losing Race." *Washington Post* (1 May).

Goodliffe, Jay. 2000. "The 1998 Utah Second Congressional District Race." In *Outside Money: Soft Money and Issue Advocacy in the 1998 Congressional Elections,* ed. David B. Magleby. Lanham, MD: Rowman & Littlefield.

Green, Donald, and Alan Gerber. 2004. *Get Out The Vote: How to Increase Voter Turnout.* Washington, DC: Brookings Institution Press.

Green, John C., and Daniel M. Shea, eds. 1999. *The State of the Parties: The Changing Role of Contemporary American Parties.* 3rd ed. Lanham, MD: Rowman & Littlefield.

Grefe, Edward A. 1998. "Can Political Candidates Afford to Allow Their Data to Be Managed by Anyone but a Professional?" *Campaigns and Elections,* December/January.

Grey, Lawrence. 1999. *How to Win a Local Election.* Rev. ed. New York: M. Evans.

Gross, Donald A., and Penny Miller. 2000. "The 1998 Kentucky Senate and Sixth District Races." In *Outside Money: Soft Money and Issue Advocacy in the 1998 Congressional Elections,* ed. David B. Magleby. Lanham, MD: Rowman & Littlefield.

Gruenwald, Juliana. 1995. "Wyden, Smith Vie for Center in Race for Packwood Seat." *Congressional Quarterly Weekly Report* 53: 3755.

Guide to Background Investigations, The. 1998. Tulsa, OK: Source Publications.

Guzzetta, S. J. 2002. *The Campaign Manual: A Definitive Study of the Modern Political Campaign Process.* 6th ed. Flat Rock, NC: Political Publications.

Halatyn, Tom. 1998. "Using Data Files to Raise More Bucks." *Campaigns and Elections,* December/January.

Hallow, Ralph Z. 1997. "Brad O'Leary's Fundraising Secrets." *Campaigns and Elections,* September.

Harris Interactive. 2005. Available at http://www.harrisinteractive.com. Accessed 10 October 2005.

Harris, John F. 1998. "Clinton's Campaign Consultants Reaped Millions from TV Ads." *Washington Post* (4 January).

Hart, Neesa. 1992. "Buddy, Can You Spare a Grand?" *Campaigns and Elections,* September.

Hathaway, T. R. 1996. "Bright Ideas from Pat Buchanan's Integrated Campaign Database." *Campaigns and Elections,* November.

Helton, Charmagne, and Kathey Pruitt. 1998. "Millner Pulls TV Ad Erroneously Reporting Barnes Parole Vote." *Atlanta Constitution* (6 August).

Herrnson, Paul S. 2000. *Congressional Elections: Campaigning at Home and in Washington.* Washington, DC: CQ Press.

———. 2004. *Congressional Elections: Campaigning at Home and in Washington.* 4th ed. Washington, DC: CQ Press.

Hershey, Marjorie R. 1984. *Running for Office: The Political Education of Campaigners.* Chatham, NJ: Chatham House.

Hewitt, John. 1999. "Sending Effective Press Releases." *Campaigns and Elections,* April.

Himes, David. 1995. "Strategy and Tactics for Candidate Fund-Raising." In *Campaigns and Elections American Style,* ed. James A. Thurber and Candice J. Nelson. Boulder, CO: Westview.

Hines, Cragg. 1992. "The Reagan–Bush Era; Reagan's Simple Message Hit the Spot." *Houston Chronicle* (16 August).

Hockaday, Tom, and Martin Edlund. 1999. "Banner Advertising as a Voter Outreach Tool." *Campaigns and Elections,* May.

Holbrook, Thomas. 1996. *Do Campaigns Matter?* Thousand Oaks, CA: Sage.

Holbrook, Thomas M. "Do Campaigns Really Matter?" In *The Electoral Challenge: Theory Meets Practice,* ed. Stephen Craig. Washington, DC: CQ Press. In press.

Hutchens, Jon. 1996. "Buying Cable Time: How to Get Your Money's Worth." *Campaigns and Elections,* June.

Institute on Money in State Politics. 2005. "Study: Money, Incumbency Hard to Beat in Legislative Races." Available at http://www.followthemoney.org/Newsroom/index. phtml?r = 199. Accessed 26 January.

Institute of Politics, John F. Kennedy School of Government, and Harvard University, eds. 2006. *Campaign for President: The Managers Look at 2004.* Lanham, MD: Rowman & Littlefield.

Jacobson, Gary. 1997. *The Politics of Congressional Elections.* 4th ed. New York: Longman, 37.

Jacobson, Gary C. 2004. *The Politics of Congressional Elections.* 6th ed. New York: Pearson Longman.

Jalonick, Mary Clare. 2000. "Greatest Hits II: Democratic House Candidate Sites." *Campaigns and Elections,* July.

Jamieson, Kathleen Hall. 1984. *Packaging the Presidency.* New York: Oxford University Press.

———. 1992. *Dirty Politics.* New York: Oxford University Press.

———. 1998. "Facing Up to It; What Those Polls Are Telling Us." *Washington Post* (22 March).

Johnson, Dennis W. 2001. *No Place for Amateurs: How Political Consultants Are Reshaping American Democracy.* New York: Routledge.

Johnson, Dick. 1995. "Victory His, Jesse Jackson Jr. Heads to Congress." *New York Times* (14 December).

Johnson, Glen. 2003. "Opposition Research Seen as Key by Presidential Rivals." *Boston Globe* (8 June).

Johnson, Wayne C. 1992. "First Do No Harm." *Campaigns and Elections,* July.

Johnson-Cartee, Karen S., and Gary A. Copeland. 1991. *Negative Political Advertising: Coming of Age.* Hillsdale, NJ: Lawrence Erlbaum Associates.

———. 1997. *Inside Political Campaigns: Theory and Practice.* Westport, CT: Praeger.

Jones, Stanley. 1964. *The Presidential Election of 1896.* Madison: University of Wisconsin Press.

Kanfer, Ron. 1991. "Direct to the Bank." *Campaigns and Elections,* July.

Kaplan, Robert L. 1991. "Psychology of Silence: Raising More Money by Psyching Out Donors." *Campaigns and Elections,* November.

———. 2000. "Getting the Most Out of Your Professional Fundraiser." *Campaigns and Elections,* February.

Katz, Benjamin A., and Cheryl Brummer. 2004. "Online Politics Is Also Local." *Campaign Guide.* Available at http://www.completecampaigns.com/article.asp?articleid = 1. Accessed 21 August 2005.

Kayden, Xandra, and Eddie Mahe Jr., eds. 1985. *The Party Goes On.* New York: Basic Books.

Key, V. O. 1966. *The Responsible Electorate.* New York: Vintage Books.

Krehbiel, Keith, and John R. Wright. 1983. "The Incumbency Effect in Congressional Elections: A Test of Two Explanations." *American Journal of Political Science* 27: 140–57.

Kurtz, Howard. 1992. "Hotline to Campaign Central; Daily Clip Sheet Keeps the Pack Ahead." *Washington Post* (29 February).

Lakely, James G. 2004. "Grass Roots Seen Key in 2004." *Washington Times*. Available at http://www.washingtontimes.com/national/20040816–124248–5854r.htm. Accessed 21 August 2005.

Larsen, Elena. 2003. "Digital Town Hall." Pew Internet and American Life Project. Working paper online at http://www.pewinternet.org/pdfs/POP_Digital_Town_Hall.pdf.

Larsen, Elena, and Lee Rainie. 2002. "Digital Town Hall: How Local Officials Use the Internet and Civic Benefits They Cite from Dealing with Constituents Online." Pew Internet and American Life Project. Available at http://www.pewinternet.org/report_display.asp?r = 74. Accessed 12 February 2006.

Lau, Richard R., and Gerald M. Pomper. 2004. *Negative Campaigning: An Analysis of U.S. Senate Elections.* Lanham, MD: Rowman & Littlefield.

Lavrakas Paul J., and Michael W. Traugott. 2000. *Election Polls, the News Media, and Democracy.* New York: Chatham House.

Lindauer, Charles. 1999. "Tactical Cartography." *Campaigns and Elections,* April.

Luntz, Frank I. 1988. *Candidates, Consultants, and Campaigns: The Style and Substance of American Electioneering.* Oxford: Basil Blackwood.

Maisel, L. Sandy. 1990. "The Incumbency Advantage." In *Money, Elections, and Democracy: Reforming Congressional Campaign Finance,* ed. Margaret Latus Nugent and John R. Johannes. Boulder, CO: Westview.

Maisel, L. Sandy, and Darrell M. West. 2004. *Running on Empty? Political Discourse in Congressional Elections.* Lanham, MD: Rowman & Littlefield.

Malbin, Michael, J., ed. 2003. *Life after Reform: When the Bipartisan Campaign Reform Act Meets Politics.* Lanham, MD: Rowman & Littlefield.

Malchow, Hal. 1990. "10 Ways to Design In House Mail That Works." *Campaigns and Elections,* June/July.

———. 1997. "The Targeting Revolution in Political Direct Contact." *Campaigns and Elections,* June.

———. 2003. *The New Political Targeting.* Washington, DC: Campaign and Elections Magazine.

Maor, Jacob. 2001. "Writing Campaign Speeches That Connect." *Campaigns and Elections,* August.

Marks, Paul. 2005. "Polls Cast the Net Wider" [online]. *The News Scientist.* Available at http://web.lexis-nexis.com. Accessed 21 August 2005.

Matalin, Mary, and James Carville. 1995. *All's Fair: Love, War, and Running for President.* New York: Touchstone.

Mayhew, David R. 1974a. *Congress: The Electoral Connection.* New Haven, CT: Yale University Press.

———. 1974b. "Congressional Elections: The Case of the Vanishing Marginals." *Polity* 6: 295–317.

McDevitt, Bob. 1996. "Fundraising: Quick Tips for Candidates." *Campaigns and Elections,* September.

McGinniss, Joe. 1969. *The Selling of the President 1968.* New York: Trident.

McIntire, Mike. 2005. "Contributions to Candidates via the Web Rise in the City." *New York Times.* Available at http://www.giffordmiller.com/press/061305_nytimes.html. Accessed 7 January 2006.

McLuhan, Marshall. 1964. *Understanding Media: The Extensions of Man.* New York: McGraw-Hill.

Medvic, Stephen M. 2003. "Professionalization in Congressional Campaigns." in *Campaign Warriors: Political Consultants in Elections,* ed. James Thurber and Candice Nelson. Washington, DC: Brookings Institution Press.

Mentzer, Bruce. 2000a. "Banner Ads: The New Entry in Paid Political Media Plans." *Campaigns and Elections,* July.

———. 2000b. "A Political Media Buying Strategy for Using Cable." *Campaigns and Elections,* June.

Meredith, Todd. 2000. "Fundraising Events: The Dollars Are in the Details." *Campaigns and Elections,* February.

———. 2004. "Open the Envelope: Getting People to Look at the Direct Mail They Receive." *Campaigns and Elections,* December/January.

Milbank, Dana. 2000. "The Year of the Latino Voter? Only in Campaign Rhetoric." *Washington Post* (21 May).

Milne, John. 2004. "State Campaigns Turn to Consultants." NHPR News. Available at http://nhpr.org/view_content/7285. Accessed 26 June.

Mitchell, Alison, and Frank Bruni. 2000. "Bush and McCain Swap Strategies for Next Battle." *New York Times* (21 February).

Morris, Dick. 1999a. *Behind the Oval Office: Getting Reelected against All the Odds.* Los Angeles: Renaissance Books.

———. 1999b. *Vote.com.* Los Angeles: Renaissance Books.

Morris, Dwight, and Murielle E. Gamache. 1994. *Gold-Plated Politics: The 1992 Congressional Races.* Washington, DC: CQ Press.

Morrow, Daniel R. 2005. "Karl Rove: Prince of the Push Poll," *The Potomac.* Available at http://www.webdelsol.com/The Potomac/politics-rove.htm. Accessed 12 October 2005.

Mostert, Mary. 2000. "Absentee Ballot Fraud among Democrats in Florida an Old Story." Available at http://www.bannerofliberty.com/OS11–00MQC/11–15–2000.1.html. Accessed 10 July 2004.

Nagourney, Adam. 2004. "Bush Campaign Manager Views the Electoral Divide." *New York Times* (19 November).

Nammour, Chris. 2005. "Presidential Campaign Fundraising Heats Up." Available at http://www.pbs.org/newshour/extra/features/july-dec03/campaign_10–20.html. Accessed 21 August 2005.

Napolitan, Joseph. 1972. *The Election Game and How to Win It.* Garden City, NY: Doubleday.

———. 1986. "Some Thoughts on the Importance of Strategy in a Political Campaign." In *The National Republican Congressional Committee Campaign Starter Manual.* Washington, DC: Republican Congressional Campaign Committee.

Nelson, Candice, David A. Dulio, and Stephen Medvic, eds. 2002. *Shades of Gray: Perspectives on Campaign Ethics.* Washington, DC: Brookings.

Newman, Bruce I. 1999. *The Handbook of Political Marketing.* New York: Sage.

Nimmo, Daniel. 1970. *The Political Persuaders.* Englewood Cliffs, NJ: Prentice Hall.

Nyden, Paul J. 2005. Common Dreams News Center. Available at http://www.commondreams.org/headlines05/0331–11.htm. Accessed 1 June 2005.

Obama for Illinois, Inc. 2004. "Obama Community Groups." Available at http://www.obamaforillinois.com/index.asp?Type = B BASIC&SEC = {4DC3B4C0-BF43–4236-AFOB-5E30E2843848}. Accessed 22 August 2005.

O'Neill, Tip, with Gary Hymel. 1994. *All Politics Is Local and Other Rules of the Game.* Holbrook, MA: Bob Adams.

O'Neill, Tip, with William Novak. 1987. *Man of the House: The Life and Political Memoirs of Speaker Tip O'Neill.* New York: Random House.

Opensecrets.org. 2005. "Money in Politics." Available at http://www.opensecrets.org. Accessed 6 January 2006.

Ouzounian, Richard. 1997. "Satellites, Feeds and Computers." *Campaigns and Elections,* August.

Panagopulos, Costas, with Preethi Dayanand. 2005. "Pack Your Bags: A Guide to International Political Consulting." *Campaigns and Elections.* April.

Persinos, John F. 1994. "Gotcha!" *Campaigns and Elections,* August.

Pew Research Center. 2000. "Internet Sapping Broadcast News Audience." Available at http://www.people-press.org/mediaoorpt.htm. Accessed 11 June.

Phillips, Gerald M. 1984. *How to Support Your Cause and Win.* Columbia: University of South Carolina Press.

Pine, Joseph B. 1993. *Mass Customization: The New Frontier in Business Competition.* Boston: Harvard Business School Press.

Pomper, Gerald M. 1974. *Elections in America.* New York: Dodd, Mead.

Randolph, Sallie G. 1989. "The Effective Press Release: Key to Free Media." In *Campaigns and Elections: A Reader in Modern American Politics,* ed. Larry Sabato. Glenview, IL: Scott, Foresman.

Reich, Brian. 2005. "E Strategies That Worked." *Campaigns and Elections.* Available at http://web.lexis-nexis.com/universe. Accessed 10 August 2005.

Riordon, William L., ed. 1995. *Plunkitt of Tammany Hall: A Series of Very Plain Talks by Ex-Senator George Washington Plunkitt.* New York: Signet.

Robberson, Tod. 1996. "Those Who Dig Dirt Are in Demand." *Washington Post* (1 November).

Robbin, Jonathan. 1989. "Geodemographics: The New Magic." In *Campaigns and Elections: A Reader in Modern American Politics,* ed. Larry Sabato. Glenview, IL: Scott, Foresman.

Sabato, Larry J. 1981. *The Rise of Political Consultants: New Way of Winning Elections.* New York: Basic Books.

———. 1989a. *Campaigns and Elections: A Reader in Modern American Politics.* Glenview, IL: Scott, Foresman.

———. 1989b. "How Direct Mail Works." In *Campaigns and Elections: A Reader in Modern American Politics,* ed. Larry J. Sabato. Glenview, IL: Scott, Foresman.

———. 1991. *Feeding Frenzy: How Attack Journalism Has Transformed American Journalism.* New York: Free Press.

Sabato, Larry, and Glenn R. Simpson. 1996. "Vote Fraud!" *Campaigns and Elections,* June.

Sabato, Larry, Mark Stencel, and S. Robert Lichter. 2000. *Peepshow: Media and Politics in an Age of Scandal.* Lanham, MD: Rowman & Littlefield.

Salmore, Barbara G., and Stephen A. Salmore. 1989. *Candidates, Parties, and Campaigns.* Washington, DC: CQ Press.

Schlesinger, Joseph A. 1991. *Political Parties and the Winning of Office.* Ann Arbor: University of Michigan Press.

Schuman, Howard, and Stanley Presser. 1981. *Questions and Answers in Attitude Surveys.* San Diego: Academic Press.

Scudder, Virgil. 1997. Interviewed in "Spin." *Campaigns and Elections,* April.

Selnow, Gary W. 1994. *High Tech Campaigns.* Westport, CT: Praeger.

Semiatin, Richard J. 2005. *Campaigns in the 21st Century.* Boston: McGraw-Hill.

Shaw, Catherine M. 2004. *The Campaign Manager: Running and Winning Local Elections.* 2nd ed. Boulder, CO: Westview.

Shea, Daniel M. 1995. *Transforming Democracy: State Legislative Campaigns and Political Parties.* Albany: State University of New York Press.

———. 1996a. *Campaign Craft: The Strategies, Tactics, and Art of Political Campaign Management.* Westport, CT: Praeger.

———. 1996b. "Issue Voting, Candidate Quality, and the Ousting of a Ten-Year Incumbent. *American Review of Politics* 17: 395–420.

———. 1999. "The Passing of Realignment and the Advent of the 'Base-Less' Party System." *American Politics Quarterly* 27(1): 33–57.

Shea, Daniel M., and Stephen C. Brooks. 1995. "How to Topple an Incumbent." *Campaigns and Elections,* June.

Shirley, Craig. 1997. Interviewed in "Spin." *Campaigns and Elections,* April.

Shrum, Robert. 1997. Interviewed in "Spin." *Campaigns and Elections,* April.

Sidlow, Edward I. 2004. *Challenging the Incumbent: An Underdog's Undertaking.* Washington, DC: CQ Press.

Sifton, Elisabeth. 1998. "The Serenity Prayer." *Yale Review* 86 (1): 16–65.

Silverberg, Carl. 2000. "The Secret Ingredient for Successful PAC Fundraising: Discipline." *Campaigns and Elections,* June.

Simon, Paul. 1995. "Capitol Hill Nine: Retiring Senators Discuss Why They Chose to Leave Public Office." Interview, CBS, *60 Minutes.* 17 December.

———. 1999. *P.S.: The Autobiography of Paul Simon.* Chicago: Bonus Books.

Simonich, Milan. 2004. "Ex-Hostage Takes Heat from GOP Foe; Ohio Campaign One of the Nation's Nastiest." *Pittsburgh Post Gazette* (30 October): A1.

Simpson, Dick. 1996. *Winning Elections: A Handbook of Modern Participatory Politics.* New York: HarperCollins.

Snider, Steve. 1990. "What Makes a Press Release Sing." *Campaigns and Elections,* January.

Sorauf, Frank J. 1988. *Money in American Elections.* Boston: Scott, Foresman.

———. 1995. "Competition, Contributions, and Money in 1992." In *Campaigns and Elections American Style,* ed. James A. Thurber and Candice J. Nelson. Boulder, CO: Westview.

Squier, Robert. 1998. Interview, PBS, *The :30 Second Candidate.* Available at http://www.pbs.org/30secondcandidate. Accessed 10 January 1999.

Stephanopoulos, George. 1999. *All Too Human: A Political Education.* Boston: Little, Brown.

Still, Edward. 2000. Listserv posting to Law-Courts Listserv. 9 December.

Stonecash, Jeffrey M. 2003. *Political Polling: Strategic Information in Campaigns.* Lanham, MD: Rowman & Littlefield.

Strachan, J. Cherie. 2003. *High-Tech Grass Roots.* Lanham, MD: Rowman & Littlefield.

Straumanis, Andris. 2004. "Campaigning on the Web Is Becoming Standard Procedure." Minnesota Public Radio. Available at http://news.minnesota.publicradio.org/features/2004/08/13_straumanisa_polsonline. Accessed 21 June 2005.

Sussman, Gerald. 2005. *Global Electioneering: Campaign Consulting, Communications, and Corporate Financing.* Lanham, MD: Rowman & Littlefield.

Sweitzer, Don. 1996. "Kill or Be Killed; Military Strategies Can Help Win Campaigns." *Campaigns and Elections,* September.

Sweitzer, Don, and David Heller. 1996. "Radio Tips: 10 Ways to Give Your Campaign Ads More Punch." *Campaigns and Elections,* May.

Swint, Kerwin C. 1998. *Political Consultants and Negative Campaigning: The Secrets of the Pros.* Lanham, MD: University Press of America.

Tapper, Jake. 2005. "Too Jewish?" Salon.com. Available at http://archive.salon.com/politics/feature/2000/08/09/lieberman/index1.html. Accessed 10 October 2005 October.

Thibodeaux, Bessie. 1999. "The Road Home: Direct Mail Fundraising." *Campaigns and Elections,* May.

Thomas, Robert J., and Doug Gowen. 1999. *How to Run for Local Office: A Complete Guide for Winning a Local Election.* Detroit: R&T Enterprise.

Thurber, James A., Robin Kolodny, and David A. Dulio. 2000. "Consultants on Candidates: Survey Taps Surprising Attitudes." *Campaigns and Elections,* May.

Thurber, James A., and Candice J. Nelson. 1995. *Campaigns and Elections American Style.* Boulder, CO: Westview.

———. 2000. *Campaign Warriors: Political Consultants in Elections.* Washington, DC: Brookings Institution Press.

Thurber, James A., Candice J. Nelson, and David Dulio. 2000. Chapter 1. *Crowded Airwaves: Campaign Advertising in Elections.* Washington, DC: Brookings Institution Press.

Traugott, Michel W., and MeeEun Kang. 2000. "Public Attention to Polls in an Election Year." In *Election Polls, the News Media, and Democracy,* ed. Paul J. Lavrakas and Michael W. Traugott. New York: Chatham House.

Trent, Judith S., and Robert V. Friedenberg. 2004. *Political Campaign Communication: Principles and Practices.* 5th ed. Lanham, MD: Rowman & Littlefield.

Trippi, Joe. 2005. *The Revolution Will Not Be Televised: Democracy, the Internet, and the Overthrow of Everything.* New York: Regan Books.

Tron, Barrie. 1996. "Staging Media Events: What We Learned from the 'Contract with America.'" *Campaigns and Elections,* December/January.

Troy, Gil. 1991. *See How They Ran: The Changing Role of the Presidential Candidate.* New York: Free Press.

Tufte, Edward R. 1975. "Determinants of the Outcomes of Midterm Congressional Elections." *American Political Science Review* 69: 812–26.

Tuttle, Stephen. 1996. "Arizona Primary of Secondary Concern." *Arizona Republic* (4 February).

U.S. Census. 2004. Available at http://www.census.gov/population/socdemo/voting/cps2004/tab04b.xls. Accessed XXX.

U.S. Census. 2005. "Voting and Registration in the Election of November 2004." Available at: http://www.census.gov/voting/cps2004.

Usher, Doug, and Mark Mellman. 2004. "Advances in Polling: Lifestyle Cluster Targeting." *Campaigns and Elections,* April.

Varoga, Craig. 1995. "The Lone Star Upset." *Campaigns and Elections,* March.

Visser, Penny S., Jon A. Krosnick, Jesse F. Marquette, and Michael F. Curtin. 2000. "Improving Election Forecasting: Allocation of Undecided Respondents, Identification of Likely Voters, and Response Order Effects." In *Election Polls, the News Media, and Democracy,* ed. Paul J. Lavrakas and Michael W. Traugott. New York: Chatham House.

Wachob, Bill, and Andrew Kennedy. 2000. "Beating B-1 Bob: Underdog Ends Conservative's Congressional Career in California's 46th District in 1996." In *Campaigns and Elections: Contemporary Case Studies,* ed. Michael A. Bailey, Ronald A. Faucheux, Paul S. Herrnson, and Clyde Wilcox. Washington, DC: CQ Press.

Wallace, Amy. 1994. "Stunning Blow for a Hired Gun." *Los Angeles Times* (14 November).

Wattenberg, Martin P. 1998. *The Decline of American Political Parties 1952–1996.* Cambridge, MA: Harvard University Press.

Wayne, Stephen. 1982. "Great Expectations: What People Want from the Presidency." In *Rethinking the Presidency,* ed. Thomas E. Cronin. Boston: Little, Brown.

Weaver, Mark. 1996. "Paid Media." In *Campaign Craft: The Strategies, Tactics, and Art of Political Campaign Management,* ed. Daniel M. Shea. Westport, CT: Praeger.

Weigel, David. 2005. *Campaigns and Elections.* Available at http://www.campaignline. com/printedition/subscribe.cfm?pageid = 726&navid = 50&redurl = /printedition/ page.cfm?pageid = 726&navid = 50. Accessed 1 October 2005.

Westneat, Danny, and Tom Brown. 1998. "Self-Funded Races Rarely Succeed." *Seattle Times* (3 September).

Whillock, Rita Kirk. 1991. *Political Empiricism: Communication Strategies in State and Regional Elections.* New York: Praeger.

White, John K., and Daniel M. Shea. 2004. *New Party Politics: From Jefferson and Hamilton to the Information Age.* 2nd ed. Belmont, CA: Wadsworth.

White, Theodore H. 1961. *The Making of the President, 1960.* New York: Atheneum.

Wilson, Chris, and Mike Burita. 2000. "Winning in Unfriendly Territory." In *Campaigns and Elections: Contemporary Case Studies,* ed. Michael A. Bailey, Ronald A. Faucheux, Paul S. Herrnson, and Clyde Wilcox. Washington, DC: CQ Press.

Yamamura, Kevin. 2005. "Matsui Easily Succeeds Late Husband in Congress," *Sacramento Bee* (8 March).

Yeutter, Clayton, Jeanie Austin, James S. Nathanson, and Jane Hershey Abraham. 1992. *The NRC Campaign Encyclopedia.* Washington, DC: Republican National Committee.

Index

About the Authors

DANIEL M. SHEA is Associate Professor of Political Science and Director of the Center for Political Participation at Allegheny College in Meadville, Pennsylvania. He has worked as a political strategist in some of New York's most challenging races, and has written widely on campaign strategy and political parties.

MICHAEL JOHN BURTON is Assistant Professor of Political Science at Ohio University in Athens. He worked in the Office of Vice President Al Gore as Special Assistant to the Chief of Staff and Assistant Political Director. Before that he spent two years on the Hill. His research is focused on political campaign strategy and White House operations.